MAKING THE BIG GAME

Tales of an Accidental Spectator

MAKING THE BIG GAME

Tales of an Accidental Spectator

JEFFREY FEKETE

TWO HARBORS
MINNEAPOLIS, MINNESOTA

Two Harbors Press
212 3rd Avenue North, Suite 290
Minneapolis, MN 55401
612.455.2293
www.TwoHarborsPress.com

ISBN - 978-1-935097-32-7
ISBN - 1-935097-32-6
LCCN - 2009900351

Book sales for North America and international:
Itasca Books, 3501 Highway 100 South, Suite 220
Minneapolis, MN 55416
Phone: 952.345.4488 (toll free 1.800.901.3480)
Fax: 952.920.0541; email to orders@itascabooks.com

Typeset by Kristeen Wegner

Printed in the United States of America

for the fans

Contents

Introduction

The name *Heisman* garners the most recognition from the trophy awarded annually at the New York Downtown Athletic Club to the nation's outstanding collegiate player.

Upon receiving the honor and the hardware in 1965, future Super Bowl champion Mike Garrett famously said, "The award is wonderful, but who's Heisman?"

Legendary coach John Heisman was a law-school graduate of the University of Pennsylvania. He never became an attorney. Instead, over thirty-six years he coached football at eight universities, compiling a record of 190–7–16 between 1891 and 1927. Heisman was an intellectual, comfortable attending the opera or banging heads on the practice field with linemen several years his junior.

Heisman revolutionized the game by introducing both the forward pass and the center snap, or *hike*. His innovative *jump shift* led to the modern day *T* and *I* formations. These advances helped transform football from a difficult-to-watch, brutal scrum into an elegant ballet of skilled movement and high drama. Heisman elevated, and may very well have saved, the prospects of American football as a modern spectator sport.

The coach was a brilliant public speaker. He frequently drew on skills honed as a Shakespearian actor. At the first team meeting of every new season, Heisman stood before his squad holding out a football for all to see, just as Hamlet might grasp and contemplate a skull. In compelling, captivating fashion, he uttered these words:

"What is this?" he asked his players rhetorically. After sufficient dramatic pause, he answered, "It is a prolate spheroid."

Heisman recruited exceptional scholar athletes, but new recruits often struggled at first to grasp the coach's train of thought. Heisman reminded his leather-helmeted students that a prolate spheroid is better suited for throwing and much harder to fumble than the conventional spherical baseball or basketball.

"It is an elongated sphere in which the outer leather casing is drawn tightly over somewhat smaller rubber tubing. Better to have died as a small boy than to fumble this football," Heisman told his players.

To John Heisman, a football player could commit no greater sin than fumbling the ball. He hated fumbles. A prolate spheroid is by nature easier to hang onto. However, the distinct shape of the football makes recovering what careless hands lose exceptionally difficult. He instilled in players an appreciation for the physics and inherent risks built into the football. A fumbled football leads to freakish caroms, ricochets, spins, and outcomes remembered as laughable or heartbreaking.

Not all such havoc comes unexpectedly. Consider the desperate intent of an onsides kick to create controlled chaos. The play is a designed attempt to negate an otherwise predictable outcome, namely, an orderly change of possession.

By design and by chance, a loose, tumbling football is a moving illustration of chaos.

Memorable game-changing plays result after a football comes to rest following unpredictable flashes of erratic movement. Franco Harris's 1972 Immaculate Reception, Herm Edwards' 1978 Miracle of the Meadowlands, Earnest Byner's 1988 Fumble, and Manning to Tyree in 2008, all owe notoriety to the handling, mishandling, and chasing of an oddly shaped ball in motion.

The most carefully constructed game plan can crumble under the consequential weight of fumbles, bobbles, and deflections. Fortunes turn on swift, instinctive reactions to the strange bounce, roll, or turn. A ball can fall squarely into unprepared hands and drop away unsecured on a crazed path to an unknown final destination.

When advancing the ball, the sure-handed ball carrier minimizes negative variables and increases the probability of victory. Heisman so believed in this principle that he even ran deceptive plays, later outlawed, where players hid the ball under their jerseys.

For ten ragged, nerve-wracking, and exciting days in late January and early February 2008, I figuratively chased a loose, moving, and sometimes hidden prolate spheroid. A seat at Super Bowl XLII, one of the most anticipated championships in the storied history of the National Football League, suddenly and unexpectedly became an attainable object of my desire. The pursuit began at my home in Sacramento, California, and moved through New York and New Jersey, into cyberspace, and finally to Phoenix, Arizona.

The chance to attend the Super Bowl did not quite land in my lap, nor did I deliberately seek it out. As a sports fan in general, I consider myself fortunate to have been present for a number of regular-season pro games, NBA and MLB play-off games, and a couple other meaningful contests. I was in the gallery on eighteen at Pebble Beach when Tiger Woods completed his blowout of the U.S. Open field in 2000 and again as he battled a painful knee injury en route to winning at Torrey Pines eight years later. I attended multiple events at the 2002 Salt Lake Winter Olympic Games. My memorable live-spectator encounters until Super Bowl XLII involved many weeks or even months of careful advance planning.

The specific timing, process, and circumstances of getting to Glendale, Arizona, the site of the big game, proved both entertaining and maddening. Internal and external obstacles required self-awareness, patience, and improvisation to work through wholly unanticipated challenges. At least one motive for writing this book is my desire to help fans understand not only the frenzied ticket market, but also the deep-seated emotions that drive the market.

At various times in my advertising career I have helped conceive, sell, and execute various sponsor-ready pieces of high-profile and second-tier sports and entertainment events. Hundreds of thousands of fans have seen some of my work. Very few ever knew it was my handiwork.

On the way to the park or stadium, you heard a particular sponsor's ad on a radio broadcast. When you arrived at the gate, someone handed you a free product sample. You wandered past a certain sponsor-branded message once inside. You took your seat as a sponsor representative tossed out the first pitch or appeared on the scoreboard. After the game started, you watched some curious stunt or contest filling the gap of a timeout. I was there also.

I do not compete on the playing field but help others compete for your attention by integrating their message into your spectator experience.

This background gave me a useful perspective but afforded no insider access to experience Super Bowl XLII any differently than another paying spectator in the upper deck. However, on other occasions, my own media and advertising work, my wife's past involvement in the music business, and her current career in law, have allowed us some access and privilege. We have received the periodic backstage pass. We have met and worked in a variety of situations with people you expect to find behind the tinted glass of limos and luxury boxes. This book does not focus on them as much as it does on our collectively evolving American spectator experience, an experience in which once passive bystanders now increasingly share in the creation and chronicling of the event itself. It is about fan engagement that transcends merely showing up, cheering, and jeering. Our national relationship to sports runs deeper than a box score or friendly fan debate. For better or for worse, our culture embeds the big game buildup in our psyche.

I hope anecdotal references to everyday life beyond football lend an otherwise football-centered story a perspective different from that of coaches, players, or sports journalists. I have taken some side roads through my own childhood, work, and leisure to put elements of this Super Bowl travelogue in broader context. I include these personal snapshots not because they are particularly remarkable, but because they may relate to your own life and our society. I have woven small stories through bigger storylines to dissect the irrational but real passion fans carry for a team, a player, a place, an event, or a game.

You may take joy in watching a small-town, minor-league game with a child or in taking your grandmother to the philharmonic. It is likely in such settings you have savored special moments with close friends alongside hundreds or thousands of perfect strangers. You shared a fleeting, intense, and collective human bond with mostly anonymous spectators until a curtain falls or designated time expires.

After the Super Bowl XLII game clock expired in Glendale, Arizona, I reached out to some of the equally elated seated around me in Giant underdog territory. I wanted to include my temporary neighbors in this story before they vanished anonymously through the exit tunnel. You might recognize aspects of yourself in some of these fans in my game day narrative.

Traditional media regularly place those in the stands and those on the field into divided camps of the watchers and the watched. The viewing public places unrealistic expectations on players and all too often excuse poor fan behavior. Sports journalists and fans build legends around singular feats of athletic skill in a critical moment and often take for granted the daily, quiet heroism of supposed ordinary people. It is easy and sometimes justifiable to be cynical about a culture of upwardly spiraling excess and greed in both modern American sport and other institutions. Off-field struggles and transgressions among players, team management, media, sponsors, and assorted profiteers corrupt the innocent pleasures of watching the game. The game reflects imperfections in other aspects of our lives and challenges us all to distinguish love from blind worship. Fans and players share a dream and urge to partake in grand things larger than ourselves. Whether playing or watching, we are more frequently participating together in making the big game.

Chances are good that you have traveled to an unfamiliar place and felt just a bit closer to home upon spying a passerby wearing a familiar logo on a cap, shirt, or jersey. Such connections seem trivial, yet in a mobile, fragmented, isolated, and alienated society, locating roots of any kind can be a comforting exercise.

The use of a spectacle as an instrument of diversion, propaganda, and power brokering has a long history encompassing the Roman Coliseum, the Olympics from Berlin to Beijing, and yes, even to the national holiday which is Super Bowl Sunday. We readily give consent for the use of pictures, descriptions, and accounts of these proceedings to distort our perceptions at least temporarily. Such use reflects our humanity more than it exposes any inherent deficiency with grand communal events that are shared to capture something memorable and inspiring.

On February 3, 2008, along with two family members and seventy-one thousand and ninety-eight fellow fans, I witnessed perhaps the greatest championship upset in the history of the National Football League. An unanticipated open window of opportunity reacquainted me with fond recollections and unpleasant memories. I saw them anew through the prism of pregame hype. I arrived at a better understanding of my appreciation for the game while placing the actors in proper perspective.

I owe a debt of gratitude to season ticket holders Howard and Herman Hoffman, whose undying loyalty to the New York Football Giants made the journey possible. My cousin, Jason Kainu, made getting to Arizona conceivable. My wife, Mindy Steuer, allayed last-minute concerns, endured my occasionally doubting ways, and made arriving at our destination, then and now, worth the effort.

I. Marking the Spot

Some people keep diaries. Others make scrapbooks, collect postcards, and archive digital photos or videos. Most of us mark life stages by referencing significant births, weddings, anniversaries, and funerals. Simple keepsakes, personal holiday traditions, family recipes passed down—any or all of these—serve as tools to mine our memory banks.

In addition to physical objects, mementos, and significant gatherings, major historical events trigger personal recollection. We attach ourselves to these trigger mechanisms, grow fond of them, despise, embrace, or avoid them. We also can exaggerate, manipulate, and even become subservient to them.

Jarring images frozen in time at irregular historical intervals shape entire generations. A flash over Hiroshima, a motorcade in Dallas, an Eagle that landed on the lunar landscape, a wall torn down in Berlin, and two towers crumbling in New York, all exist in the eye of the beholder as textbook references or personally transformative moments.

No wonder we take comfort in the more orderly history of big sporting events. Their predictability, if not always their outcomes, reassure.

In proper perspective, great games are like page numbers marking the chronological progression of lives in a place no single book, library, or database can fully explain. As seasons pass, the triumphs and defeats of our favorite players and teams serve as pins to fasten footnotes to our family and community stories. Sport offers a place to anchor small, individual joys and struggles, giving them relatable meaning and purpose.

Until by dumb luck and persistence I attended the Super Bowl in 2008, the game for me had been purely a televised affair. Memories of where and with whom I watched the game on those Super Sundays accompany my recollections of most of the contests. I suspect this is common among football fans or others who catalog years of their lives using some recurring model of sporting or cultural events. The Super Bowl is simply one of the largest and most familiar common reference points.

I could not tell you exactly when I first employed Roman numerals to anchor sections of a roughly half-written life scroll. I can tell you I grew up with the Super Bowl, and it grew up with me. My formative days as a young fan unfolded as the National Football League formally attached these elegant, imposing symbols to their annual championship game.

Immediately following the merger of the old National Football League and the upstart American Football League in 1966, the championship games only later referred to as Super Bowl I, II, and III were played under a different title. In 1970, league officials replaced the *AFL-NFL Championship Game* with the designation *Super Bowl*, thereby effectively helping to unify the perception of a reconstituted league. In 1971, the league applied a bit of historical revisionism by assigning a Roman numeral to the fifth championship game. The numerals were retroactively applied to the first four contests and used to mark the game accordingly ever since. In a practical sense, the numbering system eliminated any future historical confusion created by the NFL season's overlap of two calendar years. Hence, the Baltimore Colts are simply Super Bowl V winners. They neatly sidestep the historically fuzzy reference as 1970–1971 NFL champions.

There was another, more significant effect of the use of Roman numerals. It forever lent mystique to the game. Pete Rozelle, the imaginative NFL commissioner, found a way to give a kind of global, weighty importance to the championship game. Clark Haptonstall, an associate professor of sports management at Rice University, may have summed it up best: "Rozelle felt by using Roman numerals it kind of gave that gladiator-type Roman feel. It was something that differentiated the Super Bowl from other sporting events."

Idolized strong men play the Super Bowl today in the grandest of coliseums before both average citizens and social elite. The object, territorial nomenclature and trappings of the game are analogous to conquest, a persistent theme in Roman society. The Super Bowl spectacle projects a modern American cultural empire whether celebrated or ridiculed.

However, in midsummer 1971, none of this far-flung symbolism mattered to a nine-year-old boy whose father was taking him to a Syracuse, New York, auto dealership to meet two big-time football players.

"Who are these guys again, Pop?" I asked from the passenger seat of the massive interior of our Chevy Impala. We were cruising on thirty-five-cents-a-gallon gas along Erie Boulevard, a commercial thoroughfare of strip centers, furniture and appliance dealers, and local family-style restaurants.

"Larry Csonka and Jim Kiick," my father replied. "You'll hear a lot about these guys this season."

I cradled a football given to me a few days earlier for my birthday and a magic marker. At a tender, single-digit age, my organized sports experience revolved mostly around playing Little League baseball. My small but growing bookshelf contained stories of the glory days of past

Yankee greats Ruth, DiMaggio, and Mantle. I devoured young-reader edition biographies of baseball players dead, retired, or beyond their prime. The Bronx Bombers' original dynasty largely predated my birth. Paperback tales of pinstriped ghosts solidified the Yankees as my original favorite team in any sport. The relative geographic proximity of New York City and the presence of the Yanks' primary minor league farm team in Syracuse deepened the connection.

However, the home-state Yankees I knew firsthand from television were a struggling group that included Bobby Murcer, Mel Stottlemeyer, Horace Clarke, and my hero in left field, Roy White. An updated cast of Bronx baseball legends was still a few years off. As a boy, I liked playing the game. However, just like the Yankees of the late sixties and early seventies, I struggled with baseball. I started to favor swinging junior golf clubs over taking misguided cuts with a twenty-eight ounce bat.

As far as watching the televised game, the leisurely pace of baseball on the small screen made me fidgety.

Before cable television, football broadcasts scarcely compared in number or complexity with today's constant barrage of live-game nights and replays over ESPN Classic or NFL Network. Regular-season games now spread over four days a week. In the early seventies, Monday Night Football was a still a curious anomaly some network executives doubted had legs. The few glimpses of pro football I got as a young viewer intrigued me. No single football team captured my imagination or loyalty. As a fan, I was far less familiar with the NFL than I was with major league baseball.

Unlike the regimented mentality in today's youth sports camps, kids were encouraged to informally experiment playing different games. Though I would never take up football on any organized level, I was a stocky kid. My father never pressured, but maybe he figured I might try the game out when he suggested a weekend outing to meet two rising NFL stars. The bulky Impala rolled towards the car dealership and the promotional autograph session. My curiosity increased as we drew closer.

"What team do they play for?" I inquired while the breeze whipped around the half-open car window and cut through the humid summer air.

"The Miami Dolphins," Pop answered.

"That's in Florida isn't it?"

"Yep."

"Florida sounds nice. That's where the moon rockets blast off, and it's always warm."

"Yeah, except it gets sticky-hot down there a lot, and there's no snow to play in, son."

Pop meant well but could be a wet blanket at times. He often saw the glass as half empty. I remained undeterred in my infatuation with the Sunshine State, though I had never actually visited.

"I saw in my *Weekly Reader* at school there's going to be a *gigantic* amusement park in Florida. It's like a hundred times bigger than Suburban Park. Bigger than the New York State Fair!"

Walt Disney World in Orlando opened later that year, concluding the largest construction project to date on the planet. Disney World sprawled over two hundred and sixty acres, a scale unimaginably grander than our neighborhood kiddy park or even The Great New York State Fair, a local tradition dating to 1890.

My father's civic pride kicked in. He reeled me back north.

"Well, Larry Csonka played right here in Syracuse, just over at the college, before he went off to Miami. That's why you're getting to meet him today."

Csonka racked up nearly three-thousand yards in three seasons as a Syracuse Orangeman fullback from 1965 to 1967, breaking school records held by Ernie Davis, Jim Nance, and Floyd Little. At Syracuse, Csonka statistically eclipsed perhaps the greatest back of all, Jim Brown. In a couple of weeks, Larry Csonka would report to the Dolphins for his fourth pro campaign in Miami. He was heading into to the first of three straight thousand-yard NFL rushing seasons and consecutive appearances in Super Bowls VI, VII, and VIII.

I was completely oblivious to Csonka's already firmly established local legend and promising future prospects.

"Well, he must be good if gets to play in Florida! He's good isn't he?" I asked.

Pop rolled his eyes and sighed. "He's real good, son. Anywhere he plays."

"What about the other guy, Kick? Did he play for Syracuse too? What a cool name for football! *Kick.*"

"No, but he's pretty good too. But you know that name? He spells it a little different with one more *I*. K-i-i-c-k." My father spread his index and forefinger and pointed them towards his eyes as he guided the Impala to a customer space in the dealer parking lot.

"How do you spell *Csonka*, Pop?" I was forming an erroneous mental image of athlete autographs. I envisioned the signatures would be decipherable handwriting examples of the kind practiced in grammar school drills.

4

"C-s-o-n-k-a."

"No!"

"Yes."

"With a *C* and an *S*?"

"That's what I said."

"Kah-ick and Ka-Son-Ka."

"No. Kiick and Csonka. *Zahon-ka.*" Pop was getting testy.

Sounds like my Tonka trucks!" I exclaimed as I bounded out of the car, a bundle of energy ready for my scheduled meeting with two of football's brightest stars.

"Son!" My father grasped my arm before I could sprint into the new-car showroom.

"What?"

"Settle down. Let's get your autographs and do *not* make fun of their names. You wouldn't like it if they made fun of your name would you?"

"No," I said sheepishly. Needless to say, *Fekete* inspired plenty of improvised schoolyard variations, circa grade three.

"Then you'll call them Mr. Csonka and Mr. Kiick unless they tell you different. Now let's go in there."

Zonk, as many Syracuse area fans knew him, attracted the most attention of the duo. When we swung open the big glass entry doors, I was a tad crestfallen. My first autograph signing would not be the intimate gathering I imagined. Based on the throng of fans in the showroom, the appearance generated the car dealer's desired result of weekend floor traffic.

Years later, I would orchestrate my own ready-made events to stimulate sponsor commerce by enlisting players, tickets, and any other conceivable resource available. I once recruited two Oakland Raiderette cheerleaders for an advertiser promoting a video arcade and laser-tag arena. I anticipated the cheerleaders would fulfill their appearance obligation signing photos and posing for pictures with customers. To the delight of the largely adolescent male clientele, the women also decided to suit up for several rounds of laser tag in the Gothic-inspired play space.

Where we these promotions when I was a kid, anyway?

Once in the showroom, my father and I worked our way around people, steel, and rubber until I could crane my neck up to see Larry Csonka.

"How ya doin' there, pal?" Larry grunted. He barely saw past the items thrust at him for signature as he multitasked away scribbling and greeting. He may have been thinking how much allocated time remained before he could wrap up the appearance. He could then cash his check and maybe visit a few old friends at the SU campus.

"I'm good," I said as I looked up at Csonka's bulldog-like head. He scrawled across the face of the football and returned it to me with his massive hand.

Both Csonka and Kiick were holding out from training camp. Each hoped to squeeze new contracts from Dolphin ownership, starting with the 1971 season. Eventually, both secured deals to pay them about sixty thousand a year for the next three years. In 1972, they would appear on the cover of *Sports Illustrated* as "Miami's Dynamic Duo."

"Thank you, Mr. Csonka," I said. As I began to draw back clutching my football, Larry pointed me towards his "side Kiick."

"Be sure to get that guy to sign too, kid. He's pretty good too. You can call him Jim. I'm still Mr. Csonka."

Larry smirked knowingly at his teammate.

Jim Kiick was no slouch as an NFL running back. He provided key blocking support for "Mr. Csonka." Kiick racked up important receiving and critical short-run yardage. Coach Don Shula used him sparingly but effectively to round out a run-intensive attack that included the cagey speedster Mercury Morris.

Kiick flashed me a warm smile and humbly reached out to shake my hand and add his signature on my football.

"Nice to meet you, sir, thanks," I said as Kiick nodded and quickly turned his attention to the next fan overflowing from Csonka's minions.

"Don't touch those signatures, son," Pop said as he gathered me up to leave. "I've got some lacquer spray at home that'll keep them from fading."

Having accomplished our mission, we left the showroom and started home.

"So you gonna watch the Dolphins on TV this year? See these guys run down there in Florida?" my father inquired.

"I think so." I answered.

Watch them I did. As an impressionable lad, meeting two Dolphins from an exotic far-off place cemented a lifelong, if somewhat irrational, interest in following the Miami Dolphins from Csonka and Griese through Marino, Taylor, and beyond. Then again, what is rational about sitting on the edge of your seat pleading for helmeted and padded men to advance or repel the movement of an oddly shaped ball over a chalk line?

My father knew my football team allegiances were malleable at this point. He enjoyed sizing up where my future rooting interests might reside even if his own did not run deep. He was much less interested in following a specific NFL team than he was about checking in with Arnold Palmer, Jack Nicklaus, or Gary Player on a Sunday afternoon.

"So, do you still like the Cowboys?" Pop said as the Impala climbed up to speed.

"I guess." I answered tentatively. My heart was not quite in the notion.

A few years earlier, a close kindergarten playmate who originally hailed from Dallas had told me about his Cowboys. What five-year-old boy does not like cowboys? I later learned the upcoming young quarterback in Dallas had been in the U.S. Navy like my uncle. When my mother escorted me to the local JC Penney's department store on a shopping trip for first-grade school clothes, the distinctive star logo on a Dallas Cowboys sweatshirt caught my eye. My father looked puzzled when my mother and I arrived home and I plucked the shirt out of the bag to show him.

"Why Dallas?" he had asked me.

"I dunno. My friend Brad likes them."

"But he's *from* Dallas," Pop pointed out. "And didn't Brad's family move away from here last year?"

"Yeah," I looked down wistfully at the shirt, realizing I missed my playmate. "I guess I kinda like the star," I said to my father, rationalizing what was not really a very rational decision.

"Oh, then Dallas is your team I guess," he replied, unconvinced.

I was free to like any team, but maybe my father was making a point. Someday I would make much more important decisions, like where to live and work or whom to marry. I probably would want to be able to justify these choices first to myself and perhaps to others as well.

There may have been no profound lesson at all. I cannot say I ever recalled my father sporting the logo of any team or rooting for any one franchise in particular. He was either not emotionally invested or simply favored fitting in by remaining outwardly neutral. I understood the latter better when I first wore the new shirt to school.

The Dallas Cowboys evoked both negative reactions and compliments among my classmates. The Cowboys were winners all right, but they were far from universally popular or loved.

I was slowly getting the impression that true fans did not establish rooting interests superficially. Moreover, there was something noble in sticking by your chosen team, particularly if they played in your community.

Syracuse sat in a bit of an NFL no-man's land, over two hours from the home of the thoroughly hapless and inferior AFL Buffalo Bills. Two hours south was New York City, the home of my Yankees, and an urban center I would not set foot in for several more years. To me, the Big Apple and the surface of the moon were equidistant through the window of television. I had only seen either place through the camera lens.

"I like Joe Namath," I announced to my father as we passed from the industrial outskirts of Syracuse into the suburban, tree-lined avenues towards home.

He was silent.

I gazed at the fresh ink laid down by Csonka and Kiick.

"Joe Namath won the Super Bowl for New York right?" I added, seeking confirmation that Broadway Joe was somewhat a local icon worthy of boyhood admiration.

"Humph. Well, one person does not win any football game by himself, son. It takes a whole team."

Joe Namath was not of my father's generation. In his mind, Namath was a mouthy, longhaired playboy. Actually, a goading heckler at the Miami Touchdown Club had prompted Joe's much-ballyhooed "guarantee" of a Super Bowl III victory. No one remembered or much cared about the initial provocation. Ultimately, the media characterized Namath's brash prediction as a call-out to the NFL old guard, announcing a new day dawning. My father was as old guard as they came.

Namath broke convention in countless ways. He wrapped himself in a fur coat and sunglasses on the Jet bench one winter Sunday. In a classic commercial that first aired during Super Bowl VII, Farrah Fawcett sensually stroked Joe's face with Noxzema shave cream. The New York quarterback pitched Hanes pantyhose by wearing them over his surgery-scarred knees. Madison Avenue drafted the quarterback as a male sex symbol to reflect changing mores and cultural standards. He inexplicably earned a place on Richard Nixon's famed "enemies list."

Broadway Joe originally had signed with the Jets for the princely sum of $427,000 over three years, less than half today's league minimum. Although paltry in comparison to today's multimillion-dollar contracts, Namath's salary was still fifteen to twenty times the mortgage on the average American home, an amount that I later realized was beyond my own parents' grasp.

"I think I like the Jets," I said to my father, affirming all-inclusive appreciation for the team and their space-age moniker.

"What about the Giants? They play in New York, too." Pop was holding out for a more traditional selection.

"Are they good?" I asked.

This business of picking a team to root for felt a bit like adopting a puppy. Would I choose to follow an eventual champion or would my team be an unwanted mutt that piddled in the bottom corner of the standings every season?

"The Giants used to be a great team. They aren't so much now. I like that Fran Tarkenton as quarterback, though. He might do something good."

"Fran sounds like a girl's name," I mused as I stared at the football's laces.

"I don't know, son. Namath looks like a girl with that long hair. He's got a bad knee that might not hold up too well."

About a month later, a mail order I placed with birthday gift money arrived at our house in a cardboard packing tube. I unrolled and tacked to my wall three NFL action-shot posters. The stoic Roger Staubach stood tall in the pocket with passing arm extended. Larry Csonka rumbled ahead like a tank through a hole of his own creation. Lastly, there was Joe Namath grasping the ball with both hands up to his green number twelve. He perched cat-like on toes seemingly suspended above a field upon which mere mortals tread. I prefer to remember him this way as opposed to how I mostly watched him. In the twilight of his playing days, Namath hobbled on those creaky knees, stumbling awkwardly off the stage at the end like Mays, Ali, Unitas, and even Jordan.

As the 1971–1972 campaign progressed, my new acquaintances, Csonka and Kiick, along with their Dolphin brethren, rolled up victories. Miami finished the regular season with a mark of 10–3–1.

On Christmas Day that season, the last spent in my boyhood home, Garo Yepremian wrapped up an epic victory with a thirty-seven yard, game-winning field goal, kicked squarely through the uprights. It may well have been my favorite gift that day, when Miami, playing on the road, took down the Kansas City Chiefs in a double overtime play-off thriller. The game was the longest in NFL history.

On January 16, 1972, Super Bowl VI became the first edition of the big game I followed intently as a young fan. Wearing my Cowboys shirt and holding the Csonka-Kiick autographed football, I did not much want either team to lose at all, let alone badly. I struggled with divided loyalties as Dallas dispensed with Miami in a lopsided 24–3 contest.

In a matter of months, events divided my loyalties again.

Outside forces closed in from beyond the walls of my cozy room covered with images of sports heroes, moon landing shots, and other assorted real and fictional youthful icons. Money became a scary word at the dinner table. Night after night, angry voices, whispers, and sobs slipped out down the hall behind my parents' closed door. Eventually, the door opened.

My mother sat me down one evening for a difficult conversation. There was not enough money in the bank to keep the house and not enough love in her heart to keep Pop, who by then had fallen into a depression. The only uncertainty about the departure from our bucolic enclave in Kings Grant Estates was the actual calendar date. My mother had worked odd jobs for some time hoping to stabilize the situation. It was not enough. My father had been distant and unable to hold lasting work for months.

Pop had also been notably absent from a summer trip my mother, my younger sister Julie, and I made to Philadelphia. The announced purpose of the visit was to see my mother's dear college friend from her Syracuse University days, a man introduced to me two years earlier as Uncle Bob. Bob Scarpato was not a blood relation, but he had been my godfather since birth. We coincidentally shared the same birthday.

Bob knew my mother was becoming more miserable in her marriage and played the role of cautious matchmaker. His brother Charlie, recently widowed, would eventually become my stepfather. During a weeklong journey in the late summer of 1972, my sister and I met Charlie's kids, our future stepsister Lynn, and a stepbrother also named Charlie.

I can mark with the Roman numerals *XX* the first time the six of us spent together around a television. Over those awkward final days of summer, our soon-to-be new family watched the Games of the Twentieth Olympiad. Long before Pete Rozelle appropriated ancient symbols to designate Super Bowls, the modern Olympic movement applied them. During the hours of coverage from Munich, we all took in our share of highlights while becoming acquainted with one another and with relatives in various locations around Philadelphia.

As we watched light welterweight Ray Seales chase gold, I learned that Charlie was a former Marine welterweight boxer. Lynn and Julie marveled at Russian gymnast, Olga Korbut's incredible back flip off the uneven bars.

"Has that been done before?" Jim McKay exclaimed on ABC with a tone and cadence I admired.

"Not by any human," his telecast partner answered.

Like other kids, I dreamt of making the winning play, but I conjured other images from collected LP records of various sports highlights. I listened to the thrilling announcer calls repeatedly and pictured the action in my minds eye in lieu of video. I fancied delivering immortal calls to electrified millions tuned in.

"Havelick stole the ball!"

"Down goes Frazier! Down goes Frazier!"

"There's a new home-run champion of all time, and it's Henry Aaron!"

Although the Olympics provided common ground to get to know my newly blended family, rarely had I ever felt so shy and eager to recoil into my own private space. Everything familiar was in turmoil. I was staring at an entirely new reality of a separated and recast family. It was a life being strangely, if superficially, approximated in prime time on the network series *The Brady Bunch*. I craved a nonfictional escape from a surreal setting.

The 1972 Summer Olympics provided an entertaining celebration of the human spirit. The constant event telecasts passed the time, helped to fill pregnant pauses with conversation, and made the whirlwind of introductions to the new extended family and friends tolerable. The Games offered temporary shelter from a storm of anguish and anxiety raging inside me.

On our last full day in Philadelphia, September 4, I stole away to an upstairs guest bedroom where a small black-and-white TV promised more Olympic glory and diversion. I could deny imminent and painful future events and my disintegrating world in New York State by immersing myself right here in the present. Then, the protective shell of the sports world cracked before my eyes as well.

My mother tapped gently on the guestroom door.

"Son, are you coming downstairs soon?"

"No. I don't want to right now," I answered sharply.

She nudged the door open and peered in. At other moments during our visit, I felt like crying in self-pity. As a surly ten-year-old, I withheld little displeasure from my mother over the family situation. This feeling was different. My tears welled for the plight of others.

"Something really bad is happening, Mom," I said with my stare fixed on the small screen resting on an antique brown dresser.

"Can we have this talk later, there are people downstairs …"

"I'm not talking about *that*," I snapped at her to head off a discussion of past, present, or future family matters.

"It's this," I added softly and pointed to the screen. The television camera zoomed in on a hooded figure peering from an upper-floor athlete dormitory. My mother edged slowly into the room, and I welcomed her presence.

The bliss of the Munich Games had evaporated. A mysterious group, called *Black September*, held Israeli team members at gunpoint. Jim McKay morphed from sports commentator to news anchor. The idealistic games gave way to stark reminders of hatred among peoples and nations. The political and social context of the televised images was beyond my limited grasp of global affairs and animosities. I was trying to extract a history lesson from the coverage. This was my first introduction to international terrorism. The captors were Palestinian Arabs seeking global attention and free passage to Cairo with Israeli hostages as human travel insurance.

I hoped my mother or Jim McKay might answer my most basic question, "Why?" Over sixteen hours, neither of them could explain adequately. McKay could only tell me the next day once we returned to our old house for the last time, "They're all gone."

A failed rescue attempt and bloody firefight at a West German NATO air base claimed the lives of eleven Israelis, five terrorists, and one German police officer.

Whether raised in the time of JFK, the Challenger disaster, or 9/11, children of the developed, modern world appear destined to have their innocence claimed by televised tragedy. Munich 1972 took my innocence and gave me the gift of perspective. The events on the other side of the globe made my own struggles appear insignificant.

I started fifth grade in the familiar, sheltered village of Manlius just outside Syracuse. I would later finish the school year in the comparatively harsh, alien culture of Greater Philadelphia. Over the next several weeks, boxes were packed and a foreclosure date set on my childhood home. I would be leaving my school and young friends behind. It had been months since I playfully harassed my six-year-old sister, as older brothers seem genetically predisposed to do. The situation tormented her enough without my teasing or poking. I did what I could to console her.

On a Sunday afternoon in mid-November, my father sat weeping in the stairwell of our home. At dusk, he went out for the evening to take temporary leave from a house divided. Nearly eight years passed before I would see him again.

That night, a yellow rental moving van, driven by my soon-to-be stepfather, rolled into the driveway. With the help of two relatives, he loaded up the vehicle with our possessions. I piled into the family car with my mom, my sister, and our golden retriever, Cammy. We followed the moving van's taillights south on the interstate through tears and scattered rain showers.

Years later, this experience would resonate painfully when I read an eerie account of the Baltimore Colts' controversial 1984 move to Indianapolis. Team owner Robert Irsay and Indianapolis Mayor William Hudnut arranged for a dozen Mayflower vans to carry equipment out of the Colts' office and training complex in Owing Mills, Maryland, under the cover of darkness, on a rainy night, to a new city and a new era.

Our small family arrived in Philadelphia, where a larger adopted clan immediately swept us up. Unfamiliar, expressive relatives, joined by remarriage, swirled around me. Some of the elders spoke Italian. They punctuated their speech with sweeping hand gestures. A few of them cursed the gridiron misfortunes of the hapless Eagles, or "Iggles" as the locals still say to this day.

When they greeted me, it was with vigorous hugs, sloppy kisses, or oscillating pinches on my cheek, often as prelude to a meal drenched in exotic sauces and spices. This extended family welcomed us, and to a degree, changed us. Their love and affection was no more or less sincere than the polite, reserved variety shown by my mother's much smaller family.

Adjustments became the order of the day. Our new family of six moved to a home in a working-class neighborhood just outside the Philadelphia city limits. There was more concrete and fewer trees compared to my former street. In our old house in upstate New York, my dog had thrived on a long chain run and enjoyed unleashed excursions with me into nearby woods. Now, she shared a narrow side yard with my stepfamily's less than amicable German shepherd.

The home and lifestyle were more modest, but we were not left wanting. My mother took up full-time work as a special education teacher. Charlie, who was now simply "Dad," was a skilled technician repairing and maintaining elevators in residential and commercial buildings across the region. His work took him anywhere people ascended and descended, from shiny corporate offices to hardscrabble slum projects. He sometimes worked in opulent and miserable settings in the same day.

Eventually, I put some psychological distance between my former semirural surroundings and an environment where everything seemed a bit more dirty and cramped but also more real and alive. With each day, I was becoming a bit more of a city kid.

For a time, I shared a converted attic bedroom space with my fourteen-year-old stepbrother, Charlie. As we got used to one another in close quarters in the winter of 1972, we shared a television. From there, I continued to follow the developing perfect season of the Miami Dolphins.

"Why do you like the Dolphins?" Charlie asked me as we watched Miami eliminate the cross-state Pittsburgh Steelers from the play-offs on New Year's Eve.

"I just do," I stammered. I was not up to explaining the weird comfort I took in Miami's unblemished record. They had not lost a game since the prior Super Bowl in January. To me, that Dolphin loss was quite literally a lifetime removed. Miami winning football games was the one thing in my mind that retained sweet continuity through a disruptive year. I had a different dad, different siblings, and different friends. I lived in a different city, attended a different school, and slept in a different room. However, I could still root for the same undefeated Miami Dolphins.

Charlie remained determined to get a better answer, even if getting to know me this way entailed getting under my skin.

"Is it just because they never lose that you like Miami?" he asked.

It was a legitimate question. He wondered if I was just riding a winner's bandwagon. This time I had a more reasoned answer than when Pop had asked me, "Why Dallas?"

"It's not because they never lose," I replied as I got up, flicked off the television set, and slumped back on the bed in my corner of the room.

"Everybody loses sometimes. Miami lost last year's Super Bowl, and I wasn't too happy about that."

"But it's *Miami* and you're from *New York.*" My stepbrother was not a rabid sports fan, but he took enough casual interest to be curious.

"Yeah, but we don't have pro football in Syracuse," I answered to be geographically precise. "But Larry Csonka and my mom both went to college there. I met him and Jim Kiick the summer before last. Here, check out my football."

I scrambled under the bed, pulled out the signed football still slick to the touch from Pop's autograph preserving lacquer job, and tossed it to Charlie.

"Cool. So you do really like them I guess." In Charlie's view, the ball legitimized my appreciation for the Dolphins. "Nobody's ever won this many games in one season. I guess I can root for them in the Super Bowl. Seventeen and zero, right?" he said, handing the ball back to me with appropriate care.

"Seventeen and zero," I repeated with an approving glance.

"Do you like the Eagles?" Charlie asked me.

"I don't know that much about them, really. Maybe I should, since they're the hometown team, right?" I replied, not yet ready to call the city of Philadelphia my own hometown.

Charlie laughed. "They suck. I can't even watch them."

That was my initiation to the brutally blunt, Philadelphia sports-fan mentality. Two weeks earlier, the Eagles' season had mercifully ended in another defeat, 24–23, against the equally unwatchable St. Louis Cardinals. The Eagles finished 2–11–1 for the year. They gave up well over twice the points they scored. When I first arrived in the City of Brotherly Love, Philadelphia as a sports town was a national joke. Adding to the football woes were the struggles of the Phillies. A colossal late-season collapse in the 1964 pennant race still dogged them. The 76ers were in the midst of setting a record for basketball futility by compiling a 9–73 season. The still unproven expansion, Flyers of the NHL, offered a little reason to hope.

Over the next decade, I would make fast friendships with neighborhood kids as we waved handmade signs in the streets following two Broad Street Bullies Stanley Cup wins. I would raucously revel in a college bar in October 1980 with the son of long-time Phillies broadcaster Andy Musser. Together we watched the Phils win their long-awaited first World Series title.

Three years later, I would again celebrate a Philly title in random yet glorious fashion. On May 31, 1983, immediately after work, I dropped into the nearest convenient watering hole on the city's outskirts. The Sixers, led by "Doctor J," Julius Erving, were already in the fourth quarter and on the verge of setting down the mighty Lakers four straight in the 1983 NBA Finals. I passed through the front door of a randomly available bar I had not set foot in before and have not returned to since.

Just as I was silently lamenting not having familiar company to watch the game, I spotted three former high school classmates at a table inside. Our unexpected reunion came during the final five minutes of play. Immediately after the Sixer victory, and seemingly against better judgment, we piled into my car and drove straight across City Line Avenue into the heart of solidly African-American West Philadelphia. Wilt Chamberlain had played high-school ball here. Without a care, we crossed over to wrong side of the tracks.

Never had I personally seen Philadelphia's persistent racial divisions so dramatically bridged. Our merry band of white kids from the other side of the county line rolled windows down and exchanged high fives with exuberant West Philly fans. We slowly moved down twenty blocks of Chestnut Street through a section of the city we generally avoided or dashed through with locked doors. For one celebratory night in May, color lines gave way to Sixermania.

While a Super Bowl title continued to elude the Eagles in those years, the Birds flew high. Vermeil, Jaworski, Bergey, and company advanced to the Big Game in 1981, but fell to the Oakland Raiders. However, the Eagles of the era produced a real life "Rocky" of sorts in the person of Vince Papale, a walk-on portrayed years later in the 2006 film *Invincible*. Former Eagles' Head Coach Dick Vermeil remains a Philadelphia icon, as evidenced by continuing regional endorsement deals unheard of even for active sitting coaches in other major markets.

Philadelphia fans retain a rough exterior and a sometimes deserved reputation for intolerance. They also remain a knowledgeable lot. They idolize athletes who play hard and leave everything on the field, court, and ice. For a generation, these fans were deprived a title. The city's championship heritage faded for a quarter century following the 1983 Sixers title. A legendary curse took root just as a development renaissance, spurred initially by the American bicentennial, transformed the Philly skyline. Prior to this building boom, Philadelphia City Hall stood as the tallest building in town at five-hundred and forty-eight feet, a number cited by baseball trivia buffs as equal to the career home run total of Phillies' Hall of Famer Mike Schmidt. A gentleman's agreement among politicians and developers had maintained a tradition that no structure could rise over the statue of the city's founder, William Penn. Penn symbolically watches over Philadelphia from atop City Hall, the largest municipal building in the United States.

In 1983, money trumped sentiment. Economic stimulus required building up and over the twenty-seven-ton bronze likeness of Penn. In that year, the development firm Rouse and Associates announced plans to build Liberty Place, the first of two gleaming new skyscrapers that eventually eclipsed the top of Penn's hat by some four hundred feet. The same company, reincarnated as a publicly traded entity, completed the slightly taller Comcast Center in 2007, overshadowing the city's founder, Penn, even further. Construction workers placed a four-inch replica of the Penn statue on the highest mast of the new tower in June of 2008 in deference to the *Curse of Billy Penn*. After twenty-five years without a major sports championship in Philadelphia, local fans suggested Penn was taking a form of retribution for being passed over by a rising skyline. Four months later, as this book was being prepared for press, the Philadelphia Phillies defeated the Tampa Bay Rays in the World Series in bizarre fashion. The Phils won a decisive rain delayed game five that took two days to complete and ended the title drought in the city founded by the forgiving William Penn.

California granted me a new set of sports-anchored memories. In

1989, I celebrated in the streets of San Francisco's North Beach after the 49ers' Super Bowl XXIII victory.

Years later when traveling in Germany and Poland, I discovered that the NBA conferred international recognition to California's capital city of Sacramento. The presence of one-time European basketball stars Vlade Divac, Peja Stojakovic, and Hedo Turkoglu on the Sacramento Kings roster registered with citizens living half way around the globe.

Such anecdotes delight professional sports executives as they build the case for civic investment in addition to fans buying tickets and sponsors investing in suites and signage. Politicians eager to please likely voters ally with team owners eager to secure public subsidy for highly profitable facilities' upgrades. The policies conceived by these bedfellows underscore the importance of fans engaging as citizens first through a dispassionate understanding of sport as business.

The same small-business owner who protests a sales-tax exemption designed to lure a big-box store to town may vigorously support a tax increase to help his or her beloved team construct a new stadium. The fans' emotional connections to their hometown teams are currency for those teams negotiating with elected leaders, particularly when the prospect of moving to another city looms.

A team with a solid history can mark the spot of its home community in bold relief on the mental atlas of outsiders. A championship title, or the absence of one, becomes part of local lore. Our sporting traditions influence the ways we associate with others and identify with ourselves. As teams and fans have become increasingly mobile over the years, it is fair to ask how, whether, and at what cost and benefit these traditions will continue to tug at our hearts and our provincial sense of what home is.

II. A Home Game is Never Far Away

"Howard has tickets to the Super Bowl," Mindy casually remarked as we sat down to a late evening January dinner. Long hours were standard for both of us. This particular Wednesday night was no exception.

It was eleven days before the Big Game.

Mindy had worked initially as a clerk in Howard Hoffman's successful law practice while completing her own legal studies. When she passed the California Bar Examination, Howard hired my wife as his sole associate attorney. He continued to mentor Mindy and give her progressively larger responsibilities.

Most of her work focused on disputes over individual brokerage accounts, pension plans, and retirement savings. The clients generally were defrauded and relatively unsophisticated small investors. The people who sought the firm's help were a diverse group. They could easily have been friends, neighbors, or coworkers.

Representing asset-starved clients of average-to-below-average means required Howard to take most cases on a contingency basis. He needed to be selective. Some lawyers make a living from an hourly rate. They profit from slowing the wheels of the legal process while the meter runs. Howard's paydays came in a different manner: by efficiently winning settlements before judges or arbitration panels. Some prospective clients knowingly took on investment risk. Their cases were harder to prove. Others were hapless victims who had been manipulated and exploited by unscrupulous advisors. Howard and Mindy sorted out potential cases both on the merits and on the magnitude of financial losses.

Similar to my own profession of radio advertising, Mindy's legal work involved lots of number crunching, high-touch personal service, and being able to read people. These skills would serve us both in the days to come.

"How did Howard get Super Bowl tickets?" I asked Mindy with more than a little curiosity.

"The *lottery*," she replied.

To a professional sports season ticket holder, the word *lottery* evokes more than visions of scratch-off tickets or buckets of bobbling ping-pong balls.

The Super Bowl lottery grants ticket purchase rights to a small number of the most loyal paying fans across every NFL market. The process effectively levels the playing field to allow access beyond exceptionally well-connected league officials, corporate sponsors, and the very wealthy who bid up prices of resale seats. Each of thirty-two NFL franchises controls an allocation of available Super Bowl seats. Teams conduct fan lotteries to distribute purchase rights to randomly selected season ticket holders. The franchises notify the fortunate by letter. Team management gives fans about two weeks to exercise their rights to buy a pair of Super Bowl tickets at face value.

Each of the two teams advancing to the Super Bowl receive about one-sixth of available game tickets. Another third of the seats are split equally among each of twenty-nine remaining teams. The home-market team in the Super Bowl's host city receives a larger share: five percent of the total. In 2008, the Arizona Cardinals franchise received this extra allocation.

Mindy was already familiar with the general concept of the Super Bowl lottery. Her father's seat number had come up a winner nearly thirty years earlier.

My father-in-law, Alan, is a San Francisco Bay Area resident and a long-time 49ers season ticket holder. He is the prototypical dedicated fan through thick and thin.

In the late sixties, San Francisco magnetically drew legions of restless youth to the Haight Ashbury district of the city. In an era of hippie flower children, paisley, LSD, civil rights rallies, and antiwar sit-ins, most autumn Sundays Alan sat on hard, wooden bleachers in the old Kezar Stadium. He suffered through multiple losing Niner campaigns. Kezar crowds were much sparser than those drawn to see Jefferson Airplane and the Grateful Dead perform in nearby open public stretches of Golden Gate Park.

After years of relative mediocrity, the 49er franchise was reborn under new head coach, Bill Walsh, and a kid fresh out of Notre Dame named Joe Montana. The Niners reached Super Bowl XVI in 1982. Alan received a coveted lottery letter. Face value for two tickets was eighty dollars. He jumped at the opportunity to go and immediately booked a flight to Detroit.

The NFL scheduled the game in the glistening new Silverdome in Pontiac, Michigan. Detroit city officials offered up free use of the stadium to the league in a successful bid to attract the game to a cold-weather locale.

Whenever conversation turns to the San Francisco 49ers at our family gatherings in Northern California, someone usually acknowledges Alan having been present for San Francisco's first of five Super Bowl victories. He has not been back to the Super Bowl, but my father-in-law will forever be able to say he made the Big Game. While lottery luck may not visit him again, Alan still maintains his pair of season seats. Every year, he sends various family members, including his daughter and me, to a San Francisco home game. He carefully presides over his own game selection process, taking into consideration individual schedules and preferences. Whenever the Philadelphia Eagles travel to the City by the Bay, he thoughtfully sets aside his seats for Mindy and his avid Eagles fan son-in-law.

In an endearing way, Mindy's boss Howard is similarly generous and a touch paternalistic. A large, imposing, yet soft-spoken man, he can bear down on a witness or opposing counsel like a lineman bull rushing a quarterback. He can also be a disarming teddy bear in whom one might feel comfortable confiding.

According to Mindy, Howard summoned both personas in court as needed to grill, coax, and cajole defendants.

At dinner that evening in January 2008, I took my turn to pursue a line of questioning with my wife.

"So Howard has *purchase rights* for tickets to the game?" I said as I leaned forward across the table.

"Yes."

"How?"

The match up between the New England Patriots and New York Giants had been set only three days earlier. New England posted the first ever 16–0 regular season in league history to earn a first-round bye. The Pats knocked off Jacksonville in the divisional round, and then they locked up the AFC crown at home against San Diego for an unprecedented eighteenth victory. Meanwhile, the Giants advanced in the NFC as a fifth-seeded wild card. They won three road games at Tampa Bay, Dallas, and finally a memorable battle at Lambeau Field in Green Bay.

Unaware of all the intricacies of the lottery process, I did not know how Mindy's boss won purchase rights, particularly since local northern California teams were not involved.

"I'm not exactly sure how it happened," Mindy said of Howard's good fortune. "I think his dad has Giants' season tickets. I just found out about the whole thing from Charlene this afternoon."

Howard's legal secretary Charlene, herself a devout Pittsburgh Steelers fan, monitored both football and office news. The two had suddenly converged.

Along with a cousin on the East Coast, Howard helped maintain his aged father's New York Giants season ticket account. His cousin wanted no part of flying to Phoenix from New Jersey to see what most media and fans expected would be the crowning of the New England Patriots as Super Bowl XLII champions.

"Well, I guess if I was much of a Giants' fan, I wouldn't be that eager to see the Patriots crush my team either," I said to Mindy between forkfuls of vegetables.

New England already ruined one particular Sunday for me three years earlier. They shattered the Super Bowl championship dreams of my Philadelphia Eagles.

In 2005, I had invited a small group of good friends over to our Sacramento home to watch Super Bowl XXXIX. I had taken myself out of Philadelphia over twenty years earlier, but Philly had not left me. My mother and sister still resided in Southeastern Pennsylvania in addition to several childhood friends. Now the Eagles were making their first Big Game appearance in twenty-four years and after three consecutive seasons of falling just shy with losses in the NFC championship game.

Throughout the 2004 campaign, my anticipation grew with each passing week, watching the Birds soar through the regular season, the play-offs, and conference championship. When they reached the Super Bowl, Mindy made a plan to order up a Philadelphia delicacy for our game day guests.

Before cheesesteak outposts began to pop up around the nation, few people outside of Southeastern Pennsylvania were familiar with this sandwich creation. A proper cheesesteak consists of provolone or Cheese Whiz slathered on an Amoroso roll and stuffed with thinly shaved grilled meat. The culinary invention of hot-dog vendors Pat and Harry Olivieri has become as synonymous with the city as the Liberty Bell and Rocky Balboa.

The Olivieri brothers first served cheesesteaks in 1933 on the corner of Ninth and Passyunk in South Philadelphia. The site recently acquired formal historical landmark status. I grew up with family ties just steps away from the famous intersection located at the foot of the open-air Italian Marketplace. A piece of old cobblestone from the original street, spared from the jackhammer during an asphalt-laying renovation, sits today on my brick fireplace ledge in Sacramento.

Celebrities routinely drop into Pat's King of Steaks or Geno's Steaks. The competing establishments face opposite one another along Passyunk Avenue.

John Madden has munched on Philly cheesesteaks from the Monday Night Football broadcast booth.

Presidential candidates make Ninth and Passyunk a must-stop on the campaign trail. Philly's cheesesteak emporiums serve as backdrop for photo ops and a recurring media circus act. Reporters record every nuance of candidate pilgrimages to the famed outdoor cheesesteak stands. Political consultants agonize about ensuring that their candidate clients tersely order a sandwich at the counter like the locals.

In 2004, Massachusetts Senator, and Democratic presidential nominee, John Kerry made a major faux pas. Kerry clumsily asked for a cheesesteak with *Swiss*. No true Philadelphian ever would bastardize a cheesesteak with a Swiss twist. The blunder made Kerry cannon fodder for local media, and gave Democratic precinct walkers indigestion. Who the hell was this guy trying to get votes in South Philly? How can he be president of the United States when he can't even order a freaking cheesesteak?

A few months later, Massachusetts governor Mitt Romney fired back and crossed party lines in defense of the maligned Kerry. Romney declined a cheesesteak offer from Pennsylvania's Ed Rendell in the traditional gubernatorial Super Bowl bet. He declared the sandwich had "no nutritional value."

Like others in many other parts of the country, an entrepreneur in the Sacramento region had cast dietary prudence aside and recently established a local cheesesteak shop. While Philly's cheesesteak legend grows, attempts to recreate it elsewhere expand with mixed success. As with most nonindigenous, cheesesteak joints, the Sacramento version strives and humorously overreaches for authenticity in both menu and décor. This particular cheesesteak restaurant opened its doors just in time for Super Bowl XXXIX in 2005. I had spotted the Cheesesteak Grille a few days before the big game. I concluded it was a worthy place to send Mindy on a pregame food run while I entertained our guests at home.

Inside the Cheesesteak Grille, a weathered aerial shot of the Eagles and Phillies former home, Veterans Stadium, graces one wall. The "Vet" exemplified awful seventies-era stadiums that were completely lacking in architectural character. With scant protest or sentiment in March 2004, a demolition team blew it to bits to make way for the vastly improved Lincoln Financial Field.

On the opposite wall, a smaller framed photo establishes a tenuous connection between Philly and Northern California. The shot shows former Eagle reserve fullback Josh Parry, a San Jose State graduate, lumbering down the sideline in Eagle white and Kelly green. Parry had scribbled above his indecipherable autograph, "Best cheesesteak West of Philly!" It matters little that Parry's Eagle career and NFL tenure were both short-lived. Parry played in an Eagle uniform as a West-Coast transplant from nearby Sonora, California. His seal of approval amused me. The actual sandwich off the grill impressed me as generally true to the original.

Before Mindy returned home with the game day steaks, my own pregame preparation for watching Super Bowl XXXIX included donning the replica jersey of my favorite active NFL player, Donovan McNabb. A random combination of athletic, personal, and irrational factors drew me to follow Number Five. McNabb has yet to earn a Super Bowl ring but he had earned my respect for off-the-field conduct. Few other players have dealt so well with absurd circumstances created by fans, media, and at least one spoiled superstar.

On NFL draft day in 1999, McNabb was a standout Syracuse graduate and promising pro prospect. Philadelphia selected him in the opening round. The catcalls and boos of Eagle fans were endlessly replayed on ESPN.

Immediately after his cool draft-day reception, I felt a weird empathy with McNabb. Such is the nature of the visceral bonds that fans forge with their sports idols. When my mother, sister, and I moved from Syracuse to Philadelphia, I was a ten-year-old, worried about acceptance by new step-siblings, friends, and schoolmates. Now McNabb was making the same journey from Syracuse to Philly with an inauspicious start.

Vitriolic calls from disgruntled fans flooded the phone lines of the city's sports-talk station, 610 WIP. Many of the Philadelphia faithful preferred another name on the draft board that day: Ricky Williams.

Both Williams and McNabb produced brilliant college numbers. However, drug suspensions later marred Williams's checkered NFL career. Prior to his most recent lengthy absence from the Miami Dolphins, he took an extended sabbatical to teach yoga in the laid-back Northern California foothill town of Nevada City. Meanwhile, the Eagles' draft pick compiled impressive stats and led his team to multiple play-off wins, division titles, conference championship appearances, and a Super Bowl.

Though underestimated before he took his first professional snap, McNabb let his play do the talking. He handled the tough local media and even tougher Philadelphia fans with grace. Sadly, at times there were subtle racial undercurrents in the criticism.

In 2003, those undercurrents surfaced and placed the Eagle QB squarely in the center of controversy. Early in the season, national radio host and newly minted *NFL Sunday Countdown* commentator Rush Limbaugh carelessly created a toxic mix of sports and social commentary. On September

28, he offered up an opinion on the ESPN program that McNabb was overrated because the national media had been "very desirous that a black quarterback do well."

When the story broke, it was *topic one* at my workplace. It had been right here in Sacramento where Rush Limbaugh had laid the groundwork for his national talk radio career fifteen years earlier. I routinely toured clients through our newsroom at KFBK and always noted the main studio where *The Rush Limbaugh Show* held court as a local program in Sacramento until 1988. Rush continues to both produce phenomenal ratings and food for my table. While Limbaugh's subject matter is largely conservative political commentary, he sometimes references his affinity for pro football during his broadcasts. He offers casual predictions and analysis to break up the more partisan content on his radio show. His love of the game, along with a radio audience of twenty million, helped Rush Limbaugh secure the ESPN job.

A number of my coworkers had worked with Limbaugh in his Sacramento days. Those still at KFBK who knew Rush regarded him fondly as an amicable and even shy person off the microphone. When the McNabb flap hit, some of the talk show host's former associates already knew I was an Eagles fan. The subject eventually reached the water cooler. When inevitably asked, I said I only hoped for McNabb's sake he would not match Rush's ill-advised comments with equally misguided words. It was an inconvenient and occasionally necessary part of my job to perform damage control with advertisers following a controversial remark by a radio host. I would have been far more flustered and annoyed defending the kind of counterattack McNabb could have easily launched in the wake of Rush's comments.

Much to my relief and pleasure, McNabb bit his lip and stuck to the high road. Unlike the way he laughed off the draft day boos of Philly fans, the quarterback was subdued and candid on this occasion. He also sounded genuinely hurt.

"It's somewhat shocking to hear that on national TV from him," McNabb said. "It's not something that I can sit here and say won't bother me." Even if he may have been seething inside, McNabb avoided a verbal escalation that probably disappointed the ratings-motivated media.

Four days after his divisive racial comments, Limbaugh resigned his ESPN post and apologized. He chose the National Association of Broadcasters' convention in Philadelphia as the forum in which to do it. Two years later, in 2005, McNabb was again thrown into someone else's public maelstrom. This time the figure was a teammate who, like Rush, had once passed through Northern California. Just as in the draft day and

Limbaugh controversies, McNabb played the straight man and quiet actor in an unfolding drama featuring the talented but brooding wide receiver Terrell Owens.

In 2004, Owens parted company with the San Francisco 49ers. He wore out his welcome on the West Coast by demanding the ball and criticizing teammates and coaches. Immediately after leaving the Niners, Owens not so subtly questioned San Francisco quarterback Jeff Garcia's sexual orientation in a *Playboy* magazine interview. Terrell Owens would become equally distracting as an Eagle.

After Owens's remarkable nine-catch day in the Eagles' narrow Super Bowl loss to the Patriots, the receiver expressed doubts over McNabb's game management and heart shown in the waning minutes of the close contest. Owens implied McNabb was soft. He later publicly speculated the Eagles might be better off if they had more of a warrior at quarterback like Brett Favre. McNabb steered clear of the mud slinging.

Another dustup created by Owens during his Eagles tenure involved his desire to dabble in a different sport during the off-season. In July 2005, Eagles owner Jeffrey Lurie had rejected Owens' request to play summer league basketball with a particular NBA franchise. Neither Lurie, nor Eagles president Joe Banner, wanted to risk another devastating injury such as the one that sidelined Owens for much of the 2004 season. Geoff Petrie, a former NBA star and now West-Coast-based team executive heard these concerns. As a result, Owens' flirtation with pro basketball ended abruptly.

The wide receiver would not spend his summer shooting hoops with the Sacramento Kings. Petrie, who oversees the Kings' basketball operations, ensured that sports fans in my current hometown would not endure a second "T.O." carnival sideshow involving Northern California. Now, thanks to the New York Giants knocking off top seed Dallas in the NFC, I would also not have to endure watching Owens play his primary sport in Super Bowl XLII.

"Charlene told me if Howard doesn't go to the Super Bowl, he probably won't buy the tickets," Mindy said. She pulled my attention back to the present hot sports topic with this shocking dinner table revelation.

"That would be criminal," I said in feigned horror at Mindy's words but not without a real cringe.

"Criminal," Mindy raised her eyebrows and chuckled. "I see."

Then she reminded me of the more serious considerations her employer needed to weigh.

"Howard is still getting over from that knee-replacement surgery. I don't think he wants the hassle of flying and getting around down there. You know. We've been to big events. It involves a lot of walking and crowds. He's just not that mobile yet."

It was true Howard had slowed down and struggled of late with health issues. The taxing knee-replacement surgery kept him working primarily from home during recovery. Flying to another city, negotiating baggage, airport security, game-day crowds, and stadium steps, even with disabled accommodations, would be daunting.

I quickly suppressed a fantasy. I was rising off the bench at a critical impasse to enter the game cold after the starter goes down. The vision appeared callous, opportunistic, and unrealistic. Was it? I could not help but briefly ponder the idea of Mindy and me buying the tickets and going to the game. The trip might have been a no-brainer if the 49ers or the Eagles were playing, if the cost were less steep, the timeline less frantic, or the general economic outlook less grim.

"Couldn't Howard just get the tickets and sell them?" I asked. "I'm sure this year he could get a thousand dollars a piece for them just like that!"

I unwittingly underestimated wildly fluctuating market values in a year when the New England Patriots were driving towards a historic, undefeated season. I would soon learn the impact of technology and the sheer magnitude of this game in the resale marketplace. At that moment, the average price paid on the secondary market through third-party brokers was running anywhere from four to ten times face value.

Face value established only a market floor, and the floor had escalated over the years. For Super Bowl XLII, face value, the price paid at the box office by fans selected in the lottery, had jumped to seven hundred dollars a ticket, a near twenty-fold increase in the twenty-six years since Mindy's father had attended Super Bowl XVI. If we were to go, last-minute travel and hotel bookings would certainly send the tab of such indulgence sky high.

I quietly ate for a while and rubbed the wooden edge of our glass-topped octagonal dining table. This well-worn piece of furniture was a hand-me-down from my former Air Force supervisor. It had survived five moves since my arrival in California in the mid-1980s. Neither Mindy nor I saw any need to replace it. Our combined earnings would easily have supported a new one long ago. A fancy table just did not seem important. We were more likely to entertain our eclectic group of friends with a backyard barbeque and beers than with white-linen dinner parties. On occasion, we would indulge in something extravagant, most likely a short vacation away from both work and our less than prestigious address.

In thirteen plus years of marriage, we had taken trips to Cancun, Belize, and Europe, enabled in part because our home remained a modest place. We both believed experiences consistently outperformed material possessions. We chose the less-tethered option of renting for several years before purchasing our first home in California's capital in 2001. When we first met with a mortgage broker, she glanced quizzically over our application.

"You know you really can afford a lot more home," she said.

Mindy shrugged at the broker's observation.

I simply answered with a question, "Why?"

We were buying a fourteen-hundred-square-foot, three-bed, two-bath home, situated minutes from downtown Sacramento. Just a couple of blocks to the west of the lot were the stately grounds of William Land Park with gloriously mature trees, a nine-hole golf course, and the Sacramento Zoo. Million-dollar homes ringed the park boundary. Running north to south along the eastern edge of William Land was Freeport Boulevard. The strip hummed with redevelopment, including new Asian and Latino-owned businesses, evidence of a global migration to this relatively affordable section of town.

Across Freeport Boulevard was Hollywood Park, a small transitional neighborhood, spanning a wide socioeconomic spectrum. Low-income, Section 8 apartments and student-occupied rental properties mingled with homes of working-class families, long-time senior residents, and young, first-time homeowners.

Planned in the Roaring Twenties and built on prime farmland as the Great Depression set in, Hollywood Park was originally at Sacramento's encroaching edge of growth. When we arrived, it had become a fully surrounded urban frontier, ripe for gentrification.

"Well, you have the income for a bigger place or a different location," the broker continued. Undoubtedly, she considered us candidates for one of the more upscale adjacent enclaves with an accompanying larger mortgage.

"But you still haven't answered why we should buy 'a lot more house,'" I said, repeating her suggestion.

Secretly, I loved playing this form of perceptual roulette with people. The broker may have been privately processing her own thoughts.

I do not get you two. One is a successful advertising sales representative with above-average earnings. The other is about to finish law school, already works full-time, and has great prospects for a new career. You are thirty-nine and thirty-two year old DINKS *(dual income no kids). Why aren't you shopping for homes just a couple blocks over and clear of any riffraff?*

We moved in to the little Hollywood Park house. For the first seven months, our next-door neighbors were a single mom and her two teenage boys. The boys could have lived up to the names *Riff* and *Raff*. The mom was an odd character.

"You watch out for me, and I'll watch out for you," the family matriarch said to me after I asked my new neighbor how she liked life on our block. It was a curious response only until her income stream became more apparent.

A county probation officer checked in routinely on one of the neighbor boys. Trucks, minivans, beat-up wrecks, and well-appointed late model sports cars routinely idled out front at the sidewalk for a few minutes during suspiciously brief visits. My city-honed radar picked up a telltale clue of the business operation. Just around the corner, a pair of tied-together old sneakers hung by the laces over phone wires above. This high-flying signal let would-be customers know a transaction point was close by. The family had turned their rented house next door to us into a retail branch office for a local drug ring.

Our neighbors were neither subtle criminals nor good tenants. In a matter of months, the property owner finally cleared the last hurdles in the arduous eviction process. Several months elapsed before needy patrons of the former storefront operation finally gave up on driving by the house.

Once that adventure passed, there was plenty of evidence of an improving lot for our little street and surrounding area. Within a couple of years, the tony publication, *Sacramento Magazine,* dubbed Hollywood Park as one of the top ten up-and-coming neighborhoods of the metro region.

Formerly vacant parcels now sprouted bright investment properties, while older homes received facelifts. Small, neatly kept yards of longtime homeowners fit alongside those of younger arrivals from the San Francisco Bay Area, Los Angeles, and beyond. Kids played in the street spontaneously and autonomously absent the rigid structure of leagues, clubs, and parent-organized activities that were pervasive in the outlying suburbs.

In Sacramento's centrally located neighborhoods, there are fewer physical demarcations between class and race, relative to what I knew growing up just outside Philadelphia. Entrenched, old, agricultural money mixes with newly affluent technology moguls spilling over from Silicon Valley. Migrants from expensive coastal regions find improved purchasing power. In local cafes, galleries, parks, and shops around the tree-covered downtown and midtown districts, high-powered legislative lobbyists blend with career civil servants, artists, homeless wanderers, and ever-increasing numbers of immigrants from Latin America and the Pacific Rim. Economic and social refugees from the former Eastern Bloc and Soviet Republics, human vestiges of the Cold War, also make their way to Sacramento, a place with a military legacy of its own.

The city was one of five American communities profiled in Ken Burns's PBS television documentary that chronicled life on the domestic front during World War II. Sacramento once hosted two large Air Force installations and an Army depot that have all since been converted to civilian uses. During the war years, over five hundred major-league baseball players, including Ted Williams and Bob Feller, along with another four thousand minor leaguers, served in the American military as draftees or volunteers. Some players were not in the service and remained stateside to play in a subdued, wartime edition of the game. Among them were members of the Sacramento Solons, Pacific Coast League pennant winners in 1942.

Six years after the war, the New York Yankees made their only visit to Sacramento. The 1951 Yankee-Solon exhibition game notably featured both the upstart center fielder Mickey Mantle and the pride of San Francisco, Joe DiMaggio, in the twilight of his career.

As a sports town, then as now, Sacramento lurked in the shadows of the San Francisco Bay Area some eighty miles to the west.

In fact, in most aspects, the capital city is but a modest moon in the galaxy that is the Golden State. The brilliant stars of San Francisco refinement, Silicon Valley innovation, Hollywood entertainment, and Napa wine and cuisine surround us. From the perspective of many Californians, Sacramento merely borrows and reflects their light. Our celebrity governor, Arnold Schwarzenegger, illuminates a distinguished, yet staid Capitol Building by day then commutes home by private jet to glamorous Brentwood.

Sacramento spreads across the intersection of two critical interstates and two life-giving major rivers. Many Californians associate Sacramento with little else but school field trips to gold rush and rail museums. Considered by some outsiders to be more town than city, Sacramento is both a former Pony Express stop and a modern day fuel stop. Travelers pass through and over the place, en route to the natural wonder of the Sierra Nevada and Lake Tahoe but they seldom linger. As a Sacramentan for over two decades, I have come to appreciate all that occupants of cars zipping past the city on Interstates 80 and 5 are passing up.

Throughout the nineties, despite growing nightlife, an awakening cultural scene, and a burgeoning economy, the big-town flavor of Sacramento still largely eluded the cosmopolitan tastes of San Francisco and Los

Angeles.

The community alternately endured and embraced comparisons to Midwestern cities like Chicago, or the more accurately scaled model of Kansas City, from where our NBA Kings were imported by way of Omaha, Cincinnati, and Rochester.

Los Angeles Lakers coach and master psychological warrior, Phil Jackson, taunted Sacramento with the label *cow town*. Fans answered the visiting coach in Arco Arena with deafening cowbells. However, it was Jackson and his team that got inside the heads of our local Kings when Sacramento challenged for the NBA throne in 2002.

Oakland Raiders owner Al Davis briefly flirted with the idea of moving the Silver and Black to Sactown in 1990. For all practical purposes, Davis used prospects of a move to the River City as a bargaining chip to extend and sweeten lease terms in Los Angeles.

When the Raiders eventually returned to Northern California, pricey tickets and the questionable expansion of Oakland Coliseum conspired to guarantee nearly all home games fell under the NFL television blackout rule. Sacramento sits just inside Oakland's one hundred mile blackout radius. This drove local Raider fans batty while greatly aiding my cause of selling ad time in unaffected Raider radio broadcasts.

Sitting on the west side of the Sacramento River is the home of the Oakland A's top minor-league affiliate. The Sacramento River Cats boast multiple league titles and a tradition of funneling great talent to the Oakland parent club. Former River Cats like Cy Young winner Barry Zito figured prominently into the strategy of noted A's general manager, Billy Beane. The book, *Moneyball,* details Beane's success on a tight budget.

Hot, minor-league prospects arrive in Sacramento. After these players excel here, the nearby A's call them up for a few years' service in the *bigs.* Just as these standout players become household names, Oakland management tends to export our former local stars to other major league teams with looser purse strings. The A's opt for youthful player development on the cheap. Instead of dumping large sums of cash into the free agent market, Oakland generally buys low and sells high.

Meanwhile in Sacramento, the River Cats have outpaced all other minor-league teams in ticket sales nationally for seven out of eight years, filling a lovely little ballpark built on a foundation capable of handling expansion. The stadium was constructed to accommodate additional sections and decks at some undetermined later date. The theoretical possibility of a future Raley Field retrofit, maybe to one day host a major-league team here, reflects forward regional vision. It is one more manifestation of Sacramento's quiet yearning for grown-up-city status. In the past, when this town has dared to dream aloud, our larger sibling cities in California have generally flashed patronizing smiles to remind us of our junior-varsity status. Those attitudes began to change as the high cost of dating prom queen coastal cities sent thousands of Bay Area and Southern California residents inland to Sacramento and other less exotic Central Valley communities.

With the start of the new millennium, Sacramento looked quite good as one of the most affordable, livable, housing markets in the state. Money began to stream through banks at low interest rates. Over the next few years, the cash flow into the capital city was as rapid and mighty as mountain snowmelt filling the American River in springtime.

Soon after we bought our home, values began to rise, and then rise more, and then skyrocket. Real estate became party talk. Then, everyone started to get a little cocky.

Publicly traded homebuilders, mortgage brokers running high-volume call centers, and local home-improvement contractors became my biggest radio advertising clients.

The commercial script was simple and compelling.

"Take advantage of historically low rates now. Use your home's equity to consolidate debt, add a room, or just take a vacation."

Low starting monthly payments hooked unqualified, first-time buyers in droves. Existing owners tapped their home equity like personal ATMs to take on new, seemingly cheap, lines of credit. Banks began to pool and collateralize debt obligations, package them up, and sell them off into newly expanded mortgage-bond markets. These under-regulated, new instruments left unclear who really owed what to whom. Sacramento was at the epicenter of these activities as evidenced later by foreclosure rates relative to the rest of the nation.

During 2005, a career advertising sales year, I started to gingerly question marketing directors, loan officers, mortgage brokers, and other long-time real estate people. How sustainable was this upward spiral? The answers ranged from cautious to downright cavalier.

"It's not like prices are going down," a fresh-faced sales agent in a model home office said as I did advance work to support yet another radio promotional appearance. I was helping to keep the host of our weekend real estate show quite busy at various new home developments.

"I guess." I answered the agent and sheepishly masked my serious doubts. Why argue with the enthusiastic employee of a paying advertiser?

At meetings with senior managers, developers, or ad agencies, I would allow myself to be more critical.

"The homes in the new community you're opening next month are starting in the low five hundred thousands," I would observe, spreading my demographic and ratings data across a conference table. "The median household income in this region is just over fifty thousand a year. Even with our news-talk listeners being considerably above that income level, it seems that overall, you might run into an affordability challenge with this particular product."

"We're doing a lot with creative financing," the media planner or division marketing director would typically assert.

"So who are you seeing as the most likely buyers for these homes?" I would ask with the hope of capturing larger shares of ad budgets to reach my relatively well-heeled established audience.

"Oh, lots of first-timers and young families!" came the reply.

"We're also seeing a broader ethnic mix: Hispanics, Asians, and African Americans."

I supposed that was fair enough. A Harvard University study, widely reported by *Time* magazine, cited the Sacramento region as one of the most ethnically diverse in the nation. First- and second-generation Latinos, Asians, and Pacific Islanders were commonplace. A large Slavic population was evident, particularly in the congregations of newly erected orthodox churches. Sacramento even boasted a *Russian Yellow Pages*. Eventually, the news media revealed how unscrupulous lenders heavily targeted minority communities.

Whether native or immigrant, young or old, I could not imagine how clerical workers, skilled and semi-skilled trades people, truck drivers, teachers, nurses, and small-business owners could afford to buy. Increasingly expensive tract, production homes sprung up like weeds across the region. From what I could see in the market research, income profiles, and lifestyle data, the numbers did not add up. Lenders, builders, and buyers chased and leveraged paper gains, bid up sale prices, and tapped anticipated future equity gains to spend money today.

In early 2007, telltale signs of the unraveling to come emerged as luxury-goods advertisers began dropping off the airwaves. One of my clients, a recreational-vehicle dealer sales manager, recognized the warning signs. His normally brisk spring sales plummeted. RVs are second homes and unlikely to sell well when consumer confidence wanes.

"The toys go first," he said as he gazed at banners and balloons strung over a sales lot filled with inventory and devoid of shoppers.

Some of my other successful clients quietly began to unload collectible cars, boats, and other nonessentials.

The growing crisis eventually would become national in scope, but the impact was more pronounced in California's midsection. Fed by in-state moves plus outside immigration, both legal and otherwise, Sacramento and the Central Valley's housing bubbles expanded faster than most and burst with uglier consequences. Foreclosure activity was rampant. Bank-owned, repossessed houses competed with residential builders' unsold inventory. Recently licensed real-estate agents, drawn by the boom, fled the bust just as rapidly.

January was generally a slow advertising month in any economy, but in 2008, local radio-market revenues in Sacramento saw double-digit, year-over-year declines. My commission checks shrunk. I was working much harder and longer hours, as were my associates, managers, and clients. My sales wheels were spinning hard. I started to think aloud and tossed out a half-baked idea to my wife as we cleared the dinner table.

"Maybe I could get the tickets and sell them for Howard," I said. "I could split the profits with him. Tie in an advertiser. Find someone in the company to pick them up. Anything would be better than just letting two Super Bowl tickets go to waste."

"I guess I could ask Howard about that tomorrow," Mindy responded. "I don't think he actually has the tickets right now. He just has a couple of days left to decide. I think he kind of put the whole thing off because of the knee surgery."

"Well, where are the tickets?"

"They're probably still in New York. I think somebody has to actually pick them up." That complicated matters considerably.

The tickets were sitting three thousand miles away in East Rutherford, New Jersey, at the Meadowlands box office. It was Wednesday evening. The Giants instructed lottery winners to exercise their purchase rights in person at the box office on either Friday or Saturday. Howard and his wife Kathy had let the notification letter sit for several days. They mulled, procrastinated, and attended to more pressing issues, including the daily challenges of running a household and raising two children. Kathy at one point considered flying to New York, but the idea lost steam with Howard's waning interest and temporary physical limitations.

As Mindy and I cleaned up in the kitchen, the *Sacramento Bee* lay open on the countertop, saturated with mortgage meltdown stories. The result of years of speculation in home prices, shaky adjustable-rate financing, and high-stakes shell games was now obvious to all. The exposure and destruction of wealth on paper was already affecting consumer and investor psychology, each of which were tied directly to our respective livelihoods.

The Super Bowl, no matter how or where my wife and I might experience it, would be a welcome diversion from a gathering economic storm.

III. Footloose

On Thursday morning, Mindy told Howard of my interest in finding a buyer for his tickets. He was open to alternatives other than passive forfeiture of the purchase rights. If he did nothing, the two seats could revert to another randomly selected fan, front-office executive, player's relative, key sponsor, or other Giant insider.

Marquee sporting event tickets are valuable currency. Super Bowl seats are the gold standard. In the right hands, and with some time to plan and shop around, tickets can be parlayed into gains beyond the scalper premium of several times face value. A pair of Super Bowl tickets can cement multimillion-dollar corporate relationships or help close the sale of a major contract. Such complex business deals generally involve layers of decision-makers. They can take weeks, months, or even years to develop and consummate.

By Thursday, I had half a business day to potentially broker tickets not even in my physical possession. In an economy turned sour, I had more pressing work priorities, scraping together modest ad contracts during the slow post-holiday season.

Certainly, I knew local business owners and advertising agency principals with a likely interest in the Super Bowl and the resources to attend, given the chance. I had sold local-affiliate radio advertising inside pro football and baseball broadcasts. I knew sports-fan clients with marketing budgets. However, it was highly unlikely anyone in my local network could take the tickets on such short notice, let alone make a related, major, marketing investment.

In another time and place, finding last minute mad money was easier.

Several years earlier at the height of the dot-com boom, broadcast advertising ties to Bay Area football helped me secure an initial hundred-thousand-dollar contract with the CEO of a Sacramento Internet-service provider. At the time, simple dial-up Internet access was still a cottage industry. Two years into our relationship that was built on regional football and golf tournament sponsorships, the CEO sold his firm for a cool twenty million to an out-of-town high bidder. His Web-service subscriber base eventually became part of the Internet colossus, EarthLink. His success story was similar to those of hundreds of other *dot-commers*, particularly in

Northern California.

The big telecoms, cable operators, and DSL providers eventually consolidated the consumer online service market by bundling phone, TV, and Web offerings. In the sixties and seventies, computer scientists engineered the World Wide Web for academic research and national defense. In the past decade, giant players like AT&T and Comcast have transformed a growing array of Web-enabled consumer information services into major corporate enterprises. In between these eras, tech-oriented entrepreneurs like billionaires Mark Cuban and Paul Allen bridged the gap between the white lab coats and the Wall Street suits. These men and others were midwives for the information technology business. They tended to be geeky young males with a yen for sports. Eventually both Cuban and Allen became professional sports franchise owners. Tech mavericks initially bought into the professional game in style as sponsors. They could use luxury suites to entertain potential investors and take expense write-offs against growing taxable profits.

It was only a matter of time and cash before, industry captains like Allen and Cuban simply bought entire teams and helped finance new stadiums.

The same nerds exiled by the jocks in high school had come back and bought the playground. Once there, these neophyte owners found validation and vindication in the front row, in the locker room, and in the team photo next to star athletes. They made headlines almost as often.

For every Apple, Amazon, eBay, Yahoo, and Google, scores of other tech companies started up and sputtered out. Some fell into acquiring hands. Others sold off to bigger players. Buyouts sometimes consisted of nothing more than transferring a memorable domain name.

Throughout Northern California in the late nineties, a number of local tech startups printed money with well-executed, sound ideas. Others blew venture capital on power trappings such as luxury office furniture and foosball tables. Fancy workspaces, fat paychecks, and stock options lured a twenty-something labor force of knowledge workers as candy draws children. For a time, venture capitalists served as the indiscriminate candy men.

In 1999, an underemployed writer friend of mine was pulling in a ten-thousand–dollar-a-month salary from a startup Web site. He spent a few hours a week composing *how to* articles ranging from the mundane to the titillating. The site where his work appeared survived on investment capital that was chasing the promise of a future advertising revenue stream. The site architects envisioned a massive self-help reference library on a wide range of curious subjects ranging from *How to attend an NFL away game* to *How to get rid of a hickey.*

As new Web sites popped up, well-funded Webmasters used traditional mass media to drive eyeballs to their content. As an advertising medium with quick production turnaround, radio benefited tremendously. A twenty-five-year-old techie recently anointed with a squishy title like Creator of Marketing Magic or Developer and Idea Chief would call a radio station in San Francisco on a Friday afternoon. Within an hour or two, a station sales representative would scoot over to one of the converted warehouse office spaces south of Market Street. Here, many poorly defined, dot-com operations found cheap rent in a hip district populated by creative types. The station ad rep would receive cash in advance to book a huge schedule of local radio commercials for launch the next Monday.

Venture capital money continued to test good and bad cyber concepts in the consumer marketplace in this frantic manner until dot-com dreams crashed hard. Many tech people with good business sense saw the implosion coming. Some dumped stock options built into their compensation packages before they became worthless paper. The young workforce came to refer to these devaluing assets as "sloptions." Other employees and investors stayed latched onto eventual winning enterprises and became young multimillionaires.

In 2000, seventeen different Web site advertisers shelled out at least two-million dollars each to buy one or more thirty-second spots in Super Bowl XXXIV. Seven, including the owners of Pets.com and Computers.com, were out of business within a year. Technology reporter Terry Lefton wrote in a January 1, 2001 CNN.com online report titled Web Firms: Super Bowl Ads Not A Super Idea, "more site visits could not mask unsound business fundamentals, however entertaining the ads."

By 2008, there were no "Creators of Marketing Magic" to seduce with Super Bowl tickets. I knew it would be impractical at best, tacky at worst, to propose a quid pro quo radio time buy to more traditional local advertisers, especially without travel or accommodations lined up.

There were other procedural complications. I could not assign an unknown proxy courier to pick up Howard's tickets on either my own or someone else's behalf. I needed to give Howard a specific name so he could properly transfer the purchase rights. Only that designated person could walk up to the window at Giants Stadium and secure the tickets as a legal owner.

Whom might I enlist and trust on short notice for this responsibility? I worked for the biggest radio company in the world. Clear Channel radio stations across the country were for all purposes a connected network of branch offices. If I had a valid business reason, I could tap someone in our New York division for the task. Even if I could not personally use the situation to entice an advertiser in my own backyard, perhaps someone else could. A radically altered organizational structure in the radio industry opened up such options.

Before it evolved into a more hierarchical, corporate-driven enterprise, the radio business operated through decentralized, local, sole proprietors and small partnerships under strict, federally imposed ownership limits. Quite simply, radio stations were largely mom-and-pop businesses.

The first station owner I worked for made a fortune in Southern California real estate. His dad had founded a major technology company that produced the first generation of handheld calculators. The radio station was a mere dalliance, a tax write-off within a larger portfolio of more successful holdings. For a time, the owner allowed an underachieving son with no appreciable broadcast experience to run the place. The son made impulsive and reckless decisions about everything from the songs played to personnel hired and fired. He micromanaged the station from a market-leading ratings position straight into oblivion.

During the eighties, many station owners, particularly those in small markets, barely kept the doors open. A broadcast tower and a microphone did not always attract sufficient advertising revenue to pay staff or even stay on the air twenty-four hours a day. Undersold airtime left operators with resources to advertise their other business interests cheaply or pursue shadier arrangements like unreported barter deals. Many a commercial spot paid for an owner's personal needs, ranging from home improvement to fine dining. Such informal arrangements were tamer remnants of a radio culture that gave rise to the payola scandals of the fifties. In those days, independent music agents dropped cash and drugs in the hands of radio program directors that were willing to spin a new record for the right price or right fix.

In the seventies, the rise of the FM stations opened up new broadcast licenses. Regional ownership strategies, pursued notably in Texas by Lowry Mays and others, led radio broadcasters and their bankers to get serious about cleaning up operations and sprucing up bottom lines. A single-owner licensee still could only operate a handful of stations before running up against federal limits.

The Clinton administration and Congress, responding to the broadcast industry lobby, dramatically loosened up ownership limits. The Telecommunications Act of 1996 allowed an individual owner to operate multiple frequencies within a single city and across the country. Up to this time, the law limited any single entity to owning no more than one AM and one FM station in any given media market.

The new law opened the floodgates for local and regional owners to sell their licenses. High bidders seeking a national footprint to better influence large advertisers scooped up dozens then hundreds of stations.

Passage of the telecom act effectively put over ten thousand commercially licensed radio stations in play to be bought, sold, or swapped. Transactions spun like an out-of-control turntable through a series of progressively more active trades and buyouts. Radio companies grew larger collections of stations under common group ownership. Stations in the same city that once fiercely competed for listeners and ad revenue came under common ownership. Market share was split under fewer and bigger corporate umbrellas as fast as consolidating deals could happen. The act capped total market share that any given broadcaster could control in any city. While the Federal Communications Commission still monitored allocation of broadcast frequencies, the Department of Justice now managed a complex new set of antitrust guidelines.

Ownership of the two news-talk stations where I worked in Sacramento changed hands three times in five years between 1996 and 2001.

By the turn of the twenty-first century, new radio conglomerates like Clear Channel, Infinity, Entercom, Beasley, and Emmis, to name a few, had transformed the mom-and-pop model of radio ownership. These firms and others ran stations around the U.S. in local operating divisions consisting of three, five, ten, or more radio properties. These station clusters reported to a higher corporate office that in turn reported to shareholders who had earnings expectations. Big lenders eagerly financed the merger and acquisition activity.

In just a few short years, the decentralized industry of local radio began to resemble similar structures already prevalent in film, recording, and newspaper industries. In those media businesses, a few dominant studios, record labels, or publishers account for most of the marketplace.

In time, my job changed with the industry. I was not only selling local advertising contracts in Sacramento, but exporting revenue to stations in San Francisco, San Diego, Las Vegas, Honolulu, Boston, and New York, albeit for lower average commissions.

By January 2008, the new landscape of the radio business meant I could possibly insert a pair of Super Bowl tickets into a significant regional or national advertising deal with one phone call. Early Thursday morning, I left a voice message and an e-mail—three levels up my company's organizational chart—for our local market manager. With a little more time and a chance to focus, I might have called our Boston, New York, and Phoenix stations on my own. Instead, early Thursday afternoon, I reached Jeff Holden, who oversaw operations for all four of our Sacramento radio properties.

I initially worked for Jeff eighteen years earlier in what could best be described as my first serious radio employment with a significant station: a contemporary jazz and New Age format. We had both arrived in Sacramento around the same time in the late eighties. The broadcasting business then bore little resemblance to today's deregulated, highly consolidated industry.

When Jeff picked up, I was reasonably certain he had no immediate, hot prospects for the tickets.

"I don't think we can get any traction to turn a piece of business with tickets this late," he said.

"A couple grand hard costs to buy them, you would think someone could use it to help close something big on short notice," I replied. Certainly, somewhere in the vast company, a pending advertising contract in another market could justify the ticket purchase price and a small premium. I already knew intuitively that if we really could not justify such a deal locally, any out of market possibilities would have to be extremely obvious.

"I didn't get any Super Bowl ticket requests from local clients this year," Jeff informed me. "There's probably less interest with no California teams in it this time around. I don't know about Boston or New York. Those market managers are already pretty wired into their own requests. We've got other things to deal with here."

He was right. The local value of tickets would have soared with the Niners, Raiders, or even another West Coast team in the game. As to other markets, we could not afford to bother. With ad revenues in Sacramento tanking, our priority was capturing deals and dollars close to home.

"Yeah, I guess I'm not surprised. I figured I'd call just to see if someone was on the fence," I sighed.

Actually, I was the one on the fence. I was not particularly disappointed with the lack of an immediate business application for the tickets. I was feeling burdened by a decision now solely my own.

My boss may have sensed that indecision, too.

"Thanks for letting me know anyway," he replied. "You never know what might be out there as far as someone looking to get tickets."

From the earlier message I left, he knew about my quirky circumstance and the brief window of opportunity to access Super Bowl tickets. He could relate to it. Almost a year ago to the day, in 2007, after his hometown Chicago Bears won the NFC title, Jeff Holden was making his own arrangements for the Big Game. He took his father to Super Bowl XLI in Miami. My call turned from business to personal, just where I thought it might end up anyway.

"What was it like?" I asked Jeff.

"It was pretty amazing. Everyone who can get to see a Super Bowl really ought to do it. It's a once-in-a-lifetime deal."

That was what I was waiting to hear. As an executive, Holden was in an immediate position to confirm that the opportunity was nontransferable. As a fellow fan, he confirmed I should not let the opportunity slip away.

When I ended the call, I felt no motivation or entitlement to broker Howard's tickets outside my own company. The options narrowed. Do nothing or go to the game with Mindy. My mind raced, and I started to conjure up excuses.

The whole thing was too complicated. The time, effort, and expense would be considerable. Who would actually pick up the tickets? Howard undoubtedly had gone through some of the same considerations when he got the notification letter from the New York Football Giants.

It was a few minutes past one o'clock in the afternoon. The next morning, Giant's season ticket holders or newly assigned purchase-rights holders would line up at the Meadowlands. I had to figure out very soon—today—whether and how to exercise my option. Would I watch future Super Bowls and invariably recall this moment when I had the chance to be there but let it go?

My Blackberry vibrated in my suit pocket like a restless bullfrog. It was my wife calling from Howard's office.

I wrestled with a familiar great weight. In times of high stress, it dropped into the stream of my subconscious like a fallen petrified tree slowing and jamming free flowing current. At the trunk of this inert mass, the deep-seated roots of hesitation, fear, and indecision could paralyze me and block my progress at best or drag me underwater by the feet at worst.

Time was running out.

A bird-like tweeting replaced the initial croaky buzz of the phone.

I needed to cast aside the doubts in my head and think on my feet. My head would hold me back. My feet would carry me forward. I knew the pull of these opposing forces well. I needed my feet to triumph over my head and take me where my heart wanted to go.

I wondered if my feet were up to the task.

In sports, footwear can be your best friend or your worst

nightmare.

For example, if you are somehow possessed with the idea of strapping two long, narrow strips of fiberglass-coated wood onto your feet and careen down a slippery snow-covered mountain, you quickly discover that comfortable boots matter.

I had learned this years earlier on the second day I spent skiing on a late January morning in a spectacular setting over the largest alpine lake in North America. My feet screamed for a change of scenery from inside my ill-fitting rental boots. At Heavenly Lake Tahoe ski resort, I looked down the gentle beginner's slope called Maggie's run. I was oblivious to the smiling faces effortlessly gliding past me. The more experienced skiers— nearly everyone else—massaged the machine-made grooves in the packed powder. They cut crisply. They traversed gracefully. They floated across powder-dusted ancient contours of granite among majestic white fir, cedar, and Jeffrey pine.

The most energy I could muster inside the mid-mountain café was just enough to lift a plastic tray and the remains of lunch off a snack bar table. The simplest tasks weighed heavily. I rose up from a molded plastic chair built more for quick pit stops than for extended lounging. The unfamiliar boots clamped down on my toes as they had all morning through multiple low-speed falls, weaves, and stumbles.

I had long ago made a casual vow not to bother with skiing. After a random string of events, I was taking the sport up as an adult. Now, I felt ready to quit for the day, perhaps for good. All I could think about was waddling back to retrieve my street shoes in the main lodge. There I could remove these shackles from my painful and inflamed feet.

My girlfriend Mindy, sat across from me at the snack bar table. She eyed me sympathetically.

"Are you sure you don't want to go back?" she said as she gathered her gloves, goggles, and cap from the table. "I already did some good runs this morning. I don't mind going down the easy stuff with you the rest of the afternoon."

"I'm done." I said. "Have a good time. You should. I'll go back down to the locker to change and hang out at the base lodge. Just meet me there when you come off the mountain."

We had been dating for a couple of years now and would eventually marry. Mindy had grown up on the West Coast. She had taken numerous family ski trips to Lake Tahoe. She held low expectations this morning for my progression as a starting skier. I wished I were enjoying the experience more. Mindy and I enjoyed many pursuits together, but I was beginning to believe skiing was not going to be one of them after this day.

A few weeks earlier, I had landed an advertising contract with Mount Rose ski resort near Reno. Nancy Jesch, the mountain's marketing director, graciously offered me a complementary learn-to-ski package. I begged off at first. She gently persisted after I mentioned my girlfriend was a skier. I waffled and tried unsuccessfully to change the subject back to commercial scripts and the ad campaign.

Old fears subconsciously surfaced.

Nancy was a young mom with plans to take her toddler out to learn. She suggested there was no harm in my trying out the sport under the guidance of a trained instructor. She could arrange it all for me at no cost. If her three-year-old could get on skis, what was stopping me, a grown adult, from giving it a shot?

She told me if I accepted, the beginner bunny slope would be neither steep nor imposing. I was a goner when Nancy said she would give Mindy a complementary lift ticket to boot. Sale made. In the worst-case scenario, I would accept a nice client gesture, confirm my own ski phobia, and impress Mindy with my inside track to score at least one free day on the slopes.

I generally had a healthy relationship with snow, although up to that point it had not involved skiing. During crisp winter days as a grade-school kid in upstate New York, I noticed colorful ski-resort patches sewn on the down jackets and fuzzy parkas of my schoolmates. The patches read *Stowe, Lake Placid, Sugarloaf, Killington.* They were northeastern ski destinations where families would trek in faux-wood-paneled station wagons. Ski-patch covered jackets suggested traveler credentials like a passport filled with the stamps of many nations. Instead of border guards, lift attendants patrolled entry points to these skier nation-states.

Winter ski playgrounds were mysterious places to me. I heard secondhand tales involving straps, goggles, boots, and other gear resembling the pictures I had seen on television of the space suits the astronauts wore during the moon landing.

The resort patches were not the only visible tip-offs of ski-tripping kids. Every winter, I saw fellow school bus riders sporting freshly wrapped casts around bruised and broken limbs. I sometimes accepted invitations to practice my developing penmanship skill on these plaster sleeves. It was like signing some star-crossed yearbook. The casts and crutches quelled my desire to hitch a ride to the slopes with friends and their parents. On a good day, ski terrain in the eastern U.S. can be an unforgiving battlefield of thin cover, ice, and exposed rock.

Our own family trips to the nearby Adirondack Mountains unfolded in seasons other than winter. We spent lazy summer days on the shores of Saranac and Tupper lakes. If we were lucky enough to time an autumn drive on just the right weekend, our view through the windshield filled with the crimson and golden zenith of fall color.

Then came winter, and the studded tires went on the car. Driving turned into an unpleasant chore all around the greater Syracuse area.

My father was not about to drive to the mountains in winter. Even at my tender age, I could hardly blame him.

"Why would you want to be stuck in the car for a couple of hours, son?" Pop would say at the slightest hint of a winter ski trip. "Skiing is expensive. It takes forever to get there. There's plenty of snow to play in right out our front door!"

Then he would grin. "Hey, I've got an idea. Here's a dollar. Take this shovel and go move the snow out of the driveway. You can build a snow fort in the front yard. Go on now. Get some exercise."

Clever job assignments aside, it was true that snow forts, snowmen, snowballs, and zippy downhill sled rides were mere boot steps away. It was big stuff for a five- or six-year-old. I spent the winters of my early youth content to barrel down nearby hills or on gently sloping, snowy residential streets astride my trusty, red Flexible Flyer sled.

Weather systems passing over nearby Onondaga Lake sucked cool moisture from the water's surface and poured it back down as snow across the entire region. We measured accumulations in inches, then in feet, then in school days off.

On many early winter mornings over Froot Loops cereal and orange juice, I lingered in the kitchen and listened to a thunderous voice of authority over the AM transistor radio. I waited to hear the number *452*. That was my elementary school's snow-day closing code. The omnipotent man in the radio read a whole series of numbers corresponding to local schools.

When I was very young, I was convinced the man in the radio held sole discretion to declare my math and spelling lessons postponed for a day of snow play. I fancied being the man in the radio and wielding his awesome power.

Before bedtime, after snow-days brought snow play, my mom and I would sometimes sit in a living room bay window nook and watch the white stuff fall. From that cozy perch, we looked out into the darkness across our front yard, situated at the bottom of a hill on the lightly traveled King Road.

The busier Seneca Turnpike ran parallel to our quiet street. A narrow, rocky ditch separated the two thoroughfares. The turnpike moniker seemed to overstate the significance of this relatively minor two-lane road. My parents took to emphasizing "turnpike" to my younger sister and me as we grew out of diapers and into training wheels. Over time, earlier references to the "big road" lost significance as this paved strip shrunk in our eyes. We respected the traffic flow, particularly since we once lost a young house cat that scampered out onto the large asphalt ribbon. Few things make parents more skittish than an unattended child near a roadside.

On snowy winter nights, cars infrequently emerged from the turnpike hilltop behind a stand of trees visible from our bay window. Vehicles would cruise down the hill at a thirty-to forty-miles-per-hour clip or faster. If you did not know the road, it was easy to misjudge the downward-sloping dip immediately beyond a blind corner at the hilltop. Drivers could easily enter the descent just a bit too swiftly. Rain or snow complicated driving factors in this tricky spot. Traction could get iffy.

One evening when my mother and I were in our bay window nest, we looked out as a fierce winter storm blew and dumped piles of snow. The big plows and salt trucks had already been out in full force, but nature was having its way. Nothing other than a plow had much business to be on the roads in this weather.

As we gazed out at the growing white blanket and blowing drifts, a lone pair of headlights crested the peak of Seneca Turnpike, splitting the darkness. Suddenly the beams angled sideways towards the ditch as the car entered a slide.

The next five seconds passed in slow motion. The car buckled and skidded as the unseen driver fought gravity, ice, and hydroplaning tires. He or she was barely hanging onto control of the vehicle spinning and sliding sideways down the grade.

Slush and ice spit violently from the wheel wells. Corrective steering first drew the vehicle back on a straight line out of danger. Then the car edged back closer to the ditch. Perhaps the driver was wearing a seat belt. Such precautions were anything but customary, let alone legally enforced at the time.

When I was in the family car before child safety seats were common, my mother would sometimes instinctively reach her arm across to my passenger side seat if she needed to slow suddenly. Reason suggested this was an utterly futile attempt to protect me if we ever had the misfortune of a collision. Her reaction taught me the occasional rule of instinct over reason.

On this occasion, from the broken serenity of a safe and stationary place, my mother and I were merely helpless witnesses to a stranger's potential disaster in the making.

Our wide-eyed stares were frozen in the bay window glass and directed towards the fishtailing car fighting to stay on the turnpike. It weaved and wobbled over the center line into the opposing lane. Fortunately, there was no oncoming traffic. The driver's side front and rear wheels scraped along the upper portion of the ditch like an off-balance wide receiver tight roping the sideline desperately trying to stay in bounds.

We heard loose rocks bouncing off the car's undercarriage as it ground along the ditch's edge for perhaps twenty more yards before miraculously pulling back up onto the highway and continuing into the night.

The motorist was either incredibly lucky, a talented driver, or a bit of both. I would rather not think alcohol was involved, especially under those weather conditions, but anything was possible. In any event, the memory of the dangerous combination of snow, the hill's severe pitch, and bodies in motion remained impressed upon me, and perhaps even kept me off skis.

By my teens, our family had moved farther south to Philadelphia, where infrequent snow melted quickly and did not play heavily into local youth culture. The closest I got to winter sports was hockey played on the street. It was even easier now to swear off skiing as inaccessible, pricy, and somehow more hazardous than a flying hard rubber puck or street-hockey ball. At that time, I could hardly have conceived of becoming acquainted with ski slopes years later after moving to sunny California.

In 1992, my introductory lesson at Mount Rose worked out better than expected. The instructor was a blissfully nomadic fellow who spent winters at Lake Tahoe and summers in Australia giving surf lessons. He moved me and three or four other first-timers through the basics, starting with the hand-eye-butt coordination required for getting on a moving lift chair. With that trick somewhat mastered, we worked up to easy turns on beginner runs.

Muscle memory and balance skills imprinted from swinging a golf club and school years spent tossing a shot put and discus kicked in. The sense of equilibrium acquired in those sports seemed to help me. Heavy snow fell throughout the beginning lesson. The snowfall cut visibility just enough to compel our group to learn more from the feel of the powder below our feet. Skiers generally prefer clear days, but I was none the wiser. As far as I knew, skiing and falling snow were natural companions to the sport.

Later, I realized learning under less than ideal conditions came with some benefit. Falling snow does not bother me nearly as much as some skiers who end their day at the first sign of flurries. Perhaps the general principle applies to other sports. Maybe kids who play on sandlots and torn-up asphalt courts develop resilience to adversity better than peers who frolic on manicured fields and gleaming hardwood.

Under the instructor's watchful eye, I caught on quickly as a thirty-year-old beginner. He saw enough raw ability to suggest a promising future as a recreational skier. I felt good.

A few weeks passed before I reached day two on skis. Unlike my first outing at Mount Rose, at Heavenly I had no instructor present. It showed in my performance.

After lunch at mid-mountain, I was quite ready to cut the day short. I almost did, until I realized Mindy still had the locker key. With no cell phone or walkie-talkie to reach her and recover the key, I would have no access to my soft street shoes for three more hours unless I could catch her right now. She was well up the long flight of stairs leading from the snack bar back to the ski runs.

I cursed my absent-minded lapse and managed an awkward ascent clanking my boots up the metal staircase to the café exit as fast as I could. When I arrived at the doorway, the sun reflected brilliantly off the crystalline snow pack.

Every ligament, tendon, and joint from my thighs to my toes ached. I scanned the long lines of steel racks temporarily housing the equipment of lunching skiers. Then I spotted my girlfriend and future wife about a hundred feet away clicking her boots into her ski bindings and leaning forward to depart.

"Mindy!" I yelled across a crowded deck leading to the slopes.

She turned her head back. I waved her down and trudged over.

"Are you going back out?" she asked hopefully.

My goal had been only to get the locker key, but now the swooshing chorus of skis on snow filled the air again. I knew if I rejoined Mindy now I might only be putting more pressure on myself to finish the day. I really wanted her to have a nice time free from my own waning interest and physical pain.

"I don't think so. I just remembered you have the locker key." I said as I labored to suck in oxygen at high-altitude.

"Oh, right!" She slipped a hand into her jacket pocket and withdrew the little piece of metal separating me from my Adidas in the locker at the base lodge. I felt certain once these boots were off my feet, I would never set foot in such contraptions again. Now, as I breathed the pure mountain air, I was not as sure.

"Let's just stick with the plan to meet at the bottom around four o'clock," I said so as not to commit myself to more punishment.

"OK."

She smiled, kissed me, then set her poles and launched into the realm of happy skiers taking in the beautiful afternoon.

I watched her steadily descend the hill and smoothly round a corner out of sight. I looked down at the locker key in my hand. I looked back out again at the slopes, feeling torn. Climbing the stairs and tromping out to intercept Mindy had gotten the blood circulating in my feet and set my heart racing. It also shifted my attention away from the creature comforts of the café squarely back to the wild mountain and long ribbons of steel-cabled lifts carrying passengers skyward.

Equestrians, when thrown from a horse, insist on getting back in the saddle immediately to overcome fear. All morning long, my rental skis had thrown me repeatedly to my knees and backside. They now sat crossed, leaning upright in the rack mocking me like a mare tied to a hitching post.

I was annoyed with myself for being ready to quit. The key in my hand sang me a different tune. "*I am your escape. Take me with you to the lodge. I'll get you to those warm, comfortable shoes.*"

The rental skis snorted back, "*Whatever, dude. Make up your mind. Ride us or take us back so we can get waxed, tuned, and ready for the next victim.*"

"Damn it!" I spit out through gritted teeth and slapped a glove on the ski rack.

I remembered similar outbursts as a child when I learned the devilishly difficult game of golf. After hitting a range ball square, true, and long, I concluded I had the whole business down pat. Then, I would scuff the next shot into the ground. My father, a top amateur player and club champion in New York State, first put a toy driver in my hands when I was three-years-old. When we played or practiced together, he would sometimes shake his head while watching me battle the ball. Sometimes he would instruct and other times he would ignore me and go about taking his own shot.

On occasion, he would roll his eyes and exclaim, "You're looking at the TV cameras again, son!"

That was his euphemism for taking my eye off the ball during the swing and bringing my head up just before impact. He had a theory. He was probably right. Some kids dreamed of blasting a baseball over the fence during the World Series. I fancied stiffing a three wood to within five feet to win the Masters. I had yet to attend a pro-golf event in person. The childhood fantasy was television induced.

The dominating presence of Tiger Woods elevates and expands the appeal of golf today. When I was growing up, pros like Arnold Palmer and Lee Trevino did the same for the game but with a decidedly different style. Woods' stern, almost hypnotic countenance contrasts with the magnetic personality of Palmer, the jocular Trevino, and later, the carefree, hard-charging John Daly, and chummy Phil Mickelson. Over time, more golfers became performers and personalities as the camera picked up every gesture and grimace.

My father came of age in the largely pre-televised dark ages of Sam Snead and Ben Hogan. He cared little if Palmer's demeanor lifted viewer ratings. At the end of day, substance trumped style. Playing to the television cameras did not make Palmer great. His scorecard result did. How many people watched you or loved you was irrelevant.

For many ordinary people and even extraordinary athletes, good things do not come from being hyperconscious of spectators and camera crews. For evidence, look no farther than to young Lindsay Jacobellis, the American snowboard rider who tossed away a big lead and certain Olympic gold at Torino in 2006. An unnecessary airborne showboat move over a final jump caused her to fall and tumble to silver.

Although we were in Tahoe, not Torino, it was best for me that Mindy was on another part of the mountain. Her eyes may as well have been television cameras. They made me self-conscious. Now, I could fall anonymously among strangers and forget about how foolish I looked.

I tried summoning the patience and focus instilled years earlier on the driving range. I eventually achieved respectable competence with a golf club. Perhaps similar effort would pay off, one turn at a time, as I gripped the ski poles. Giving in to the siren call of the locker key and quitting now would be my permanent exit from this sport and its unique sensations. I resolved to take on another run, then another, and then one more. My turns were wobbly. My thighs burned, but I was regaining confidence. Within the space of an hour, I went from the brink of hanging everything up to knowing there would be many more ski days to come.

Within a couple of seasons, steep, advanced runs were navigable and, like the Seneca Turnpike, shrank in my mind's eye. The sport had me in its icy grasp. In any activity, there is nearly always someone much better, but today I enjoy every chance to better myself on skis. Now and then, I even take a carefully considered plunge into some expert terrain.

Skiing has become a passion for me that I could have easily walked away from one frustrating afternoon. Perhaps it was a buried passion accidentally awakened. My late grandfather's family emigrated from Finland, a nation with a great ski tradition. One winter, my cousin Jason and I ventured down into the cellar of our grandfather's house. We pulled out two old pairs of antique wooden skis. We marveled at the flimsy leather straps and considerable girth. We tried to imagine how anyone stayed upright on these dusty relics. The sport skipped a generation in our clan. Our parents had taken no interest. Jason and I both did.

In time, my wife Mindy and I purchased a vacation condominium on Lake Tahoe's South Shore. It overlooked the mountain runs where I overcame the urge to give up when cutting a path seemed neither easy nor obvious. I sometimes wonder how things might have been different had I listened to the locker key that second day out and turned back to the lodge. It only begs a bigger question. What other possibly enriching experiences do we forfeit daily with our small and apparently safe choices? Establishing a nothing-ventured-nothing-gained mind-set means constantly overcoming a fear of failure, seizing the opportunity, and getting out of a personal comfort zone. The principle applies whether swinging a club, turning a ski, closing a deal, or finding a mate.

There were plenty of perfectly good reasons to opt out of cobbling together a spontaneous trip to Super Bowl XLII. In the next nine days, I would curse unforeseen complications, large and small, resulting from chasing the Big Game.

During this time, some people around me would become sounding boards. Marsha, a co-worker who was also putting in long hours during these soft economic times, reminded me of what was important. One evening, she looked up from the glow of her computer screen and peered over the cubicle wall. "It's just *life*, Jeff. You *have* to go to the game!"

This trip would be unlike any other Mindy and I routinely and carefully planned. Normally, we saved our money, paid cash, and lined up most details well in advance. This time we were not so much going to the game as going after it. Like the wild card Giants, our appearance was unanticipated. At least the team had been striving to get to the Super Bowl since training camp the previous summer. I had only seriously kicked around going as a fan for the past twenty minutes.

The Blackberry rang out a third time. My analytical right brain wrapped around probabilities. There are about 6.6 billion people on the planet, 150 million Super Bowl television viewers, and 71,101 seats for those who could get to Arizona and see it in person. What were the chances an opportunity like this would come again? I had far better odds for successfully getting to the two tickets now three thousand miles away than I had of going to some future Super Bowl.

I picked my phone out of my pocket and answered the call from Mindy. She was quick to the point.

"Howard needs to know what we're going to do about the tickets."

"I think we should go," I said. "But I need one more hour."

IV. Family Meeting

I stared at the faxed copy of the letter from the New York Football Giants. The original had been mailed to Mindy's boss Howard from Giants Stadium in East Rutherford, New Jersey. She had faxed the document from her office to mine on Thursday morning so I would know exactly what was required. The correspondence explicitly detailed the terms and conditions of securing two seats to Super Bowl XLII. The club had sent notifications prior to the Giants upset NFC Championship victory over Green Bay on January 20. Howard's transferable purchase rights were conditioned on the Giants advancing to the meet the AFC Champions in Glendale, Arizona. He had only known for four days that the letter now had real value. I was no longer measuring the value purely in dollars. If I could somehow turn Howard's rights into actual tickets dispensed by a Meadowlands box office agent a continent away...I might attend an event I never thought I could realistically ever expect to see in person.

Of all the various conditions stated in the notification letter, the last one made me laugh aloud. It advised lottery selected rights holders with no intention to buy tickets to return the letter to the Ticket Office with a cancellation marking. I wondered if on Sunday morning, there would be any original, returned notifications at the Giants' Ticket Office with "Cancel" written across the front. I conjured an image of some overly conscientious soul personally delivering notice of intention *not* to exercise the right to buy Super Bowl tickets.

Getting to the Meadowlands requires navigating one of America's most frantic stretches of six-lane highway, the New Jersey Turnpike. I imagined a ticket holder passing through multiple toll stations along the choked artery dotted with chemical storage tanks, belching smokestacks, and industrial warehouses. The gritty opening credits of *The Sopranos* television series depict this forlorn stretch of highway as fictional mob boss Tony Soprano's daily commute route.

Exit 16W leads to the Meadowlands Sports Complex. This is where urban legend suggests that the body of missing Teamsters boss Jimmy Hoffa rests under tons of concrete foundation that supports the massive, sixty-four-million-cubic feet stadium, second largest in the National Football League.

In my imagination, a fan transported an official letter safely secured in the car's glove box. Descending the 16W ramp would deposit said fan into the Meadowlands' sprawling parking area. Here in the toxic heart of North Jersey, he or she would find a parking space and purposefully approach the Ticket Office. Perhaps he would seek assistance from a lot attendant or other stadium worker for directions to the appropriate box-office agent.

I pictured my fantasy Giant booster arriving at the ticket window to fulfill his assigned duty. The diligent fan would declare purpose and intent in language much like that of the notification letter itself. "Excuse me, sir or madam, I wish to properly return my notification letter so I may forfeit my ticket purchase rights to Super Bowl XLII. I regret that I cannot attend the Championship due to other pressing obligations. As you see, I have clearly marked across the front of the letter "Cancel" so the tickets can revert to the Club. Since the notice was unclear regarding the return method, I wished not to leave anything to chance in consideration of your kind invitation. I thought it best to deliver this in person. Please extend my regrets and best wishes to the team for a favorable outcome in the Big Game."

Figments of my active imagination aside, I needed to find someone reliable who could make a similar trek to the Meadowlands and actually secure Howard's two tickets. The specific person who carried out this task would have to be the owner of the tickets by virtue of legally transferred purchase rights.

Days earlier, Howard and his wife ruled out flying to New Jersey given Howard's recovery from surgery and the need to attend to their two children. For Mindy and me to buy the tickets, we needed a trustworthy courier on the shortest of notice. Fortunately, my East Coast ties created a few possible options.

My sixty-eight old year mother lives in the countryside west of Philadelphia and still works the night shift full-time as a pharmacy technician. Like most any parent, she would do almost anything for her children, including making a three-hour drive on little or no sleep. I could not imagine asking her to complete the task, especially in the dead of winter and with her nocturnal hours. If she even knew about my chance to go to the game, she probably would insist on trying anyway. I chose not call her until game day.

My sister, Julie, works near the suburban Philadelphia community where we spent our teen years. It had been almost exactly a year, New Year's Eve 2006, since I splurged on a gift and took her and Mindy to attend our first live Philadelphia Eagles home game at Lincoln Financial Field. Ticket broker prices for club-level seats set me back several hundred dollars. Such an expense would have been unfathomable when Julie and I were in our late teens and early twenties. Our single mom was struggling then to make ends meet after she and our stepfather divorced. Having the financial means years later, it was worth every penny to enjoy a special day at *The Linc* with family. Eagles' coach Andy Reid pulled most of the starters that day after the first series when word came in of a Detroit upset over Dallas. With that early result, the Eagles captured the NFC East division title. We celebrated for the rest of the game along with 69,338 other delighted fans. The Eagles' second-string players trounced the Falcons in a game more lopsided than the 24–17 result suggested.

There would be a postscript to the game. Unbeknownst to anyone at the time, star quarterback Michael Vick played in what would be his last appearance for Atlanta. In 2007, a jury convicted Vick of running a brutally cruel, dogfighting ring at his home. He was sentenced to two years in prison, effectively ensuring that even my slim odds of reaching the Super Bowl as a fan would be better than Vick's getting there as a player.

My sister lives closer to I-95 than my mother, making Julie's travel time to the Meadowlands manageable but a grind nonetheless. I held the thought of calling her as a backup and then shifted focus to one more geographically closer family connection.

My aunt Debby, uncle Rick, and cousin Jason live in the home of my late grandparents in Middletown, New York, about sixty miles northwest of New York City. The home holds fond memories and a singular sense of my childhood roots. I remember my grandfather had a passing interest in football. In a way, he had a deep connection to the game. While avid football fans might turn the television on in time for kickoff, my grandfather made his game day appointment for halftime. He was a music teacher, skilled trumpeter, and leader of the Middletown High School marching band. After retiring, he still took great pleasure in watching intricate drills and formations unfold on the gridiron. The Xs and Os on his clipboard did not represent linemen, receivers, and backs but brass, woodwinds, and majorettes.

Mindy and I had just visited Middletown five weeks earlier. My uncle Rick, also a night-shift worker, must share the same nocturnal gene with my mother. In mid-afternoon, Rick was likely asleep or just rising and groggy. I spared engaging him in my hot pursuit for a numbered envelope sitting in East Rutherford and instead called my aunt at work.

I reached Debby at the Middletown area psychiatric hospital where she works in an administrative position. With thousands of miles between us, calendar years measured the intervals between our personal visits. We scattered periodic e-mail contact in between. The last occasion when I called Debby at work, outside of announcing my arrival in town for a visit, was several years ago in the midst of a family crisis. The first thing I did when she picked up the phone was to assure her everything was fine. I gave her a shorthand account of my ticket quest. The significance was not lost on her. It was surrounding her.

Giant's fever was palpable in the greater New York City area. Only four days had elapsed since a stunning NFC Championship road victory over the Green Bay Packers occurred at Lambeau Field. The Cinderella Giants fanned the flames of regional animosity between New York and Boston. New Yorkers were still smarting from a second blow dealt to the historical supremacy of Yankee baseball by their perpetually derided rival, the Boston Red Sox. Barely two months had passed since the Sox's 2007 World Series win proved for Bostonians the 2004 snapping of the "Curse of the Bambino" was no fluke. Now, it was widely expected the Patriots would trounce the Giants to give Boston even greater bragging rights across two sports. New York played the unaccustomed role of underdog.

As I spoke to my aunt that afternoon, the Giants' head coach, Tom Coughlin, resumed the team's practices in East Rutherford. He instructed his players to take care of all of the minor details unrelated to their task on the field for the next week so nothing else would be on their minds when the Giants traveled to Arizona for the game. I had ample details to work out before I knew if I would also be in Arizona on February 3.

Debby, a capable improviser herself, was a good sounding board for the strategy forming in my head, a strategy in which her son could be a key player.

"Sounds exciting!" Debby said as I laid out a game plan. "You can reach Jason on his cell at the firehouse. He's there now," she said and wished me luck.

I had come to regard Jason as the younger brother I never had. He is a bit of a quiet adventurer: a licensed pilot, skydiver, skier, and part of generational line of firefighters. He first followed in the footsteps of both his dad and our grandfather serving as a volunteer. Later, he became the first in the family to become a professional firefighter, making his living through long stretches of mundane routine punctuated by moments of modest to severe emergency.

Several years ago when he was just out of school, Jason made a cross-country trek. He made multiple stops to skydive in as many states as possible. At the western end of his journey, Mindy and I hosted him for a few days. Jason was our first East Coast family guest at our new Sacramento home. The three of us have ridden cable cars together in San Francisco. We have flagged down cabs in midtown Manhattan. Since miles separated us between infrequent and brief visits, nearly every moment Jason, Mindy, and I spent together passed in some way on the go.

When I reached my cousin on his cell phone Thursday afternoon at Middletown Engine Company Number 4, he was hunkering down for what he hoped would be an uneventful sleepover at the station.

"Hey, what's up?"

"Well, I've got kind of an interesting and fun situation, I guess." I could think of no other way to preface the conversation. "What are you doing tomorrow?" I asked.

"I'm here at the fire station tonight until around six in the morning. After that, I'm off all day Friday." Jason generally worked twenty-four shifts at the firehouse.

"You're off on Saturday too?"

"Yup."

"Then I've got a little errand I'm hoping you can run for me."

I explained the courier duty to Jason. If I could just get him a personally delivered overnight package with a cashier's check and the additional required documentation in his hands by Friday morning, he would be within striking distance.

"Can you make it down to Jersey?" I asked.

"Sure, I could do that," he said without hesitation.

A chill went down my spine. The clock was running down, but we were very much in the game. I started to think ahead, carefully.

"That's awesome, Jay."

We made a little small talk about the game itself. We agreed the Giants would probably be outmatched. I was mindful not to dwell on the fact that whatever the outcome, Super Bowl XLII would likely go down as one of the most historic games ever played in the NFL.

As I spoke with Jason, I felt a tad guilty for not offering anything more lasting than a game day souvenir. I knew the feeling was irrational. His immediately affirmative reply to my unexpected request came unconditionally. I insisted on promising him a couple hundred dollars for his time and expense.

Though the stadium was an hour away on a good day, I anticipated Jason would face the heavy drumbeat of New York area traffic. There would likely be a bottleneck at the ticket office created by several thousand Giant fans. I was asking my cousin to blow off a full day on my behalf. He would spend a good chunk of Saturday standing outside the Giants Stadium concourse in windy conditions and nasty subfreezing cold. I was asking him to be there with the thrilled Giants season ticket holders, the core of the fan base, to retrieve tickets to a sporting event that was the talk of the city and the nation. An agent would hand him two beautifully embossed, glossy, highly collectible tickets with raised hologram images of the Vince Lombardi trophy. At that moment, he would technically be the legal owner of the two seats.

After returning to Middletown, he planned to snap a digital photo of himself holding the same tickets as proof of his brush with the Big Game. Then he would seal them in an overnight package and ship them out to me. It was a simple set of tasks on the face of it for Jason, but quite a selfless mission as well. I started to gingerly venture towards a thought that had crossed my mind earlier. I had alluded to it with Jason's mother Debby on my previous call.

"So, Jason, I don't think I've ever asked you before but are you much of Giants fan?"

"You know, I'm not a die-hard fan. I catch a game on TV sometimes and look at the sports section here and there. Other than a couple of the big-name players, I couldn't tell you a lot about the team, unlike some people I know around here."

He was like the vast majority of casual fans: more interested in the final score than the box-score trivia. People who are otherwise completely disengaged from sports still make time for the spectacle and social event that is Super Bowl Sunday. Marketers estimate nearly twenty percent of the television audience watches the game for the entertaining commercials alone. Others watch alternative programming created exclusively for game day.

In 2005, the Animal Planet cable network premiered a highly successful counter-programming broadcast. Their alternative program, *Puppy Bowl I,* featured cuddly pups bounding around a mock stadium. The fourth edition was scheduled to air for the first time in high definition on February 3, 2008 during Super Bowl XLII. It would draw a record eight million viewers. With so many people watching TV, some take advantage of thinner crowds during the Super Bowl telecast by visiting parks, theaters, or other gathering places.

Jason would not be at the movies or watching the *Puppy Bowl* in nine days. Whether he saw the game at the firehouse, at home, or elsewhere, he would have a story to share. The extent of that story depended in part on my silent calculation of a grief-to-dollar ratio. How much added expense would a third ticket be? How much of a hassle would it be to obtain? How committed was Mindy to the game? Mindy and I still had not fully discussed, or even absorbed, the notion of going to the Super Bowl ourselves.

Jason was idling at the firehouse and not particularly pressed for time. I decided to probe a bit more to learn the extent of his availability, commitment, and resources. My cousin might make my hypothetical questions irrelevant before I even asked them.

"So where do you think you'll watch the game?" I asked.

"I don't know yet. Probably with some friends, I guess. If you have room in your bag, I might ask you to pick up some extra trinkets for them."

"No problem," I said. "I want to hear about all those Giant fans you're going to come across at the Meadowlands tomorrow. I guess some local TV news crews will get out there. It's a pretty big story even in jaded New York City."

Jason anticipated both the vicarious thrill of the ticket trip and the playful taunting rights it would earn him at work.

"I know a few guys here at the firehouse that will be pissed off when I tell them I've got family going to the game," he said.

I knew he would jab at them in a fraternal kidding manner since his close-knit coworkers routinely called each other "brothers." They were all willing to enter burning buildings to rescue strangers or each other if needed. That reality sunk in with the public at large following the September 11 attacks.

In the fall of 2001, many Middletown firefighters, including Jason and his father Rick, reached out in large and small ways to Manhattan fire companies, offering condolences and support. During our holiday trip east that year, Mindy and I compelled ourselves to visit Ground Zero. We watched a grim and constant parade of semitrailer trucks rumble down the streets of Lower Manhattan, hauling out rubble a full three-and-a-half months after the disaster.

Soon after the Twin Towers collapsed, in tribute, New York pro ballplayers spontaneously donned FDNY caps and patches on their game day uniforms. September 11 put ballgames in the proper perspective for sports fans and athletes everywhere, particularly those whose game day lexicons included shallow references to contests as *war* and players as *soldiers*. Firefighters already had the proper perspective. Jason would not attach disproportionate importance to a football game, not even the Super Bowl. I knew him well enough to think he would harbor no false expectations if I dangled the wholly uncertain prospect of him going to the game.

"Jason, have you ever thought about going to the Super Bowl?"

"Can't say I have, but I'm sure it would be pretty amazing. Maybe someday."

Maybe sooner than he thought.

"Well, I've got to say first this is not an *offer*, just a suggestion for something we might look into."

"Sure."

I was certain if I had not already set Jason's internal wheels turning by now, I would shortly.

"The purchase rights belong to Howard," I said. "He signs over the rights to you to buy two tickets at face value. I send you the signed letter and fourteen hundred dollars for the pair. If you think you might want to go to the game, let me know. I'm pretty sure Mindy probably will want to go. We haven't really had a chance to talk about it or plan on much of anything. So let me ask you: Do you think you might want to go to the Super Bowl this year?"

"I'm sure it would be exciting. I guess if I had the chance to go it would be worth thinking about."

Now Jason was in the same quasi-dream state I had been in at the dinner table the night before. He was trying to wrap his arms around the concept along with a litany of possibilities and obstacles.

"What's your work schedule, Jason?" If duty called him, I would probably not even bother to relay this point of conversation to Mindy.

"I'm already off three days from the second to the fourth. I could probably swing a little bit extra if I needed to."

I continued down my mental checklist.

"It wouldn't be cheap, Jason, with short notice on the air and hotel. We should check out some travel Web sites. I still don't know if Mindy wants to go. Assuming she does, we would need to go into the broker market for a third ticket. That could get costly. We would have to talk about splitting everything three ways before doing anything."

"It can't hurt to look into it, anyway," Jason said.

"How's your cash situation?" I asked so as not to be overly personal about Jason's financial means and priorities.

"Well, it so happens I'm getting my annual uniform allowance in a few days. That's a lump sum of about six hundred bucks coming."

While Jason calculated, I contemplated. What I was going to say to Mindy? I had just potentially made matters considerably more complicated. The night before, I had whimsically speculated about her and me going to the game. She had replied then something to the effect of, "If you wanted to go, I guess I would. I'm kind of indifferent about it, but I know you love football."

Now the reality of the situation was taking shape. I would gently test her claim of indifference. How much more cost would be involved in buying a third ticket at scalpers' prices to the most anticipated Super Bowl in a generation or more? How many future family gatherings on either or both coasts would I have to endure recounting and ruminating over this affair if I fouled up something from this point forward? I thought about the potential for misunderstanding, distraction, and tension. A careless step could strain my relationship with my wife, her employer, my cousin, or all three, all over a football game.

Between these competing thoughts, I threw myself back into the present moment and task.

"Jay, look into airline schedules to see if you even can even get anything out to Phoenix at this point. If Mindy definitely wants to go, a third game ticket could be ridiculously expensive. I haven't even checked on that."

Jason knew the potential obstacles and remained focused. "We'll try to take this thing one step at a time. It might just work out. I can bounce around the 'Net a little and see what I find. Right now, the main thing is taking care of getting you the two tickets you already know are there."

"Thanks, Jay. I'll talk with Mindy. First, I'll find out if she wants to go, then I'll check on what we would be looking at for a third ticket. You understand I can't say yes to anything right now even if I wanted to."

"I know."

Jason was single himself, but he was well aware I could not advance plans any farther until I consulted my partner. We agreed it would be best for the three of us to regroup by phone over the weekend.

After I hung up, I scurried to the bank and took a fourteen-hundred-dollar cashier's check advance from my credit card. Only a few days ago, I had taken great satisfaction in retiring my full, outstanding card balance. Months before, I had planned for the rapidly slowing economy and seasonal advertising drop-off. The fallout from Sacramento's slumping housing market looked more severe every day. My January commissions would be nonexistent. I was accustomed to irregular income that came with sales cycles, but January 2008 set up to be my worst month in five years. Under the circumstances, it was painful to pull plastic out of my wallet. I hate debt almost as much as I love football.

My next stop was Howard's house about twenty miles outside of town. He was working at home that day.

I called Mindy at her office from my car to let her know Jason would pick up Howard's two tickets at the box office in New Jersey. I chose immediate, abbreviated, disclosure about the talk with my cousin instead of waiting until dinner to go over it with her. Attorneys and spouses both appreciate full disclosure, and the conversation with Jason was still fresh. I wanted her to know the highlights before they got fuzzy, since he and I were clear on the entire matter. I suspected Mindy's casual demeanor from the night before would give way to enthusiasm for going to the game. Now I wanted to know for certain.

If she wanted to go to the game as I certainly did, we would look into costs, discuss options like the adults we all were, and rationally make a plan based on all the information. It sounded simple enough—love, family, and sport not withstanding.

For all I knew, Jason could already be learning there were no seats left on flights from New York to Phoenix. A third ticket in the open scalper broker market might command an astronomical price. Hotel rooms might be booked solid. The whole thing was still an unfinished deal in progress and loaded with uncertainty, a state of affairs lawyers despise and sales professionals expect. It was that nebulous point before all parties are satisfied and a contract either consummates or comes unraveled.

Mindy and I had yet to digest the events or address important details. We are excellent travel planners and had spent months putting together a 2002 trip to the Salt Lake City Winter Games. We addressed nearly every aspect of getting around, setting priorities, studying venues, and organizing our time to take in as many events as possible. That journey had been an intricately scripted play. Right now, I was calling audible signals at the line, changing the game plan, reacting to outside factors in motion, and hoping for the best.

Her words from the other end of my cell phone rang in my ear like those of an apoplectic coach in the helmet radio receiver of the quarterback.

"You offered Jason one of the tickets?"

"No, I did *not* offer him one of the tickets, Mindy," I said over the rumbling whoosh of freeway traffic. "I asked him if he was interested in going to the game. Let's talk at home tonight about what you and I want to do. Right now I'm driving and trying to get Howard's letter and a check out in time so Jason has it in Middletown tomorrow."

I arrived at Howard's home in the Sacramento suburb of Granite

Bay around five in the afternoon. The past twenty-four hours had drained me.

Howard's wife Kathy answered the door.

"Hi, Jeff. Come on in." Kathy was always the gracious host whether it was here at her home or at the family's summer cabin where my wife and I had been guests. She worked for Hewlett Packard, and the job allowed her to telecommute from home, which came in handy as Howard recuperated.

"Howard will be out a minute. He's a little bit slow to his feet about now."

"I understand. I'm sorry you two can't go the game, Kathy. I guess it was pretty surprising for you that the Giants even made it to the Super Bowl this year."

"They looked awfully good against Green Bay. Great defense. We watched it here. I think they'll give the Patriots a run for their money." Kathy was obviously in tune with the play-offs and following the action. She and Howard would certainly have gone to Phoenix if circumstances had been different.

"Hello, Jeff."

Howard stepped slowly into the foyer using a cane to take the pressure off the bone, muscle, and tissue that was wrapped and fused to the new titanium insert in his knee. Next year, he planned to get the other knee replaced. The technology was impressive, but recovery required considerable rehabilitative therapy. In fact, similar and more drastic medical advances were creating new legal questions in sport.

Just ten days earlier in Paris on January 14, 2008, the International Association of Athletics Federation (IAAF) had ruled that South African Paralympics champion Oscar Pistorius was ineligible to compete in the Beijing Summer Olympics. The IAAF determined artificial legs could give a runner an unfair advantage in a competition involving able-bodied athletes. Pistorius, a double amputee below the knees, runs the 400 meter with carbon-fiber blades in place of his severed feet. His personal best times are just shy of the Olympic qualifying standard. Pistorius later won an appeal in the Court of Arbitration for Sport, a body established by the International Olympic Committee (IOC) for resolving eligibility disputes. It is only a matter of time before the issue of athletes competing with synthetic joints, knees, and limbs requires comprehensive review. New rules will be needed to govern desegregated competition between so called able-bodied athletes and physically challenged competitors aided by medical science.

"How is the knee, Howard?" I asked.

"Oh, you know, it's no fun, but I'm starting to get around a little. Come sit down."

We sat at the dining room table while Kathy went to get her husband his reading glasses and the paperwork. It allowed Howard time to wax philosophic as he enjoys doing from time to time. He has a sharp and inquisitive mind and speaks in measured, balanced, and thoughtful tones.

"You know, Jeff, travel really requires four things."

I knew he would enumerate them using some combination of wise observations and possibly a wisecrack or two.

"First, you've got to have *time*. I always wonder about you and Mindy. You take these whirlwind quick trips and cram more than I can imagine into such narrow schedules."

It was true for Mindy to an extent, but particularly the case for me. Our typical vacation usually consisted of little more than a day or two tacked onto a long holiday weekend like Memorial Day, Independence Day or Thanksgiving. Sometimes our only agenda is stationary relaxation on a beach or lounging at a quiet bed and breakfast. However, we could also strategically pack into one calendar date hiking in the sun through a rustic national park and club hopping through a cosmopolitan cityscape after nightfall.
Seattle and Vancouver in four days including flight from Sacramento? A cinch. One week during the holidays on the East Coast to see friends and family in D.C., Philly, and New York? A bit hectic but doable. Mindy and I never feel rushed, but efficiency is a trademark of our quick vacations. Our travel style baffles Howard.

"Besides time," Howard continued, "you've got to have *money*. Those two things, time and money, do not always go hand in hand. There are plenty of people with lots of money and no time. There's a bunch of people with no money and all the time in the world."

Sure enough, our jobs paid well, but often at the expense of long hours, weekend commitments to prepare cases and presentations, and attend client events or other employer-required social functions.

The third item on Howard's list he personally lacked. I knew it hurt for him to say it, but he said it anyway.

"You have to have your *health.*" He extended three fingers and tapped on the table edge for emphasis. I sensed he delivered the words with a touch of remorse and a quiet resolve that I take his message to heart.

"It's important for you and Mindy to do and see as much as you can *while* you can."

Kathy returned to the living room with a manila folder in hand.

63

"The fourth thing you need to travel is companionship," he added. I accepted this as an acknowledgement that even the single traveler does not journey in total isolation.

Howard opened the folder and pulled out the original notification letter from the New York Football Giants inviting him to attend as the Club sought its seventh championship of all time. He wrote in precise longhand across the letter his authorization for my cousin Jason to purchase the tickets, and then he signed at the bottom, *H. Hoffman.*

The first time I had ever been in Howard and Kathy's home was for a gathering honoring Howard's dad soon after Mindy went to work for the law firm. Herman Hoffman had first taken his son to see the Giants when the team played in Yankee Stadium in the fifties. Names of Giant greats of an earlier era rolled off Howard's tongue with ease: Charlie Conerly, Sam Huff, Frank Gifford, Pat Summerall.

There is another name inextricably tied to the team, a family name: Mara. Howard and his father were attending games when the Giants' founding owner was still alive. The New York Football Giants, so designated to distinguish them at the time from the baseball Giants, owe their very existence to a colorful promoter, dealmaker, and bookie named Tim Mara.

In 1925, Mara, who took legal betting action at New York area horse tracks, made a five-hundred-dollar bet of his own by starting a football team. The sum was the reported price Mara paid to a fledgling National Football League eager to establish a foothold in the nation's largest city. In 2003, *Forbes Magazine* pegged the value of the New York Giants franchise at $573 million. By 2007, the same source estimated the value had crested over one billion dollars.

The first professional football game ever played in New York City took place on October 18, 1925, at the old Polo Grounds. The Giants fell 14–0 to the Frankford Yellow Jackets, a team that would later become the Philadelphia Eagles. The fortunes of the young Giants franchise turned rapidly. In 1927, in just their third season in existence, the New York Giants claimed their first NFL title.

In a defensive financial move at the outset of the Depression, Tim Mara transferred legal ownership of the Giants to his two sons, Jack, 22, and Wellington, age 14. The boys eventually guided the team into the modern era. The elder Mara would see three more championships in his lifetime in 1934, 1938, and 1956.

Less than two months after the Giants' heart wrenching 23–17 sudden death overtime loss to Baltimore in the 1958 NFL title game, Tim

Mara passed away. He was seventy-one. The Giants had been on the losing end of a contest still known to football fans as the Greatest Game Ever Played. Seventeen future Hall of Fame inductees played on the field or patrolled the sidelines that day, including the Colts' Johnny Unitas and Raymond Berry along with Giants' assistant coaches Tom Landry and Vince Lombardi. The 1958 title game attracted a substantial national television audience. It is widely credited as the catalyst for the exponential growth of televised football.

With a big broadcast rights deal knocking, Wellington Mara sacrificed tremendous potential financial gain for the long-term health of the league. At Commissioner Pete Rozelle's urging, Mara endorsed a revenue-sharing model that helped ensure small-market teams could remain competitive. Media money poured in equally to NFL teams, regardless of market size.

When Wellington Mara died in 2005, he was the last of the old breed of team owners. Control of the Giants still rests with the Mara family who retain a fifty-percent interest in the club. One of Wellington's eleven children, John Mara, directs operations as the team's chief executive.

As Howard slid the signed letter across the table to me, I received temporary custody of the Hoffman family's personal Giant fan legacy that spanned over fifty years. I promised myself I would treat that legacy with respect.

V. Trick Plays

After picking up the tickets at Howard's on Thursday evening, I dashed out to FedEx to overnight Jason a package containing the Giants' lottery letter and the cashier's check. Mindy and I still had no air or hotel reservations. We had little, if any, plan for how or whether we might actually make the Big Game. If airfare or hotel rooms proved too difficult to secure, we could still sell the tickets, but only if we had to. The issue of a possible third ticket for Jason loomed large, but that could wait at least one day for resolution. With little time to make large decisions, mouse and modem served as primary tools to get a sense of the actual financial outlay for our Phoenix follies.

On Friday morning, January 25, 2008 Neil Best filed a story in *Newsday* titled "Prepare to Break the Bank for Super Bowl Tickets." The story referenced average prices in excess of four thousand dollars at the major Internet broker sites like Stubhub and Razor Gator. End-zone corners fielded prices in the high two thousands. Best reported on a suite for eight, up for auction on eBay, for two hundred thousand dollars, the approximate median price of an American single family home. At that price, an investor could have picked up a couple of the fifty or so bank-owned properties listed within a two-mile radius of our Sacramento address.

Local home values had plummeted by about twenty percent in the past year. The Sacramento area absorbed some of the fiercest backlash after the speculative national housing bubble burst. Over five thousand home foreclosures in January alone across the eight county region accounted for an unhealthy chunk of the fifty thousand statewide. Gasoline prices surged towards four dollars a gallon at an alarming inflation rate reminiscent of an unstable Third World nation.

While Mindy and I were more fortunate than many, the headlines and frugal ways still affected our shopping psychology. We were not about to buy another Super Bowl ticket without a hard look at costs, trends, and general market forces.

On Friday night, Mindy and I scoured the Web for information. We could have auditioned for a MasterCard commercial as we scrolled through travel sites online. Airfare from Sacramento to Phoenix for two: $642. Two nights at an economy motor lodge: $590. Third ticket: Ouch. Common sense to hold off on the last piece of the puzzle for at least a couple of days: *priceless*. We booked our own travel and hotel. We postponed the ticket purchase. Certainly, Giants fans were making last-minute travel arrangements from New York. Jason would face fierce competition for flights. We did not want to leave that detail hanging long.

My package had arrived at Jason's doorstep Friday morning.

He drove to New Jersey and, as expected, stood waiting in the January chill outside Giants Stadium, along with several thousand fans. After about two hours, a facilities manager, or perhaps a member of the Giants staff, likely realized the weather and better public relations dictated opening up the inner concourse to allow fans to line up inside.

Listening to the chatter of the excited Giant faithful, Jason absorbed a full dose of pregame armchair analysis without the armchairs. He finally got up to the box office window, where an agent handed him two tickets in Section 430, Row 5. By then, it was nearly seven in the evening, just past the deadline to get the tickets out for Saturday delivery to Sacramento. Any wheeling and dealing with tickets in hand would have to wait until the following Monday.

When Jason returned home to Middletown, he snapped a photo of himself holding the tickets for keepsake and precaution. On Saturday morning, he slipped the coveted cargo into a slim shipping envelope and sent it westward. Then he went online to see if he could stitch together a crazy quilt of connecting flights from the New York area to Phoenix. Mindy and I planned to call Jason Sunday night to plan our next steps and determine conclusively if he was able and willing to make the trip.

The ticket market crested over the weekend of January 26-27, arguably the best time to sell and the worst time to buy. Many media outlets, spurred on by coordinated press releases from the League and ticket brokers, reported average prices paid. Counterfeiters and various swindles operated to separate the would-be game goers from their cash and had a chilling effect on private-party transactions with strangers. The largest ticket resellers advised fans not to travel to Phoenix without tickets already secured.

During the same weekend, the Giants' and Patriots' organizations dispensed nearly twenty-five thousand tickets—over a third of the capacity at University of Phoenix Stadium—at a collective face value of around 17.5 million dollars.

Some of the very people Jason huddled with in the cold outside the Meadowlands box office would be putting their seats up for sale immediately and influencing prices. Lottery selected buyers read and heard news reports of tickets attracting big money. Many did the math. For this historic game, a ticket holder could turn a profit of three to four hundred percent or more.

Season ticket subscribers would be divided among personally witnessing sports history in the making or running to a computer to turn seats into gold. On eBay, sellers fetched up to the mid-three thousands for upper-level seats. The Internet had changed everything, including the resale ticket market.

A generation ago, the world moved at a different pace. The World Wide Web existed only as an arcane information-sharing system with strange protocols and codes indecipherable to the average person. For example, information access gave travel agents far more relevance as personal advisors for even the most routine air trips and hotel bookings. Now, travelers handle the basics themselves online and turn to travel agents for advanced consultation on complex or exotic destinations.

Today, the same architecture behind sites like Hotwire, Travelocity, and Orbitz, to name a few, enables both easier travel booking and high-tech ticket scalping.

Just over twenty years ago, a ticket to Super Bowl XXII, if you could get one at face value, cost one hundred dollars. Parking-lot sellers operated in the shadows, as some still do today. Legal ticket brokers profited primarily from local knowledge. Human instinct about market conditions and demand for specific events to buy and sell tickets governed the resale market.

Professional brokers acquired tickets to events like field workers picking cotton by hand. In 1988, a tiny California based firm called Ticket Trader introduced the industry equivalent of the cotton gin. The company ramped up a crude central-computer system linking just five in-state subscriber brokers, much the same way travel agents connect to airline and hotel reservation systems. The secondary ticket market would never be the same.

Ticket Trader delivered what software developers commonly call a "killer application." A transformative practical use of technology can sometimes rapidly fill a need, find a market, and remake standard practices quickly and permanently. Over three hundred American and Canadian brokers plugged into a new system that greatly streamlined the wholesale ticket trade, allowing individual brokers to scoop up large blocks of seats for resale.

By 1995, Ticket Trader established e-commerce through TicketTrader. com. Consumer Internet access was still rare, but the move effectively provided an international retail outlet for ticket brokers.

The most successful Web driven enterprises were proving to be auction based. In the late nineties, premature Web centric businesses like San Francisco Bay Area grocery delivery service, Webvan, miserably misjudged both operating costs and consumer purchasing behavior. Shoppers still wanted the tactile experience of inspecting produce in their local grocery store. An event ticket, while perishable, required no such inspection, assuming the ticket was authentic.

A June 18, 2002 a press release from Intuitive Solutions announced an upgrade of the widely used MasterBroker software. Company spokesperson Patrick Toole declared in the release circulated by *Business Wire*, "The secondary ticket industry is poised to go through significant change in the coming months as more and more people, brokers and consumers alike, continue to discover the convenience of the internet in buying and selling premium tickets on the secondary market."

"These changes are expected to impact professional ticket brokers most significantly as the demand for premium tickets to events of all kinds is outpacing supply by a significant margin," Toole continued.

Today, the major online broker Razor Gator owns the Ticket Trader software platform.

On the Sunday before Super Bowl XLII, I scrawled Razor Gator, Stubhub, eBay, and a handful of other mega Web site names on a dry-erase board. I propped the board up next to my home computer.

Like many football fans who dream of going to the Super Bowl, I would have sat with an obstructed view atop a girder supporting the dome just to be in the stadium. At the same time, I did not want to be an irrational buyer in a market that punished the desperate and the hasty. I started to make some informal calculations and estimates and shared them with Mindy.

With the game seven days away, we agreed that if Jason decided to come to Phoenix, a sensible goal would be to secure a third ticket at about fifteen-hundred dollars, just over twice face value. Well before we called my cousin Sunday evening, I knew Mindy had understated her true feelings in saying she would be "a little disappointed" if she did not go to the game.

As a youth, Mindy showed little interest when her father Alan took her to 49er games. By her teen years, Alan was generally hosting other family, friends, or business associates for Sunday outings at Candlestick Park.

After Mindy wedded a football fan, her appreciation for the game grew through renewed association. Two weeks after we married in September 1994, Mindy and I attended our first 49er-Eagles game, courtesy of her father. Alan had upgraded his season tickets during the seventies when the Niners were often the doormats of the National Football League. My bride and I took our seats at midfield about twenty rows behind the Niner bench.

Philly handed San Francisco their worst home loss in fourteen years, a 40–8 drubbing. Coach George Seifert yanked Steve Young in the third quarter. Young stormed off the field with helmet off and bad temper on. We were within earshot as the normally cerebral, levelheaded quarterback spewed obscenities in Seifert's direction. Young hit a professional low point with the uncharacteristic display.

"You know I married into your Niner tickets, Mindy." I kidded.

In the waning moments of the game, we claimed long vacated seats closer to field level behind the home sideline.

A hearty chorus of boos cascaded down from the highest reaches of Candlestick to the dejected San Francisco squad watching from the bench. The clock expired. The Eagles joyfully skipped off the field. The fans' expectations had soared with the Niners remarkable fifteen-year run of success. The home crowd was wholly unaccustomed to seeing the current team struggle like the sixties and seventies editions had.

"Yeah, if it weren't for these tickets, I'd probably still be single." Mindy answered. We were building upon what would be a long-running inside joke. Our row was nearly empty but I was still basking in the post-game glow.

"Then I wouldn't be here to see Randall Cunningham and the Eagles' *D* embarrass your team," I said as I flipped through the game day program and we rose to leave.

"What's *that* all about?" Mindy poked back. "My dad gives us these great tickets. You come in here and root for other team. You haven't even lived in Philadelphia for ten years."

"Well, don't think watching this blowout is easy for me, Mindy. What's not to love about the Niners? Maybe this just isn't their year," I said. After a decade in Northern California, the 49ers had become my adopted hometown team just as the Eagles had been in my youth.

The next week Mindy and I took our honeymoon about three hours north of San Francisco. We rented a house along the isolated cliffs of the Mendocino Coast overlooking the Pacific. The outside world took a back seat. Our one diversion from the splendid solitude and seaside soundtrack came on Sunday afternoon. We turned on the television for the first and only time during our getaway. The 49ers were in Detroit playing the Lions in the same stadium where Alan had watched them win their first Super Bowl.

For much of the first half, the Niners looked as ugly and flat as we had seen them against Philadelphia the week before. Barry Sanders ran roughshod over a confused San Francisco defense and the Lions went up 14–0.

That particular week George Seifert kept Steve Young in the game, but the punishing Lions defenders nearly knocked the San Francisco quarterback out of the contest early. As Detroit drove downfield to widen their lead, 49er safety Merton Hanks picked off a Scott Mitchell pass and ran it back deep into Detroit territory. Moments later, rookie San Francisco running back William Floyd powered ahead for a one-yard touchdown run. Then the young Floyd released the pent-up frustration of an entire franchise.

He ripped off his helmet in the end zone and screamed at the top of his lungs. Anyone turning on a television at that juncture would have thought Floyd had just won the game. He had moved the team just one yard ahead. The Niners were still seven points behind. His overreaching statement was as out of touch with the 49ers methodical, businesslike image as Young's sideline rant the week prior.

NFL Films later edited Floyd's outburst out of the season's retrospective highlight package, but the play and the gesture survived the cutting room floor to mark an emotional turning point. The Niners would eventually take down the Lions that day, 27–21. They forged ahead, winning ten straight on the way to a fifth Super Bowl title. Steve Young would earn MVP honors by tossing a record six touchdown passes including a five-yard strike to William Floyd.

As the years passed, Mindy would periodically sit in and watch portions of 49ers games with me. Over time, her general understanding and enjoyment of football grew. Even if the Niners were not going to be part of Super Bowl XLII, she wanted to be.

That fact sunk in with me when I had been at Howard's house on Thursday night. When I mentioned the narrow possibility Mindy might choose to forgo the game while Jason and I used the two tickets, he drolly opined without hesitation.

"She'll kill you, Jeff."

At the very least, she would cry a lot inside, which may as well have killed me.

Now with my cousin's help, two tickets would be in my hands on Monday. If Jason wanted to join us in Phoenix, we definitely would need a third seat. It was time to take the next step and confirm if he was coming to Arizona.

When Mindy and I called Jason from our kitchen on Sunday night, I depressed the speaker button on the phone. I wanted to be sure that all three of us were simultaneously establishing a plan and some basic, agreeable plan.

After we thanked Jason for successfully completing his super errand,

I asked him the question.

"So do you think you want to do this thing, Jay?" I said as I looked over the speaker into Mindy's eyes.

"Well, the flight plan is a little wacky but I think I can get to Phoenix. If I book something now I could be there by Saturday night."

Figuratively speaking, my cousin was already taxiing on the runway. It was up to me to give him clearance to take off.

Mindy and I knew fares would only escalate and options diminish if Jason delayed any longer. We also knew if we told him to book the flight, we needed to ensure without a doubt that he would have a ticket. We shared with Jason our educated guess about the trip's total cost.

Given the added expense of his longer travel, Mindy and I proposed he buy one of the two, seven hundred dollar face-value tickets and share lodging expenses. If I were right in projecting the price movement of a single Super Bowl ticket on the open market, we could spend an average of just under a thousand dollars a seat by splitting the total cost three ways.

I did not want to think about the consequences of significant miscalculation. We were eight days out from the game. Tickets from brokers were running four to six times face value from the high two thousands to low fours. Private-seller transactions might cost less but would probably be tricky for a variety of reasons. I was taking a risk and taking on a challenge at the same time. I knew it would be only right for me to bear the difference of an inaccurate projection to avoid the emotional cost of Mindy or me not going.

As a couple, we have always given each other independence in our individual financial decisions. We also have always collaborated well on shared major purchases. As Mindy had correctly observed, I was the one who created any potential math problem by opening up the prospect of our valued ticket courier joining us on game day.

"Is there anything else that would keep you from coming out, Jay?" I asked expecting I already knew the answer.

"I've got the time off work. I guess I'm still trying to think of a reason *not* to go."

"It sounds like you *want* to go, Jason." Mindy said with a smile and encouraging tone.

Just five weeks earlier, we had visited him in Middletown. The three of us went bowling. Now, out of nowhere, we were tossing around the prospect of going to the Super Bowl.

"We'll crunch the numbers and make it work, Jason." I said. "Book that flight and we'll see you next Saturday night."

I had just signed on to being a Super Bowl ticket prospector. Over the next week, snapshots of price movements filled my simple dry erase board, reflecting more complex and extensive movement across another much bigger board. The big board exists in cyberspace as part of a highly developed professional ticket broker network.

The Super Bowl has no peer in the sporting world as far as stimulating trading activity on a sophisticated scale. The most active ticket buyers and sellers follow trends as closely as on any major stock or commodity exchange. Average fans can glean a sense of the market for the Super Bowl or other sold-out major events. Ticket broker Web sites are reasonably easy to navigate and frequently updated.

However, unlike public commodity exchanges that anyone can follow from a computer or a curbside, real-time ticket price data remains partially shrouded. Limited access to proprietary software reduces transparency for the average consumer.

Every professional ticket broker who hopes to profit from Super Bowl buy and sell transactions can access the same big board. A virtual trading floor spreads around the world. Physical possession of game tickets is not a prerequisite to participation. The electronic exchange of buy and sell contracts drives a market supported by satellite offices, phone banks, and contract runners in the field, at hotel suites, and eventually at the stadium gates, right up to game time. The infrastructure, human behavior, even the jargon, closely resembles the investment world. Playing this game requires a trained mind to cope with and exploit the frantic, perilous, and unpredictable nature of the market. This relentless, profit-driven exchange can easily consume, damage, and victimize the uninitiated.

The resale market for desirable event tickets is small enough potentially to control and manipulate under the right circumstances. Outside the most obvious instances of fraud and petty transgressions, secondary ticket sales remain largely unregulated. As is the general case in business, isolating the tipping point where consumer protection ends and counterproductive government interference begins can be like herding cats. Policymakers have devoted some attention to average fans and the pitfalls associated with limited supply and fervent demand for the big game. Lawmakers' scrutiny tends to focus mostly on the informal parking-lot scalper. Such focus has produced mostly local ordinances, restrictions, and prohibitions related to street-level scalping.

A voluntary industry group, the National Association of Ticket

Brokers, puts forth some basic professional standards. These standards help legitimize brokers and foster good relations between resale agents, event venues, and promoters. However, the NATB membership are fierce competitors first and the guardians of public interest second. Their agendas and concerns vary, but they garner little notice and even less public sympathy. Ticket resellers work in a business with image issues. The prospect of a quick buck attracts shady characters, counterfeiters, and, more recently, cyber criminals. The classic scalper image is an unkempt rogue with a handwritten *need tickets* sign in the arena parking lot on game day. I would learn this figure is an unjustly maligned tip of the ticket-resale iceberg.

Modern-day Super Bowl scalpers employ MIT engineers and Stanford MBAs to monitor and trade on the constantly moving dollar values of every section, row, and seat. As countdown to kickoff rolls, some of the craftiest business brains in the nation play a continuous game as intense, calculated, and passionate as the finite sixty minutes contested on the field. At any moment, the aggregated love, fear, jealousy, greed, and status consciousness motivating every participant in the market is measurable in dollars. Participants can be buyers, sellers, attendees, or all three.

Brokers typically collect ten to fifteen percent in commissions on each retail transaction, but commissions are not the only profit center. For Super Bowl XLII, any broker in the New York, Boston, or Phoenix area could best capitalize on the physical proximity of season ticket lottery winners in their respective home markets.

Every NFL team awards purchase rights to the Super Bowl to a small percentage of season ticket holders. Brokers in each team's market can choose to amass seats for resale the old-fashioned way by taking physical possession of the tickets. Appealing to residents in the immediate area, local brokers advertise themselves as top dollar cash buyers. They can acquire seats and resell them at a significant premium over their cost if they gauge the market well. Since tickets for future events can't produce profit until resold, brokers prefer to not tie up capital by holding onto inventory for very long.

Local brokers and fans can also sell to large national brokers. Perhaps a Baltimore Ravens season ticket holder receives a lottery purchase rights notification letter. He weighs total travel costs and decides against going to Phoenix to see a Super Bowl that does not involve his home team. At the same time, an Arizona resident might be shopping for seats at a Super Bowl game within driving distance. The Baltimore fan might elect to exercise face-value purchase rights and head directly to a local "brick and mortar" broker to cash in for a few-hundred bucks over face value. In the past, the Baltimore broker might rely primarily on a local broker in Phoenix to find a buyer. Today that same broker has more options to resell the seats online. In recent years, many fans with a small quantity of tickets to sell have been turning to online only brokers or selling tickets on their own, directly over the Web.

Unfortunately, human beings have discovered the ease of virtual mugging with a mouse click. Illegitimate sellers flood the Internet. Putting my own want ad online would increase the likelihood of finding purchase options for a third ticket. I knew it would also make me a potential target for thieves.

On Monday morning, the two tickets Jason mailed arrived at my workplace in Sacramento. I brushed my fingers over the raised silvery images of the Lombardi Trophy on the ticket faces. Two birds were in hand. One was out there somewhere in the bush.

Resale values varied from section to section. Our two seats located in Section 430 were square to an end zone with a closer view than end zone corners. Our row location was quite low and well-positioned within the expansive upper deck. Perhaps I could exchange two adjacent seats and a smaller cash sum for three stray singles spread out over less premium spots. None of us would sit together after such an exchange but it might be the most expedient way to get all three of us in the game.

One of my first stops in cyberspace was the virtual garage sale that is craigslist.com. I wrote and posted my ad on the popular exchange site in the San Francisco Bay Area section. Jason did the same on the New York section.

> *Want 1 super bowl ticket or will exchange 2 for 3 - $1,500*
> *Reply to: sale-XXXXXX@craigslist.org*
> *Date: 2008-01-29, X:XX AM MST*
> *I am looking to buy one Super Bowl ticket and will pay $1,500 from a reliable private seller or NATB member broker. I have two tickets to the game through the Giants' lottery and want to attend with another family member. I would also be willing to exchange these two tickets plus $1,500 for 3 seats located separately or together anywhere in the stadium. I can meet in Northern California until this Friday 2/1 or in Phoenix on Saturday 2/2.*

On Monday afternoon, I tried working another possible inside ticket angle. A former employee at my company now represented a firm called Custom Travel Incentives (CTI). The bulk of Larry Karg's job revolved around arranging luxury sports and special event getaway packages for individuals and companies seeking first-class entertainment.

A Friday night, CTI-hosted celebrity event enlisted former NFL receiver Shannon Sharpe and a handful of other athletes to mingle with VIPs or at least very important wallets. The event was one of dozens if not hundreds of similar pregame activities scheduled throughout the week in Phoenix. Larry had recently helped me with packaging a U.S. Open golf getaway for a local oil distributor. If nothing else, Larry was heading to Phoenix and would have some sense of the ticket market. I e-mailed Larry and referenced my fifteen-hundred-dollar target price. His reply was encouraging.

> *Hi Jeff,*
> *I am off to Phoenix tomorrow and appreciate your e-mail. The ticket market has not quite gotten down to that level yet. Let's plan to stay in touch the next few days. Larry.*

I zeroed in on the word *yet*. Larry had attended multiple Super Bowl games. He understood the nature of the event. His message confirmed my sense that the stiff prices I had gasped at over the weekend would in fact come down.

While the big-broker Web sites offered one purchase channel, an apparently better deal involved online private sellers online with the associated high fraud risk. Suspicious replies to my online inquiries hit my inbox and often went something like this

> *Hi there,*
> *The Tickets are still available, my name it's CT and i'm located in --, California. I hope you are still interested and we can make the deal happen right away. Obviously, we need a safe way to complete this deal that will allow us to make sure we receive what we are after so, if you are still interested please reply back. I will ship the tickets via TNT. They will provide assistance in handling the payment and delivery of the tickets. With this procedure, you will be able to check the tickets before I receive the payment. If you agree, please e-mail me your full name and exact shipping address in order to start the procedure. The shipping fees & insurance are included in the price and the tickets will be shipped overnight.*

The flimsy attempt to gain my confidence by referencing a nearby town was laughable. *Making the deal right away* meant to suggest a shared sense of urgency. The TNT payment verification procedure outlined was simply a ploy to acquire information potentially useful for identity theft. I called the Houston customer service center of global shipping giant TNT N.V. There was no such procedure.

"You didn't give the guy any money, right?" the helpful agent said when I called.

"No."

"Good."

The center had already received similar calls from other would-be victims who had received similar e-mails.

I responded to the e-mail anyway on the off chance the message was legitimate. The sender claimed he was in the San Francisco Bay Area. I was due there Thursday for an industry trade show. Maybe my new friend would show up for a meeting.

> *Dear CT,*
>
> *I reside in Sacramento and can purchase your tickets with a bank-issued credit card check. We can verify account balance in person at a bank branch location near you. I can then make payment and receive the tickets in person. I will not make advance payment before shipping or buy without an in-person meeting. I am already in your area Thursday but can drive down earlier this week if needed. I am checking other sources as well, so please, if you are serious about this transaction, e-mail me your local phone number, and I will call back promptly. You can also phone me today at XXX XXX-XXXX.*
>
> *Jeff Fekete, Sacramento, CA*

Any ticket seller unwilling to establish phone contact was not worth dealing with. I never heard back from CT. I reread the helpful advice posted by the Craigslist management team for avoiding fraudulent sellers. The thieves did not require the formal invitation of a classified ad to find me.

On Monday night, I clicked a link from an online auction site posting and received a message with familiar language. This appeal had more sophisticated detail than the earlier message from CT.

> *Hello,*
>
> *I have these tickets in hand and they are still for sale. My name is D-- and I am in------, United Kingdom. I am looking to sell these tickets because I am not in the US at this time and I will not be there for the game. I work for the travel agency------ in ------ and I am selling the tickets for my company. My company will pay for the delivery fee and we will use the overnight delivery service to get you*

the tickets in less than two days. We bought the tickets because we tried to make them part of a vacation package and sell the tickets along with a vacation to the US. Unfortunately, the idea did not catch up so we are now selling the tickets. If you are still interested, I am ready to move forward with this sale as soon as we reach terms. Obviously we need a safe way to complete this deal, one that will allow each one of us to make sure we receive what we are after as fast as possible and as easily as internet deals can be. I have found a way for us to complete the deal safely and fast, and in this way, you will receive the tickets in less than two days, if you can take care of your part of the deal the same day as well. An international shipping company called TNT, which is similar to FedEx, DHL or UPS, provides the solution. They will handle and delivery of the tickets as well as the payment part. With this procedure, I will only receive the payment for the tickets after the game, after you receive them and see that they are genuine. Please click on the link below to the TNT Website to see how we can complete the deal safely and fast directly from the Website of the company where the procedure is explained. Like I said, I will pay for an overnight delivery so you will receive them in time. Let me know what you think.

D. used the name of a legitimate UK travel agency that does in fact have a location in the city he referenced. I checked the Web domain he provided. There was D's Web site all right, since discontinued, but at the time, built from carefully lifted graphics taken from a real travel agency Web site. There was even a bio, photo, and corporate officer title for D. It took me about five minutes with a search engine to uncover the ploy. Still I could not resist responding with my own message I knew would attract no reply but would at least let D know his methods were tired.

D--, I would like to trust your suggestion but have some difficulty. I have been to your site and to TNT's international and domestic Web sites. I also already called TNT's customer service center to inquire about secured transactions of the type you describe. Their representative indicated this form of transfer did not seem to be a legitimate or secure means of delivery. I also noted that a photo clearly displaying your tickets does not accompany your offer. I cannot access your seller history through the auction site you used to contact me. What is your position at the travel agency and could I receive a telephone call from a company representative? My direct line phone number at my U.S. employment site is xxx-xxx xxxx. I would be happy to add a sum of $25 U.S. to the final sale price presuming we can consummate a sale. Your e-mail domain name is not linked to the travel agency site. I am an honest buyer looking to work with an honest *seller. The substance and format of your offer appears problematic. This could influence other potential buyers as it already has influenced me. Please reply with a simple return e-mail acknowledgement explaining this offer and its origination further. In the absence of a reply, I will need to notify the auction site as well as the agency represented at the Web address shown above.*

Soon after I reported D's bogus Super Bowl ticket listing to eBay customer support, it was removed from the site. The same or similar swindle continued operating online for months. A hockey fan in Mississauga, Ontario, reported to a consumer watchdog Web site that he lost $880 paid for four nonexistent tickets to the 2008 Stanley Cup Finals. The fan posted as a warning to others samples of the same misleading correspondence I had encountered.

Early in the week, legitimate Super Bowl tickets changed hands from the League to lottery fans to other fans to brokers and back again. The ticket resale business was brisk. Since the advertising business was much less brisk, I was putting in extended hours between working for a living and working to find a ticket.

The Big Game was immune to these economic ills. In Sacramento, and across the nation, a different big game was driving one of the few healthy sectors of broadcast advertising: political spending.

On Thursday January 31, 2008, Arnold Schwarzenegger endorsed John McCain for president, a day after former New York mayor Rudy Giuliani withdrew from the Republican race. In 2007, Governor Schwarzenegger moved up the California presidential primary from June to February 5. Many other states followed suit in an effort to be more relevant to the selection process. Within hours of the governor's announcement backing McCain, Republican challenger Mitt Romney's advertising people snapped up as much time on our Sacramento stations as possible for the weekend and into Monday.

A few steps from the advertising sales department, our newsroom moved at a hectic pace. The frontloaded primary season collided with the run-up to the Super Bowl. Suddenly, there were not enough superlatives to go around the airwaves. Anticipating Super Sunday and Super Tuesday simultaneously was an unprecedented event and a news editor's dream. Thursday evening, the remaining Democratic heavyweights, Barack Obama and Hillary Clinton, squared off in a major televised debate. As the Patriots readied a shot at 19–0, two of the last remaining applicants for the nation's highest office took shots at one another.

Around three thirty in the afternoon, I took a moment out to make a rare bid on eBay. I mostly only watched bidding activity from the sidelines to see where prices were moving. Nimble, computer-savvy bidders were quick to click in last second winning sums anyway. Hovering over the final seconds of individual auctions was impractical and of little use to me. Professional volume sellers parceled out tickets in systematic patterns in order to test the demand.

I tapped out a twenty-five-hundred-and-one-dollar offer for a pair of Super Bowl upper-level tickets. Though I only needed one ticket, finding a taker for a second would be no trouble. The bid stood for over an hour before someone upped the ante by fifty dollars. Earlier in the week, similar auction listings for upper deck pairs fetched offers in the high three and low four thousands. The price moved only slightly higher over the next hour before bidding closed. I later sighted a flat rate seventeen-hundred-dollar price for an upper-deck single on a major broker site. With about seventy hours to kickoff, the market showed signs of softening.

Just before six, I slipped out of my cubicle and headed home.

Thursday evening, I did my best to hide my stress from Mindy but was not very successful. Stress from any source, positive or negative, accumulates. In my case, the adrenaline rush of anticipating a Super Bowl and anxiety over uncertain expenses combined in a toxic mix. The aggregate effects showed. A few hours before, I had absent-mindedly abandoned my bankcard in a convenience mart ATM halfway between Sacramento and San Francisco. Fortunately, a woman in line behind me flagged me down before I left the scene. In my present sleepless state of mind, bringing the whole business of securing a third ticket to a conclusion held tremendous appeal.

I booted up our home computer and scribbled a few notes on the trusty dry erase board while Mindy prepared dinner. Coast to Coast Tickets had a single upper-level ticket at seventeen hundred thirty-four dollars excluding broker commissions. The final cost was two thousand sixty-seven dollars. The lowest total price at Stubhub.com for a comparable seat was remarkably close at two thousand seventy-five or about five hundred dollars more than I really wanted to spend. Private-party transactions continued to circulate with lower asking prices.

From my desktop vessel, I spotted more pirates trolling the high seas of the World Wide Web. I could now identify their flags, crude manner, and false treasure from the porthole of my e-mail Inbox.

Hi.

The price I'm selling the tickets is ...I live in Arizona but currently I am with work in UK... ...Anyway, there shouldn't be any problem, because I am using (FedEx, UPS, MoneyBookers...) ...I left the tickets at their warehouse before leaving... They will take care of the delivery... If you want to purchase the tickets, let me know and I will explain how we can move forward... waiting your e-mail. Thanks.

I scrolled through the junk messages and scam attempts then closed out my e-mail for the evening. The inviting scent of spices wafted from the kitchen. Mindy called me to dinner.

Our long-time house cat, Harriet, meowed and sniffed at her largely uneaten bowl of kibble. In addition to annoyances super and mundane, our adored, aged feline was reacting badly to medication for a thyroid condition. Harriet was family and our first shared responsibility predating our wedding engagement. Now, Mindy and I wondered how long our kitten was for this earth.

"I think we should try to buy a third ticket on Friday," I remarked flatly into the computer screen and in the general vicinity of my wife. "It might cost a couple hundred dollars more than we expected but at least it would be finished," I shut down the computer and coaxed Harriet to her food dish.

Mindy glanced up from a magazine resting on the kitchen counter next to a simmering pot of pasta. As the ticket search dragged on, my late-night keyboard finger dances just off the master bedroom progressively took a toll on her sleep. She longed for resolution as well.

"Yeah, that would be good," she said wearily. "Then we wouldn't have to worry about it and could just enjoy the weekend in Phoenix."

Some Super Bowl revelers were already enjoying the host city in the highest of style.

That afternoon, the entourage of rap star Sean "Diddy" Combs cleaned out an Arizona wine distributor's supply of eight-hundred-dollar-a-bottle Cristal for a pre-Super Bowl champagne party at a Phoenix nightclub. The club thumped with deejay beats and filled with guests who paid up to an eleven-hundred-dollar VIP cover charge.

Somewhere a Cristal public relations firm was giddy over Diddy. Tabloid reporters from the *New York Post* to the Bay Area's SFGate.com dutifully reported the rapper's run on the expensive bubbly and resulting shortage. Although Cristal was available just over the border in Mexico for about a quarter the price, the press coverage alone might send up the bidding for smuggled spare bottles among the super rich who would not be denied any available luxury.

Other demands the host city could not fully meet without imported help included working girls. Phoenix area strip clubs hired hundreds of additional dancers to accommodate the desires of incoming visitors.

After a much quieter night in back in Sacramento, I dragged myself to the office Friday morning and attended only to the most pressing of work-related issues. My tasks included completing an ugly January sales report. Around two in the afternoon, I ducked out of the cubicle farm for a late lunch at home and one last, undistracted survey of about six large broker Web sites.

I fixed myself a bowl of soup and sat once more across from my computer. My cell phone would beckon me if the world beyond cyberspace called.

To my pleasant surprise, the floor pricing for upper-level singles had fallen into the mid-sixteen hundreds before commissions and fees at the largest of the online secondary brokers, Stubhub. A decade ago, Stubhub did not exist.

In 2000, two Stanford Business School students, Jeff Fluhr and Eric Baker, launched Liquid Seats. Within a year, 49er quarterback Steve Young signed on as an investor and advisor to Liquid Seats. Young, a law-school graduate and long-time admirer of Silicon Valley entrepreneurial culture, brought money, connections, and credibility to the company that would become Stubhub.

Soon after going into business together, Fluhr and Baker forged a deal with the Phoenix Coyotes of the National Hockey League (NHL). They secured exclusive rights to solicit Coyotes season ticket holders for unwanted seats. The deal served as a groundbreaking prototype for an increasingly close relationship between teams and broker resellers.

Baker eventually left the company to start up a European-based rival. In early 2007, eBay bought out Fluhr's interest for just over three hundred million dollars. The sale consummated not long after an aggressive radio campaign indelibly branded Stubhub in the minds of the fans. The effective audio signature of Stubhub was a familiar blare of an arena bullhorn followed by a call out of "Stubhub!" The voice evoked the cadence of a ballpark hot dog vendor, a universally recognized shout-out to sports fans. Today, Stubhub is the largest secondary-market ticket broker in the country. According to CNNMoney.com, Stubhub handled five million individual transactions in 2007, more than in the prior combined six years of the company's brief history.

Eight months after eBay acquired Stubhub, the new management team reached an exclusive deal with major league baseball (MLB). The arrangement gave Stubhub a direct marketing pipeline to season ticket holders across the league. MLB got a piece of the combined twenty-five percent in commissions Stubhub earns on either end of a ticket buy and sell transaction. The partnership effectively thawed the sometimes icy relations between the American pastime and a ticket reseller by linking their interests.

While Stubhub bills itself as a fan-to-fan exchange, the company also exercises volume purchasing power to acquire tickets held by independent brokers. Local agencies may trade smaller profit margins from selling to a larger volume reseller rather than risk not finding a retail buyer for the same ticket.

Some fans consider independent resale brokers no more than opportunistic scalpers with a business license. This perception presumes ticket values for sold-out events ascend in a straight line. All brokers assume risk each time they buy a ticket. Falling market values may force them to sell a seat for less than they paid.

Some brokers fear the current trend, wherein professional leagues secure exclusive resale partners, may upset the competitive balance of the resale industry and ultimately limit options for individual fans. Resellers currently are not required to disclose to buyers where they originally acquired the ticket.

Stephen Happel, an economics professor at Arizona State University and noted authority on the subject of ticket scalping, wrote in the *Cato Journal*, "With strict licensing, a possible means of control would be to require scalpers to disclose all ticket sources. In scalping, competitors and consumer groups might scrutinize sources."

Forcing sellers to disclose how they acquired a ticket may not necessarily be a pro-consumer measure. In fact, such a requirement could aid leagues or teams seeking to enforce their exclusive ticket resale deals and restrict exchanges between their season ticket holders and other resellers. At least one pro team has already readied subpoenas to try to compel independent brokers to release customer lists.

With about forty-eight hours to the kickoff of Super Bowl XLII, my right to freely shop and compare remained intact. If Mindy and I flew into Phoenix on Saturday morning, we planned to locate a locally owned and operated ticket broker. I still saw an upside to the convenience and certainty of closing a deal before we left Sacramento. I had not even packed my bags for Phoenix. Our flight would leave in about fourteen hours.

On Friday afternoon, a major online broker with a high volume of seat offers caught my attention. All week long, they appeared to be just slightly undercutting the prevailing prices, perhaps systematically testing the market's bottom. I had not heard of the company before my Super Bowl ticket search but bookmarked their site in my Web browser along with a handful of competitors. I noted an upper-level single in section 433 listed at sixteen hundred dollars. With the broker's commission, the total would be eighteen hundred fifty-four dollars. I could live with that price if I could get it. The amount exceeded the per capita gross domestic product of forty-four nations as reported by the Central Intelligence Agency's 2004 *World Fact Book*.

With the monitor screen displaying the seat offer, I clicked *buy*, entered my credit card information, and dug my cell phone out of my pocket. At this late date, there would be no shipping of tickets, only a designated Phoenix area pickup point for confirmed orders. I wanted to confirm the details with a real human being.

As I punched in the customer support number, an e-mail detailing my order arrived in my Inbox.

> *Thank you for shopping at ----. We have received your order for Super Bowl tickets. We will send you an e-mail (usually within 48 hours) that will confirm your order and will contain other important order information. For any questions regarding this order, please call our Customer Care team. Please keep this e-mail as it contains your Web Order ID number. All orders are subject to availability and all sales are final.*

Everything appeared to be a go. I reached a young agent I will call Jerry and gave him my order number.

"Yes sir, I have it right here. Eighteen hundred fifty-four dollars on your Visa. Can I get your address? Thank you. Now for security purposes, I'll need the three-digit code on the back of your card."

I could hear the buzz of the call center behind his voice. It actually sounded soothing. There would be no nightmare scenario on Sunday afternoon of three people with two tickets and no way to avoid crushing disappointment.

"Thank you, sir. Now we will also need a photocopy of both your credit card front and back side and your driver's license to complete the transaction," Jerry instructed.

I looked to my right at my dated Hewlett Packard printer scanner, then below to my Dell desktop with a paltry 256k RAM of processing power.

"Oh, boy," I exclaimed. "Would you mind holding the line for a minute, Jerry? I'm not sure I can do this conveniently from this workstation."

"No problem, sir."

I placed my driver's license and credit card on the glass top of the scanner. I fiddled and fumbled with the controls. I did not use this function often on this particular machine. I had installed a late-model scanner interface at my work cubicle. I could have belted out what I needed in about twenty seconds if I was sitting there instead of here at home with a less-than-user-friendly device.

The scanner whirred and hummed. A neon green light passed at an agonizingly slow pace below the hood's plastic cover. I had mistakenly left the settings in high-resolution mode.

"How's it coming, sir?" Jerry asked from the other end of the cell connection.

"Crap. It's a ten megabyte file. I don't even know if I can send this over from here. I'm at home right now. Can I send this to you from my workplace? It just takes a minute from there to do this."

"Well, sir we have the tickets on hold right now. I need the information to confirm your order."

I sensed hesitation in Jerry's voice.

"I don't understand," I replied. "I know you need the backup information but what are you saying?"

"Basically, we have fifteen minutes to complete this transaction before the ticket is released."

The last thing I wanted to do was to give Jerry my sad tale of technology gone awry. I had encountered enough contrived stories online all week long. Excuses, covers, little white lies, and big fabrications had littered so many buy-and-sell offers from private parties. They were amusing at first, then just tiresome. Some personal facts and circumstances were heart-wrenching if they could be believed. A son tried to find a ticket for his eighty-two-year-old Marine veteran dad. Parents living in the shadow of the stadium offered up their home and personal cooking services if someone had a ticket for their teenage son. Mom is having surgery. Last chance to see a Super Bowl. Will swap jet skis, sports memorabilia, and loosely defined escort services for a seat. On and on it went. I had no sob story, only a need for some basic consideration to get into the Big Game.

"So, Jerry, you're telling me even though you have my credit card number, my address, and my consent to give you any other personal information you need over this phone line, you can't guarantee me this ticket?"

"That's right, sir. I have to have photocopies of the credit card and the driver's license. It's for your protection."

I could not see how this specific sequence of events was protecting my security. If I had just been clubbed in an alleyway and separated from my wallet, the assailant would had have a leg up on getting my ticket as long as they were a few paces from a Kinko's. Of course, that did not matter. I took the first of many deep breaths.

"OK. I understand the rules, Jerry," I said with a firm tone. I really want to complete this transaction. All I am asking for is some reasonable accommodation. I am in front of my home computer. I need at least fifteen more minutes to get in my car, get on the freeway, and get to a decent photocopier and fax machine to get this stuff to you. If you can help make that happen, I can get my ticket. If not, can you please escalate this matter to a supervisor?"

Jerry agreed and left me for about ten minutes as ear-splitting, bad grunge music blasted through the receiver while I was on hold. I was doing a slow burn sitting there staring at my screen's message, "Your Order for Super Bowl Tickets Has Been Received." I hoped a voice of reason would prevail.

Jerry returned to the line with his own story about ticket representatives in the field at the physical pickup point who needed to approve any extension. I had real trouble believing this explanation. The ticket I thought was mine was no more than a contract at a specified price. It was about to re-enter the free-agent market if only for a matter of minutes. I was beginning to smell bait, switch, and up-sell. It was four fifteen in the west. On the East Coast, afternoon commuters would soon arrive home. Some would be New York and Boston area partisans. They would settle in behind home computers and by cruising for tickets, spike traffic on the information superhighway.

Finally, after I prodded his supervisor, Leo, Jerry came back to the phone. He told me I had more time to get the documents to him and secure the ticket. I thanked him and rushed out the door to beat Friday rush hour traffic. Within twenty minutes, I had returned to my office, faxed out the copies of my credit card and driver's license, and e-mailed to Jerry from my cubicle. I could not help being a tad caustic.

Jerry – Hopefully, Leo is now confirming the sale. Please reference the sale

number from my online booking. I am glad we can get this thing done at the price point provided. Your office, not the person out in the field, should be able to arrange for reasonable fax time if needed ...
Jeff

Of course, I had not delved into the fine print disclosures about the broker's transaction practices. I was certain there was adequate cover buried within the company Web site to insulate against any grievance. Perhaps good faith would prevail or the market would hold at the specified price. After a few more minutes without a reply from Jerry, I phoned customer support and reached Denise.

"Yes, the fax is coming in now," she said. "It will just take us a few minutes to verify and we'll contact you."

Maybe the documents were still downloading or sitting in a tray somewhere.

I waited about ten more minutes before calling Denise back. Now it was after five in the West. Empty cubicles surrounded me. This time, she confirmed my documents had been received and verified. As far as the company was concerned, I was not a fraud. However, it fell to Denise to deliver the full message I had been anticipating. I had enough business experience in limited inventory and dynamic pricing models to recognize the game was already in progress.

"Well, Mr. Fekete, I have good news and bad news."

"OK," I said.

"We found you a ticket."

"Great."

"But it's in a different location."

"You know that's all right, Denise. I understand there is plenty of Super Bowl ticket activity right now. Any seat location is fine," I spoke in a level tone, but I sensed there was more bad news on the way.

The whole transaction smelled bad. Every momentary fluctuation of the market, every call and click, every new posting and confirmed sale, created an opportunity to make relentless, real-time adjustments in pricing and profit, all of which is unseen by the average buyer.

"I presume it's at the same eighteen-hundred-and- fifty-four dollar price on the original e-mail message I received?"

"It's not," Denise answered.

Her words inflamed me like sparks in dry tinder. It was not about the money anymore. I staunchly advocate free markets. I had been on the other end of supply-and-demand realities in my daily work. I would no more apologize for high rates levied on a procrastinating advertiser than not applaud a great bargain secured through advance booking. Fortunately, radio ad rates had yet to succumb to continuous, computer-modeled price modification.

The more distance from the tangible product and the end user, the colder, more impersonal, and more subject to abuse the marketplace. The forces driving the Super Bowl ticket market on the Friday before game day had no regard or sympathy for me. This was all right with me up to a point, a point just passed right now.

"Well, how about that?" I answered bitterly. "And tell me please, Denise, what would that *new* price be?"

"After all fees, twenty-one-hundred and six dollars" she answered mechanically.

I had watched the movements of the Super Bowl ticket market intently for more than a week. I knew a double-digit percentage price jump in an hour was technically possible. I also suspected it was highly unlikely a volume broker interested at all in fostering customer goodwill could not have locked up the ticket under the circumstance at the original quote. I wondered aloud if the company imposed the extra costs either out of arrogance or because of my being a royal pain-in-the-ass by insisting on extra time to transmit documents.

"You know, Denise, I think I need to be connected with your supervisor." I said. She drew the duty of breaking the news. Someone in a senior position could listen to my wrath.

My conversation with a fourth company representative, Tammy, lasted about ninety minutes. I vented, railed, and questioned the very core of the company business practices. I said the unlicensed, and likely unwashed, shady scalper in the parking lot had more credibility than this organization.

When Tammy explained that her understanding of the ticket was as a commodity, I pushed the boundaries of proper decorum and launched into a tirade. If she believed her product was a commodity, she was going to get an earful.

I pointed out the absence of any serious independent oversight in the ticket-broker industry and suggested that might need to change. Perhaps fans needed to raise concerns with the Commodities Futures Trading Commission, Federal Trade Commission, or Securities and Exchange Commission.

What problems might occur with the rapid swapping of buy-and-sell contracts for Super Bowl tickets in a market with such a small amount of tradable inventory? What potential exists for a few dominant brokers to collude and orchestrate phantom auctions for tickets within blocks they control to create the appearance of escalating demand? How might exclusive resale contracts with pro leagues indirectly enable such abuse? Should sports franchises try to restrict where and to whom season ticket holders resold their seats? Are there any politicians out there who might jump on a populist issue, raise antitrust questions, or even overreact with bad public policy in response?

A few feet away from me, one of our local evening talk-show hosts prepared for his upcoming broadcast. He shook his head bemused as he listened to my rant with more than casual interest.

I asked Tammy if she was aware of a new Web-based futures market. At Yoonew.com, fans place bets on Fantasy Seats to major title games, based on odds a specific team actually advances to the contest. The concept cleverly extends the traditional *football futures* betting model. In football futures, a bettor gambles at the start of the NFL season on whether a given team will win a division, conference, or Super Bowl. In Fantasy Seat futures, the payoff for a correct bet is an actual ticket to the big game.

So you think the Packers are going to next year's Super Bowl, Tammy? Do you want to spend less for a ticket? Just purchase an option-futures-style contract for a couple of hundred bucks or more based on your team's projected chances to advance. If the Pack does not make it, you are out your money. If you guessed right, the house buys you a ticket from proceeds collected from less fortunate fans and fellow gamblers. However, the house hedges the bet. If for some reason they cannot convert your Fantasy Seat to a real one, you may only get triple your money back. That means if you make a cheap wager on a long shot to advance to the big game, your three-to-one substituted cash payout probably will not cover even a face-value price ticket to the sold-out event. A true gambler would be far better off simply placing the cash bet for a higher return. As with any casino, the house has done the math necessary to guarantee victory for itself.

The Fantasy Seat proposition skews the numbers even more in favor of the bookie. The same skills required to calculate risk and make odds in the fantasy seat business apply in managing a hedge fund, trading derivatives, and pricing real seats dynamically in real time. Ownership is no longer a strategy, but an inconvenient step to be avoided if possible through leverage and short sale. Profits are much less earned than they are extracted, not unlike flipping real estate while disregarding the long term fundamentals necessary to sustain a neighborhood. Ticket brokers have a vested stake in a limited amount of seat inventory changing hands as often and as rapidly as possible since they make a fee on every transaction. For example, 70,000 Super Bowl tickets bought and sold an average of three times each equates to over 200,000 potentially commissioned sales and a turnover rate of three hundred percent. The U.S. stock market reached historically high turnover levels in 1929 immediately before the crash and Great Depression.

The hot, ticket-resale business now emulates our national preoccupation to buy low, sell high, and hold nothing. We scramble to extract wealth through cracks and fissures in the market rather than earning it on a solidly built foundation.

Short-term packaging and trading of risk rapidly gave rise to no-documentation mortgages that rolled into mortgage bonds and blew up into a credit crisis. Ticket brokers and mortgage brokers operate in different arenas but they are both agents in a wider infrastructure that benefits from a particular trading psychology. An environment of speculation, urgency, speed, and fear of loss rules over investment, patience, deliberation, and the resolve to say no.

As the big game approaches, the perfect storm of passionate buyers, calculating sellers, and tracking technology sends prices spiraling upward. Having vented passionately for nearly two hours to no avail, I remained the calculating buyer.

"I'm flying to Phoenix in the morning, one ticket short, Tammy." I finally said. "I know broker press materials discourage people from going to a Super Bowl host city without a ticket. I also know I can find another licensed broker I can work with face-to-face. Meanwhile, I would appreciate it if you keep my credit card information and leave my order open in case you do find that ticket at the price your company posted."

"That's not a problem, sir," Tammy answered, perhaps sensing an end, if not a resolution, to our stalemate. I left this patient, but powerless, gatekeeper with something to contemplate.

"I hardly expect anyone there will find that ticket for me, especially after all the grief I've given you, Tammy. You have been as good a customer service agent as someone else allowed you to be. I am very sorry no one gave you the authority to do what is right. Someday you will remember this phone call. It will remind you of why you decided to leave and work somewhere else. I will promise you this. I'll have the decency to contact your company tomorrow to close that order out when I get a ticket from another source."

"I've held the order open, sir. Is there anything else?"

"No, thank you. Have a nice evening."

With that, I hung up the phone, shut off my computer, and drove home.

VI. Festival in the Desert

A thin, sweeping strip of ivory white light divided the darkened expanse on the upper level inside Reno's Club Cal Neva sports book. I ascended the last carpeted step rising above tightly packed rows of colorful slots and video poker games beeping and flashing on the casino floor below. A sea of plush, velvety chairs and mostly empty, round cocktail tables separated me from the light source, a long counter stretching the length of the room.

It was a few minutes before the eight o'clock weeknight closing time for a quiet corner of this historic well-worn gambling house. In about forty-eight hours, a caravan of Labor Day budget travelers from Northern California would spill into Reno from beyond the Sierra Nevada mountain range. They would trace in reverse the paved-over path of nineteenth century pioneer wagon trains.

The Club Cal Neva opened in Reno in 1948, exactly a century after the discovery of gold in California spurred massive western migration. The Reno site is a younger sister property to the original Cal Neva perched about forty miles to the southwest, smack on the California-Nevada border at the shore of Lake Tahoe. The first Cal Neva opened a generation earlier in the heady days immediately preceding the great stock market crash.

In July, 1960, Frank Sinatra, with alleged behind the scenes backing of New York and Chicago mob figures, applied to the state of Nevada to take over the Cal Neva's gaming license. Dean Martin, part of the legendary Rat Pack, backed out of the partnership early. The whole gaming business and the characters it attracted did not sit well with Martin. Over the next couple of years, the famous, the beautiful and the powerful attended lavish parties at the sleepy little lodge on the lake.

J. Edgar Hoover's FBI kept close tabs on the Cal Neva. Agents suspected Sinatra was merely fronting for mafia bosses Anthony Salerno and Sam Giancana. It was not long before Sinatra's brash demeanor and shady associates alienated Nevada's tightly knit political and business establishment. In time, the state ran Ol' Blue Eyes out of the gaming business.

There is much fodder for conspiracy theorists and amateur detectives that is wrapped up in this sliver of the Cal Neva's long history. The paths of many players in mob folklore, pre-Castro era gaming in Cuba, and even the Bay of Pigs invasion, can be traced to Lake Tahoe in the early sixties.

Both Robert and John Kennedy spent some time at the Cal Neva.

Rumors of Marilyn Monroe's affair with JFK center on the Cal Neva's private bungalows. They are connected to the main lodge by discreet underground passageways that tourists can see today. Enough years may have elapsed for current Cal Neva ownership to start trading on these legends.

A new generation of young visitors has revived some of the styles and fashions of the era. Martinis and lounge music have made a comeback. To those born and raised since the hotel's nefarious heyday and exposed to the Clinton-Lewinsky scandal, whispers of a Kennedy-Monroe affair are quaint by comparison. The times are ripe to bring at least some of Cal Neva's storied past out of the shadows.

Today, the casino runs a significant legal sport betting operation large enough to serve as a subcontractor for other gambling houses throughout Nevada. Under this arrangement, hotel and casino properties can capture a piece of the lucrative sports gaming revenue segment without employing resident analysts to set spreads across a dizzying array of games. The Cal Neva staff create a multitude of thoroughly researched propositions and exports their expertise to client casinos across the state.

Pro football wagering is a big part of the action. My Club Cal Neva visit fell just a few days before the start of the 2007 NFL season. As I crossed the lounge area toward the sports book, a ticket gurgled up from a narrow slot in the counter. The lone agent taking wagers flipped it off the dispenser. He handed the slip of paper to a customer he hoped would be his last before the shift formally ended in about ten minutes. The agent's body language revealed disappointment as I approached his station and casually picked up a *Football Futures* printout from a clear plastic rack mounted on the wall. His countenance fit that of a Nevada bookmaker. A little grizzled and edgy, the fellow could have walked straight out of central casting to play an extra in *Casino* or *Oceans Eleven*. He wore no nametag.

A nickname like Stash or Little Joey might fit him well.

Right now, he was just the man on a mission to get the hell out this darkened hole as soon as possible. I was on a little mission of sorts myself to toss a comparatively pitiful sum against a multimillion-dollar odds making machine. I was now the agent's probable last customer of the day. His money had been on scoring an earlier exit. I did not terribly mind troubling him to hang around until his appointed quitting time.

"I'm shutting down," the agent grumbled.

I lifted an eyebrow just slightly, pursed my lips, and glanced down at my watch. It ran a bit fast but read 7:52.

He ruefully conceded the point before words could form on my lips in response.

"Ya got five minutes," he said.

He knew instinctively I was not a regular, a local, or a serious gamer. In sports book parlance, I was a "square," bookie talk for a novice, a nobody, a rookie. I did not pour over lines and stats, at least not in sports betting parlors. I just made an occasional bet for entertainment. He was right on all counts. I was not a professional gamer. Reno was neither home nor final destination but a way station and jumping off point to somewhere else.

I offered a weak and less than sincere smile of gratitude for the privilege of picking out a stubby pencil and making my selections.

Futures are a relatively new entry in the sports betting world and involve the house laying odds on outcome likelihoods of not just one game but an entire season. The futures concept was also gaining a foothold in the secondary ticket market as a thinly masked gambling proposition.

The Cal Neva pegged the New York Giants as a forty-to-one shot to win Super Bowl XLII on this evening. I passed over them and scanned the odds sheet outlining chances for various other teams to win respective division, conference, and the league titles.

My wife has always been amused by my modest command of pro football trivia and likely relieved by the equally modest investment I put into season futures. In late summer, I often spoke of investing a few dollars in football futures figuring it would be a fun way to follow the fortunes of a few teams throughout the year. Even if my favorite teams fell out of the play-off race, I could keep a betting interest and root for my wallet if nothing else.

After much talk and no action, I finally had gotten around on this night to playing the futures for the first time. I put sixty dollars on the agent's counter.

Mindy's mere presence in this decidedly male domain certainly tipped off my "square" credentials. She appeared annoyed by the restless agent waiting for my completed sheet and wager. I quickly checked off twelve predictions and bet five dollars on each. Eventually about a third of the money came back to me thanks to play-off runs by Seattle and San Diego. As for the rest, the Cal Neva could thank me for offsetting what was likely about five minutes of their electric bill.

With wager tickets in hand, I headed back downstairs with Mindy. We crossed Virginia Street under the famed neon arch proclaiming Reno the Biggest Little City in the World.

Many professional marketing people in Reno work feverishly to polish the faded image of the main boulevard running through the old downtown. Virginia Street touts a wedding chapel, pawnshops, and t-shirt joints interspersed among the gaming houses. Mostly downscale tourists meander around a scattered few lost souls that have likely seen their share of detox clinics and jail cells.

Capital investment for renovation certainly found a way to the landmark stretch of Virginia Street in recent years. The Carano family's hotel triad consisting of the Eldorado, Circus Circus, and the newer Silver Legacy, did brisk business as did the publicly traded Harrah's. Additionally, Reno events like Hot August Nights, a car collector celebration attracting five thousand vintage American automobiles to the city and surrounding area annually, made a generally positive mark.

Civic leaders in the area try hard and receive all too little credit from the outside world for their efforts to promote the town and stimulate a culture beyond gambling. Having lived in Sacramento and Philadelphia, places where San Francisco and New York cast respectively long shadows, I could empathize with the challenges Reno faced. Finding an identity beyond that of Nevada's other gaming Mecca is no easy task.

Many of Reno's downtown revitalization efforts had sputtered in the face of recently introduced Indian gaming in neighboring California. Condominium conversions of old properties like the Comstock struggled to find buyers in the rapidly cooling housing market. In 2002, a Canadian hotel group bought out the former Flamingo Hilton intending to continue operating as a gaming venue. I attended the grand reopening media party, a lavish public relations exercise that new management hoped would garner press interest. Shortly after rechristening the property the *Golden Phoenix*, this venture also sputtered, struggled, and finally flamed out just like its namesake. The casino now sat boarded up, its fate uncertain.

My football prognostication completed, Mindy and I walked past the shuttered Golden Phoenix. An illuminated neon Leprechaun beckoned us into the neighboring entrance of Fitzgerald's, a reasonably nice but also financially troubled property. A decent room at "The Fitz" was ours that night for just forty bucks, hardly a pot of gold.

We glided through light casino floor traffic and found a small bar staffed by a happy, sixty-something gent. He was pouring large, seven-dollar frozen margaritas into tall plastic souvenir glasses bearing the hotel's shamrock logo. A perfectly natural Mexican-Irish mix, we supposed.

"The price includes the glass," the bartender cheerily informed us.

"Look at this," he said as he reached under the plastic base of the vessel and flicked a tiny switch.

The container lit up. A flashing array of green, red, and blue lights danced across the paneled surfaces of the container. The cups were cheesy, festive, and attractive accessories for consuming alcohol.

We ordered two of the frothy, frozen drinks.

With his clean-shaven face, crisp white shirt, black bow tie, and neatly styled gray hair, the bartender looked the classic part of an earlier time.

Perhaps he had worked the region long enough to serve the iconic figures of the past.

"Would you like the usual Jack Daniels and water on the rocks, Mr. Sinatra? Or, you know we did just get a wonderful cabernet delivered up this week from Napa Valley."

Tonight, instead of serving martinis to the Rat Pack, this bartender handed two slightly bored tourists a couple of blended margaritas in strange, flashing plastic cups. The designer probably built in the psychedelic light show to enhance other mind-altering activity.

"These cups would fit right in on the playa," I said to Mindy after our server set out the drinks and turned away towards the cash register.

"You must be going to Burning Man," the jovial, weathered barman said as he returned with our change.

Wherever time warp he came from, I knew the fellow was hip to evolutionary art, cultural expression, and Reno's significance as a launching pad to the Burning Man Arts Festival.

"Yes," Mindy answered slightly startled by the perceptive server.

The bartender restored our faith in the credibility of a relatively new Reno marketing slogan, America's Adventure Place. We were indeed on an adventure as were many other people in Reno en route to Burning Man.

A hundred physical miles and a million psychological light years separated where we sat from the *playa*, the broad desert wash in the town of Gerlach, Nevada where the festival was already throbbing.

The Burning Man Arts Festival is an eight-day gathering in the harsh, unforgiving middle of nowhere. In 2007, over 45,000 attendees or "burners" brought in everything needed to survive on a barren, flat, largely waterless ancient lakebed known as Black Rock Desert.

For one week a year leading into Labor Day, this vast, empty space maintained by the U.S. Bureau of Land Management, becomes Black Rock City, the sixth largest population center in the state of Nevada. The playa extends for miles and clearly shows up on satellite imagery as a chalky smudge ringed by rugged mountains. The remarkably flat surface and open expanse at Black Rock make it an ideal testing ground for experimental high-speed vehicles and even private-venture space rocket launches.

Burning Man and the Super Bowl share the common traits of large crowds, high admission price, and sheer spectacle. Suggesting more profound similarities to attendees of either event might prompt calls for a reality check. How could a desert arts festival bear any resemblance to a football game? Somebody throw a flag! I can hear the zebra-striped referee on the public address system now.

Illegal use of association ... A freaky countercultural gathering and an American sports tradition used in the same sentence. By conventional rule, these events may not be linked in any substantive manner. Replay the down from the spot of the infraction!

OK, let us review. I speculate that relatively few human beings have been to both Burning Man and the Super Bowl. As part of a presumably select club, I feel curiously obligated to fans of either event. Attendees may not appreciate the suggested kinship between these two gatherings of modern popular culture. However, the two mega-events are evolving in unexpected ways. In the process, they are perhaps becoming more alike.

The origins of Burning Man can be traced to June 21, 1986 on a beach near San Francisco's Golden Gate Bridge. A small group of friends spontaneously built an eight-foot tall abstract wooden sculpture, a figure of a man. They ceremonially burned the man as the Pacific Ocean's waves steadily rumbled under the night sky. Motivated by one man's desire to gather with friends as he exorcised sadness over a lost love, the event bonded both its invited participants and complete strangers. The participants resolved to return the next year at the same spot to repeat the act as a kind of cleansing ritual.

By 1990, the Burning Man crowd numbered in the hundreds and became a law enforcement concern. The *man* had grown to forty feet. The event had outgrown the beach. Police and event organizers forged an agreement on the spot. The crowd could erect the wooden statue but could not burn it. This impromptu pact was consistent with city ordinances and narrowly averted a small riot. Out of safety concerns, the event moved the following year to the desert.

At Black Rock Desert, Burning Man exponentially grew to a ticketed, week-long "happening" increasingly drawing thousands of people. A disclaimer on the tickets states that every attendee must bring all the essential survival gear needed for a harsh environment. With a few angry gusts, afternoon dust storms lift all but the sturdiest rebar tent stakes.

With the exception of portable toilets, there are few services. Ice and coffee are available for purchase at a center camp, but otherwise no monies exchange hands at Burning Man. A barter system thrives inside a sprawling temporary tent city. Easy navigation is facilitated by a semicircular alphabetical street system that follows from the center outwards in the pattern of a clock.

Ticket revenue supports the site's preparation and cleanup. Proceeds also flow back into community development projects in the economically challenged Gerlach area. The economic impact fosters a positive relationship between full-time residents and the huge migratory influx of "burners."

Burning Man operates as a nonprofit entity with a small paid staff, an army of volunteers, surprisingly few rules, and remarkable self-governance. The Bureau of Land Management issues a permit to the organizers for a substantial fee and with a key condition. Participants and organizers must restore the land to its original state of unspoiled and resplendent nothingness immediately following Labor Day. The *leave no trace* ethos influences attendees and helps keep the massive cleanup relatively manageable.

The admission cost, approximately two hundred dollars per person, does not buy attendees a seat. It simply permits passage through a gate.

Most attendees drive in and park in a fixed spot for the week in what might be the ultimate tailgate party. Over 150 private planes fly in for the event, negotiating tricky winds over a makeshift airstrip staked out on the dry lakebed. Vehicular movement other than entry and exit is restricted. Along with event staff vehicles, intricately decorated art cars and buses receive special permits to move about all week. For most attendees, bicycles become a primary mode of transportation over an area of several square miles.

The festival engulfs the senses with large-scale art exhibits, fire dancers, deejays, musicians, poets, clowns, costumed characters, body paint and participatory installations from full-scale roller rinks to pirate ships. Black Rock City has been called a form of "radical self-expression," in a first-timers event guide posted on BurningMan.com. In fact, the City produces its own newspaper and low-power radio and television broadcasts during the week. Hundreds of Web sites chronicle individual camps and facilitate social hubs throughout the year.

Participants apply their own time, money, and impressive engineering and design skills to create Black Rock City. Among those who find Burning Man a constructive outlet: a few early escapees from the late nineties tech bubble. Some fled before the dot com crash with stock option riches. Now they spend time, sweat, and cash building elaborate structures in the desert, including many that highlight innovative technologies.

For all who go, the Black Rock Desert venue demands active

participation. Safety goggles, masks, hiking boots, and large reserves of sun block and water all combat blowing sand and lack of shade. You work to get to this place. You invest. The sun and desert physically and mentally challenge you.

The reward for getting to the remote location and making camp at Burning Man is Mardi Gras, Carnival, Woodstock, and do-it-yourself street theater all rolled into one. Hundreds of elaborate theme camps unfurl each year on the playa as the product of collaborative groups from various cities and countries. These groups grow in number every year through online networking and local organizing events. Many toil for months building displays and making plans for the annual journey into the desert.

My wife and I have attended Burning Man twice and kept with the spirit of the festival by creating our own mini-themed camp. In 2007, we converted an open-sided, ten-by-twelve tent into The Black Rock Watery. We put out all the trappings of a winery tasting room complete with fake medals, plaques, and award ribbons, tasting notes, a bar, and palette cleansing crackers. Instead of serving alcohol, we snootily poured small samples of purportedly designer bottled water. We labeled and branded our own attractive bottles with enticing names like Serene Stream, Antarctica, and Kilimanjaro, to parody the mammoth bottled water business. Our temporary installation in the desert made an ecological point without being preachy or strident.

Social and political commentary and satire abound in camps with names like, Al Gore's Presidential Fitness Test, Mutant Audio Outpost, and Safer Sex Camp. Words cannot do these installations justice.

As visual spectacle and social phenomenon, Burning Man engages the outside media. Festival organizers and attending press use each other in pursuit of common and competing interests. Reporters who receive press credentials operate under a strict set of guidelines including obtaining permission from subjects for any photography. Much is made of the relatively small number of attendees who exercise the option to forgo clothing for part or all of the festival. The event promoters seek to balance media access with a desire to keep gawking to a minimum.

While not created to advance an agenda specifically, the festival has developed into a platform for new ideas encouraging participation around broad, central themes, including free thought, environmental awareness, and a loose kind of live and let live ethic. To plenty of people, Burning Man is simply a party on the grandest scale. What started as a very private event is rapidly becoming something else entirely, much to the consternation of some long-time participants.

Burning Man endeavors to be a noncommercial activity existing outside the conventional mainstream. The event's evolution to Super Bowl-sized proportions becomes harder to contain with each passing year. The vast desert space assures the capacity to expand and attendance will certainly top fifty thousand. The festival's sheer scope attracts enough disengaged onlookers to trouble many actively involved attendees.

Like counterculture movements preceding it, Burning Man may be destined to have some of its elements adopted by mainstream society. The playa offers fertile ground for mass marketers who are paid to identify emerging trends. As the event leaves an imprint on popular culture, popular culture seeps into the event. In 2008, the satellite channel Current TV broadcast the "burn," a development laced with irony for a gathering founded on the principle of "no spectators." Burning Man rejects passive viewing and encourages creative participation. This may become a losing battle as the festival continues to grow and attendees' coping strategies against the harsh elements improve.

A dispute among the festival's founders over the use of the Burning Man logo and brand has surfaced. At issue is fair use of the event name and marks for purposes beyond the festival itself. A legal tussle over the Burning Man logo contrasts strangely with artwork and installations displayed each year on the playa that skewer omnipresent corporate brand symbols in the most unfavorable light.

The central event remains the burning of the immense "man" near the end of the festival. However, the weeklong revelry, the entertainment, the camaraderie, and the opportunity to meet stimulating individuals from across the country and around the world are arguably bigger than the "burn" itself.

Whereas the Super Bowl was once simply a game day, it too is now a weeklong happening complete with entertainment, special events and activities. Many observers inside and outside of sports contend the extracurricular activity collectively transcends the game on the field.

The participatory factor in today's NFL stadiums spills from the stands to the parking lot and beyond. Tailgating has become both art form and subculture even represented by a formal national association. Some fan clubs use their common bonds to do good works in their communities or raise money for charitable causes.

Radically self-expressive burners are not terribly different from passionate Oakland Raider fans seen Sunday afternoons in full costume and body paint cheering from the depths of the Black Hole at the Coliseum. These fans and others like them drawn by the game, in fact become part of the show. They are *participant-spectators*. Television has integrated them into the game coverage. An outlandish costume is not required to be a participant-spectator.

Fans amplify their cheers and jeers by posting on blogs, texting from their seats as the game unfolds, and venting opinions on sports talk radio to the point of becoming part of the fabric of the broadcast. Fans no longer just watch. They reinvent, redistribute, and redefine the game itself.

The game extends beyond the end zones and sidelines to encompass and facilitate the creation of something larger.

Fantasy football leagues actively engage fans and make anyone a coach. Software developers and professional leagues effectively produce joint marketing ventures through highly anticipated releases of realistic video games. Professional athletes take notice of the skill levels that have been programmed into their on-screen incarnations, or *avatars*, as depicted in NFL licensed electronic games. Fans watch games between real players and teams and then reinvent the same contests and match-ups in a virtual world.

Gambling, while hardly new, has joined the trend towards greater fan engagement by luring bettors with increasingly complex propositions and modes of participation. Offshore sports books sprout in cyberspace. Poker tournaments become events for ESPN. Broadcasters provide fans with online venues to draft fantasy teams or pick the perfect tournament bracket. Fans earn cash, promotional merchandise, and bragging rights for defeating thousands of online opponents.

The modern notion of audience participation to make the event more spectacular has roots in the Nevada desert.

For fifty-one weeks a year, Black Rock Desert is both desolate wilderness and dormant coliseum. For one week, nearly 50,000 people gather here in anticipation of a pyrotechnic display. What attendees share and create around the campfire transcends the purported main attraction or even the week of festivities. From this central event, subcultures, fan clubs if you will, emerge and thrive throughout the year. The "burn," like the game, becomes incidental to the event, the fellowship, and the chosen paths of the participant-spectators.

Burning Man rebels against a limited menu of predigested entertainment served up at an appointed hour from a centralized source. The festival is a backlash to the classic network television model that indoctrinated the baby boomer founders of Burning Man. A prescribed, narrowed choice of only three major networks demanded that passive, nonparticipating viewers fully engage their attention in a linear presentation of content interspersed with commercials. Technology obliterates this dated model.

Network audience ratings have plummeted. The evening news of Rather, Jennings, and Brokaw gave way to an incessant twenty-four-hour cable news crawl beginning notably during the Gulf War. Daily newspapers bleed circulation and fail to attract new readers in the wake of electronic immediacy. Even as consolidated local monopolies, the lone remaining daily paper barely reaches a third of the households in most big cities.

Radio and TV remain pervasive in our lives but less as delivery vehicles for mass simultaneous programming events. Today, these mainstream media serve subdivided and isolated format niches. Special interest programming ranges from Home and Garden Television available on most cable and satellite systems to *Good Morning San Jose,* a Vietnamese language radio program heard on the AM dial in the heart of California's Silicon Valley. A fragmented viewer base motivates large broadcasters to consolidate by gobbling up additional pieces of an ever more thinly sliced pie.

Contrary to the views of some critics, more electronic outlets, enabled by cable, satellite, and the Web, have created greater programming diversity and broader choice. Along the way, we have also lost much of the shared common experience dictated by narrower options served up to past generations.

Super Bowl XLII was the most watched edition of the Big Game ever. *TV Guide* and Fox Television reported 97.5 million viewers on average at any single point in the broadcast. Overall, the game drew the second largest simultaneous American television audience in history.

What broadcast moment is the current national record holder for audience share? It is not *American Idol, Survivor, Dancing with the Stars,* or *Oprah.* It is not a reality blockbuster, sporting event, or anything else on the current television schedule.

The broadcast that attracted the most viewers at one time in American television history took place over twenty-five years ago. The final episode of *M*A*S*H* aired in 1983. *M*A*S*H* tallied 106 million viewers back when Ronald Reagan was in office. Nothing has topped it since. *American Idol,* a smash hit by today's standard, typically draws fewer than thirty million viewers or less than one in ten Americans.

Between nine-thirty and ten at night, eastern standard time, on February 3, 2008, when Eli Manning marched the Giants downfield for the late winning score, viewer totals peaked about 300,000 short of the *M*A*S*H* finale. The resiliency of Hawkeye Pierce and the gang is remarkable given the growth in the number of U.S. television households since the program signed off the air.

Possibly the last time the nation collectively and simultaneously watched the same televised images was the morning of September 11, 2001, as dozens of different outlets broke from regular programming to cover the breaking, tragic news.

As a population, we choose increasingly divergent viewing paths as quickly as media offers them. The Super Bowl commands $2.7 million for a thirty-second commercial, in part because the game is our last regularly scheduled communal television experience.

The disintegration of mass audiences scares the daylights out of marketers and media executives. Traditional media scramble to keep advertising patrons in front of as many consumers as possible. Radio, TV, and newspapers are not dead, but they are racing to become marketable by digitally streaming on-demand content. Localism is making a welcome comeback. The media now respond to the lives, schedules, and whims of audience members, not vice versa. The consumer has spoken. Evolve or die. Run it on my time. Upload the highlights online. Give me shortcuts. Give me the hometown angle. Let me talk back to the box.

In the listener's mind, a sixty-second radio script drags on for an eternity. These days I mostly contract thirty- or fifteen-second messages. Time once spent repeating phone numbers and storefront street directions goes back into the substance of the message. Busy listeners will not bother with *"now write this number down. That number again is ..."* or *"Turn left on Madison. We're right behind Arby's."* Advertisers need not give us what GPS navigation or a Mapquest search readily provides. Yellow page directories from multiple carriers gather dust next to landline phones where landlines still exist.

In recent years, I entirely stopped soliciting advertisers that lack serviceable Web sites. Short-form advertising now directs interested customers to supplemental information online or complete virtual storefronts. Those same customers access the Web for on-demand virtual tours and comments from other users. The same listener or viewer texting a vote for their favorite *American Idol* contestant is also meaningfully interacting with an embedded sponsor message. Such interaction trumps simple mass exposure alone in the new interplay between media and audience.

Competition for attention forces better service for a media consumer who is now increasingly empowered as a media *creator* via digital cameras and Web access. As mass audiences fragment, individual pieces share, copy, and exchange content among friends in small, networked communities.

However, a text message or My Space page has yet to replace larger scale connections that mass media once routinely provided. The physically connected experience a full movie house offers still has no online equivalent. However, the debut of Sony's Grand Theft Auto game grossed four hundred million dollars in the opening week of release, far outpacing the biggest motion picture numbers. While people still gather at the movie theater, a family night at home with a debut DVD release represents an increasingly competitive alternative that narrows, even isolates, the social experience. A night out at the movies has also become a fragmented affair with the rise of the multiplex. Human beings still seek and find common bonds on a greater scale in Black Rock Desert around a Burning Man or on the streets of a Super Bowl host city. What has changed about these large communal spectator events, is that those in physical attendance can report unfiltered from the scene to those virtually engaged beyond the main gate. Spectators can instantly share the event community, and thereby alter it, with a cell phone or digital camera.

There is other evidence to support the idea that technology can bring people together in new and meaningful ways. Web networking and discussion groups have the potential to prompt civic reengagement in churches, schools, and community groups. Political analysts marveled at the Web fundraising machines of Ron Paul and Barack Obama in the 2008 presidential campaign and that of Howard Dean in 2004. Such contributions may yet challenge the high-powered, lobby-based financing and prove healthy for the democratic process. This is a radical paradigm shift from knocking on doors and walking precincts.

To quote the lyrics of musician Gil Scott-Heron, later reprised by the popular rap group Public Enemy, "The Revolution Will Not Be Televised." At least not in traditional sense.

Increasingly, the revolution is blogged, You Tubed, and iPodded.

All of these new media are participatory, not passive. Users must actively select and interact. They can also opt to add their own content and attract their own audience in the process.

Even as the Super Bowl continues to command a mass audience viewing in real time, the traditional role of spectator as a one-way receiver of entertainment erodes.

The average fan is evolving into more than a lone voice in the crowd. Increasingly, "Making the Big Game" is about more than just arriving in the stands or turning on the television. It is becoming a creative act, the sum total of the fans contributing to a richer spectator experience. In the future, interactive technologies stand to shape the way we experience the Super Bowl both as a game and as a spectacle. As we evolve into participant-spectators, the spectacle itself will change.

Next time you find yourself in Reno, bet on it.

VII. Super Saturday

We originally considered that a scheduled early Saturday morning touchdown in Phoenix would be a plus. A nine forty in the morning arrival into Sky Harbor International would give Mindy and me a full day to avail ourselves of the Super Bowl pregame festivities. Of course, a pleasant Saturday in the Valley of the Sun presumed we already had a third ticket in hand or ready to pick up. We would still have neither when our plane rolled into the terminal.

Unlike the two-and-a-half-hour hop the two of us would make from Sacramento to Phoenix, Jason would be in transit over twenty-four hours. He patiently cobbled together a patchwork of remaining available flights so he could stutter step indirectly across the country.

My cousin was all-in for the game. He had come through for us. We still had to come through for him. We would be one ticket short with one day to go before kickoff. Late Friday night, Jason departed from Newburgh, New York on the opening leg of a marathon multiple connection flight. Earlier that evening, I put a price on allowing my nagging dread to persist one more day. If the hype and anticipation of Super Bowl XLII sent tickets on one last steep ascent, acquiring a third seat could be a personal financial headache. Holding two seats until kickoff risked a potential family rift and emotional heartache. From my perspective, a few more hours of uncertainty were an acceptable cost for not accepting price escalation at the very moment my purchase was being confirmed.

The substantial last-minute price boost that the online megabroker demanded both dismayed and utterly outraged me. Any stockbroker knows that market price movements indeed can happen in the time elapsed between the funds' verification and order execution. The premium sports ticket market was certainly behaving like that of any other volatile commodity even if not subject to the comparable outside scrutiny.

Whether or not the brokering company engaged in opportunistic manipulation or responded to simple market forces, it mattered little to me now. I believed I had seen enough over eight days to distinguish between honest fluctuations and badly disguised ransom. I ended my cyberspace chase for a third seat. On Friday night, after arguing vigorously with a whole series of phone agents and supervisors, my trust in buying with the click of a mouse vanished. From here forward, the Internet would serve only as a tool towards consummating a transaction in person.

The market had stabilized at anywhere from fifteen hundred to two thousand dollars. Translated into sixty minutes of actual football action, a ticket in the upper deck would run about fifty cents a second. Some fans would be paying over ten dollars for every tick of the regulation length game. That kind of money warranted some personal service.

My experience by week's end convinced me there was no longer a complete substitute for in- person contact. I was ready to test the theory on the street or at least with a reputable professional broker in a brick-and-mortar location. We would attempt to buy our third ticket on the ground in Phoenix rather than on the Web.

Meanwhile, our original plan for a quiet Friday evening in Sacramento went up in flames. Mindy and I had envisioned some decompression time from our stressful week of work and haphazard trip planning. Perhaps after a pleasant dinner and glass of wine, we would settle in for early lights out and much needed rest. Instead, by the time my telephone tussle and unsuccessful appeal for just treatment ended at my cubicle, it was after eight. I packed up and drove home where my wife had been waiting for about an hour. We dined late and in a less celebratory fashion than I had hoped. My adrenaline churned from agitation and the imminent trip to Arizona.

Mindy kept matters in perspective. After all, I was grumbling over a few hundred dollars and a principle. The proverbial once-in-a-lifetime experience precipitated the growing dent in our credit cards. Eventually, we would pay off the balance due fueled by our plastic indulgence. The financial conundrums Mindy routinely saw on a daily basis were far more serious and lasting.

Her work revolved around individuals often ruined by bad advice and unsuitable investments pushed hard by brokers seeking the highest possible commissions. Her clients were fighting for their financial lives.

She routinely dealt with obstructionist, opposing attorneys that threw anything and everything at her and Howard in order to reduce or deny compensation to defrauded pensioners. She sometimes vented about the constant stream of irrelevant or redundant motions, delay tactics, and other diversions hurled by well-financed insurance company defense teams.

My wife could relate to the source, if not the scale, of my ire over the ticket price lost on a technicality. After a frustrating workday, Mindy would often describe for me some contrived procedural roadblock she needed to get through. Her opposition hoped to avoid settlement no matter how egregious the violation. Early in her law career, she could not fathom these behaviors. I could.

"How can you expect your opponent to play by the rules on all these procedural things when they know the evidence is so stacked against them?" I finally asked my wife one evening. "Because the rules for what you can and can't do before a court are so clear and obvious," she insisted. "These insurance defense firms know the judge is going to reject the crap they put out there. They do it anyway to force a later hearing date or trip us up on some buried technicality or make us miss a deadline. It drives me nuts."

"Exactly," I replied.

"What?"

"It's just like Hack-a-Shaq," I shrugged and yawned.

"What are you talking about?" Mindy was exasperated at my sudden indifference to her plight. I did not need legal training to advance the conversation. In fact, my detachment probably helped. That and the fact we had watched a bit of basketball together over the years. Shaquille O'Neal's well-documented, free-throw struggles inspired the late game strategy named after him.

"Don't you get it?" I said. "You have the big, strong case. Your side is on the way to a slam dunk judgment in your favor. You're Shaquille O'Neal. The only hope the defense has is to foul you before you get to the bucket."

"That doesn't make any sense, Jeff"

"Sure it does. Think about it. Your opponents argue for crooked stockbrokers. They defend so-called financial advisors with iffy credentials and questionable products. Someone has to do it, right? They know you have them outscored and outmatched on the merits of the case. They know they can't win in a clean proceeding so they try to extend the game. They probably hope you'll just tire out and give up if they poke and jab you enough. If you don't, well they can foul you and force you to make your case on the line, or in this case, in court."

"And hope we miss."

"Yes."

"Well, Howard and I are lot better in front of a judge than Shaq is on the free throw line."

"Show me a one hundred percent free throw shooter and I'll show you a defense that won't try to foul when they're desperate late in the game. I can't tell you how to practice law but don't let these people get under your skin. They do what the client pays them to do. They want you to come unglued. If you react to them with your heart instead of your head, you'll pay for it. From what you tell me about judges, they can sanction you if don't respond professionally even to stupid arguments and motions. Even if you're right. It's just like getting a technical foul."

Ever since that conversation, whenever Mindy gets upset over some blatant stalling move by the defense, I just remind her of Shaquille O'Neal and Hack-a-Shaq. It helps defuse her anger.

Now, on this night before we were to leave Sacramento for Phoenix, Shaq also was about to be Phoenix bound. Quiet negotiations to move O'Neal from the Miami Heat to the Phoenix Suns were wrapping up. A resulting trade would soon be made public.

As for my irritation over the difficult online broker and still unsecured ticket, Mindy reminded me of my own advice to her. She was my teammate extolling me to put a horrific call behind me and keep my head in the game. Step up to the line. Make the shot you already know you are prepared to take.

"Everything will be fine. We'll get a ticket in the morning. Let's go to bed."

After much tossing and turning and much less sleep, the bedside alarm clock buzzer sounded just before five in the morning. Our quest for the elusive third ticket was going on the road and into overtime. We had a plane to catch.

After we landed in Phoenix, Mindy and I dragged ourselves over to the ground transportation area. We dropped our carry-on bags to the floor with a dull thud. In front of us was a long bank of white courtesy phones to local hotels and inns. I scanned bleary eyed for a placard designating a connection to our reserved airport motor lodge. Our inn had a location in Tempe just eight minutes from the Sky Harbor terminal. The lodging would be nothing fancy. We did not need fancy but we could use a ride.

"What's the matter?" Mindy asked after I frowned at the colorful backlit displays for various hotel and private shuttle services.

"Is your cell phone handy?"

I called the front desk at the inn and reconfirmed our reservation. Like every other room in town, the nightly rates were triple the norm or more.

"Have you guys got a free airport shuttle?" I asked the desk clerk.

The voice at the other end was friendly but absent the desired response.

"Oh, I'm sorry, sir. We don't have a courtesy van. It helps us keep our rates down. Would you like me to call a cab for you?" he said.

"Yes, please."

Welcome to Super Bowl XLII where three hundred dollars a night at the airport lodge assures no free ride from the airport. To the property's credit, our room was ready for early check in.

"The sooner we get this ticket thing done the better," I said to Mindy as we tossed our bags on the bed. "Did you bring your air card?"

"Right here," Mindy produced a slim black device from her purse. I slipped it into my laptop now unfolded on the bed.

After watching me monitor the market online all week long, Mindy knew the drill. She plucked the Phoenix yellow pages out from the bedside drawer and started calling local ticket brokers.

"Hi, what's your price for a single upper deck Super Bowl ticket? Sure I can hold."

My Mac Book hummed to life. I connected to the Web, clacking away at the keyboard to report my findings to her as she did phone duty.

"Lowest price at Stubhub is about eighteen twenty-six now, Mindy. That's after service fees, taxes, commissions, everything." The market already had dipped below the level claimed by the broker from hell on Friday night.

Mindy turned her attention back to her Blackberry as the agent returned to the phone.

"Yes, I'm here. Seventeen hundred? What is it "out the door?" Nineteen thirty-six twenty. Thank you." Click. Next.

" ... Right ... any section ... lowest price ... wow, that's a bit more than what we're seeing online ..."

We went back and forth like this for about twenty minutes. I surfed the national sites for real-time pricing. I dropped in on a couple of local broker Web pages to verify membership in the National Association of Ticket Brokers.

We required a nearby physical office. I quickly dismissed online-only vendors. Many used search term logic to cleverly masquerade as Phoenix-based. Mindy deftly worked her way through the low-tech yellow pages. She used a friendly phone manner I could no longer muster. She retrieved quotes and asked for callbacks if tickets came available.

"Uh huh, sure, we just talked with that company. They were working on eighteen hundred but couldn't confirm yet .... Yeah, we might be able to check back later if we haven't found anything."

I listened in as Mindy spoke with multiple agents. Now and then, I silently mouthed brief instructions or sent her nonverbal cues, passing a hand across my throat to reject less than competitive quotes, rolling my fingers in a loop if agents seemed to string her out too long.

"Yes, is this Front Row Tickets? I need one Super Bowl upper. Any location is good. Do you have anything? Sure I can wait."

I surveyed my screen, tapped away at the keys, and bounced from site to site. "Coast to Coast is over two grand, Razor Gator might have something in the seventeen hundreds. These guys you've got on the phone have an office about three miles away."

"Hello? Yes. What section? ... One seat, right ... Sixteen hundred?"

My eyes widened. I waited for the official signal. We had likely reached the approximate market bottom at least from a source that could guarantee an authentic ticket.

"Out the door? Sixteen hundred even." Mindy repeated.

I flipped both thumbs up.

"Yes, we'll definitely take it."

I wanted to spike my laptop, or at least the phone book, on the motel room floor and do a victory dance right there.

Being patient for a week and a day saved us about twelve hundred dollars.

"We've got our third ticket. Let's go get some lunch and have fun," Mindy said after she hung up.

"Let me make just two quick calls." I said.

The first call I made to Jason. He was airborne. I left a message confirming we had found the third ticket.

I placed the second call to the online broker that had been so indifferent to my complaint the night before.

"Yes, I'm calling to cancel the open order suspended last night. Yes, I have the confirmation number. No, I won't need a call back if something lower comes up. Just please verify my card is not being charged. Thank you."

I doubted any representative would have bothered to call me back even though the broker had posted lower offers on their Web site since the night before. My own sales career relied on keeping promises. I had promised the company a call back. I just considered it good business even in the absence of respect or trust earned.

We still had to wait a couple of hours before taking physical delivery of the third seat. Locally based runners were moving tickets back and forth across the region including one with our name on it.

Though we offered to provide a credit card over the phone, the broker representative did not take or run the card number until we were at their office. The local staff at Front Row could not have been more pleasant. They were supported by, not hidden in, cyberspace. They were not only NATB members, but also independently owned and members of the Tempe Chamber of Commerce. I liked that because it probably meant local reputation and relationships mattered to them.

We walked into a tiny lobby located in a corner office complex in Tempe. I peered through the open upper half of a split door that doubled as a small service counter. A little cubicle farm housed about ten workstations. The three or four agents still on duty smiled, joked, and talked about the game. Rather than running orders to the last moment, the shop would shut down in a couple of hours and would not be open on Sunday. One employee obliged our request to take a photo of Mindy and me holding our tickets. I wondered about the company's future prospects. Consolidated secondary market brokers, cyber trading, and sweetheart exclusive deals with promoters, venues, and leagues could make it hard for local brokers like these to compete for future business.

We perched ourselves on a low-rise concrete wall outside the Front Row office and waited for our cab. The brilliant desert sun reflected off the holographic imprint of our now complete set of Super Bowl tickets. Mindy pulled out her phone and made a call.

"Hi, Dad. Jeff and I are in Arizona. We're going to the Super Bowl."

She had postponed calling Alan for over a week with any news of our trip plans whatsoever. Only now did she feel confident telling her father she would be at the Big Game twenty-six years after his own Super Bowl encounter. I was relieved, tired, and grinning ear to ear when the cab rolled up to take us back to our motel.

With just over twenty-four hours to kickoff, Mindy and I could start enjoying our surroundings. We could greet Jason with ticket in hand when he arrived that night. Neither of us felt like sleeping. Instead, we headed into the heart of Tempe, a lively college community and home to the Arizona State Sun Devils. Nearly a decade earlier, an airline mishap deposited us in this very place and squarely into another festive football atmosphere.

Our return flight following an East Coast family visit in January 1999 departed late from Philadelphia. An unfortunate attendant assigned to our plane collided with a heavy baggage cart that rolled over her foot. While the airline recruited a replacement for the injured crewmember, our postponed takeoff lingered just long enough for us to miss a connecting flight in Phoenix. We would spend the day and evening of January 4 that year as distressed travelers in Tempe.

With the better part of a day to kill until our rescheduled flight, we decided to stroll around the Arizona State University campus. I had noticed ASU Sun Devil stadium on the approach into Sky Harbor International. Since I did not meticulously follow the college game, I knew the venue primarily as the Arizona Cardinals' temporary home stadium. Mindy and I figured we would have a largely deserted campus to ourselves on this Sunday after New Year's Day. School was out of session. Obviously, I had not paid attention to the sports page that day.

As we edged nearer the stadium and the district known as Tempe Town, we were engulfed in a sea of orange that wrapped around tens of thousands of Tennessee Volunteer and Florida State Seminole fans. Tempe was playing host to the Fiesta Bowl at Sun Devil Stadium. The game was for the Bowl Championship Series national collegiate title. An otherwise dull airline layover day instantly turned into a fun afternoon of people watching.

Before eventually catching a flight back home, we absorbed the full pregame revelry of the biggest college game of the year along the thriving avenues of Tempe. All because an errant baggage cart ran over some poor flight attendant's foot. Now Howard's bad knee meant lower-body pain had again bizarrely propelled Mindy and me to a big football game in Arizona.

On the second pass, we already knew Tempe was a fun place to visit. We made the central district of Tempe Town our Saturday night destination. We could finally embrace and enjoy Super Bowl mania.

On Mill Avenue, the main thoroughfare, the dominant orange of a Fiesta Bowl long past yielded to Patriot navy and Giant royal blue. Judging by the fans' apparel, the underdog Giants attracted more boosters. Inside the Tavern on Mill, we soaked up the scene with locals and visitors alike. I laid out my own pregame spin and analysis for my wife.

"I'd love to see the Giants win, but the Patriots are just dominant. It could be a blowout. New England's due for that." I pontificated as we waited for two cold beers at our table.

The Pats perfect season to date had featured overwhelming early victories over San Diego, Dallas, Washington, and Buffalo. As the regular season wound down, New England narrowly escaped a loss at home against Philadelphia. In the waning moments, only a late interception tossed by Eagle backup A. J. Feeley saved the Pats. The lowly Baltimore Ravens also got close to the year's biggest upset save for a late second chance created after a drive-stopping fourth down play. An ill-advised Baltimore defensive time-out prior to the snap nullified a critical Ravens stop. New England forged ahead on offense and squeaked out a three-point victory.

In the final week of the regular season, the Patriots took their 15–0 record to East Rutherford, New Jersey and Giants Stadium. The game proved significant on many levels. The Patriots were chasing history by seeking to become the first team since the 1972 Dolphins to finish the regular season unbeaten.

Normally, one of the four free national broadcast networks would have automatically picked up the game. However, the fledgling, league-owned NFL Network held sole rights to the game. The network reached only 35 million American households primarily through the satellite provider DirecTV. The NFL heavily promoted the season ending matchup. This in turn exhorted livid fans who were unfamiliar with the nuances of television programming and broadcast rights to bombard cable providers with complaints. While Time Warner, the largest cable operator, and the NFL haggled over distribution fees, two prominent United States senators got in the act.

Both the NFL and Major League Baseball enjoy an extraordinary exemption from federal regulation, specifically antitrust laws. In a December 19, 2007 letter that was sure to score political points back home, Pennsylvania Senator Arlen Specter and Vermont Senator Patrick Leahy fired a warning shot directly over the antitrust exemption and NFL Commissioner Roger Goodell.

In the letter released to media and posted publicly on each of the senator's official Web sites, the two elected officials relayed concerns of constituents, namely, New York Giants and New England Patriots football fans. The teams were scheduled to meet in the final regular season week of the 2007 season with New England angling for an unprecedented perfect 16–0 record. Something else would have been unprecedented without the intervention of Specter and Leahy. Fans without the DirecTV satellite service would have no access to telecasts of either the Giants-Patriots game and a second contest with play-off implications featuring the Pittsburgh Steelers and St. Louis Rams. The NFL Network owned exclusive television rights to each of these key games and with that ownership a seemingly golden marketing opportunity to drive paid subscription revenue on behalf of its broadcast partner, DirecTV. These revenues would come either directly from new DirecTV customers or from competitor cable and satellite providers paying DirecTV to rebroadcast NFL Network content. Time Warner Cable was already actively disputing these requested fees with the league. For the first time in the annals of televised American professional football, the NFL was creating the equivalent of a pay-per-view situation.

The senators captured the attention of Commissioner Goodell and the league's thirty-two team owners. They questioned the restriction of game telecasts that any of the free broadcast networks with NFL contracts would certainly have otherwise carried. They further suggested that limiting access to the specific games might prompt them to question a special privilege enjoyed by the league. The NFL's antitrust exemption bestowed by Congress allows the league to operate for all practical purposes as a monopoly. Specter and Leahy were senior members of the Senate Judiciary Committee with the influence necessary to bring the entire exemption into question before the full legislature.

The league quickly gave in to the senators' request to make the game more broadly available on free commercial television. CBS and NBC simulcast the Giants-Patriots contest nationwide along with the NFL Network. A thrilling 38–35 Patriot victory capping a perfect regular season also captured the highest recorded television ratings since the 2007 Oscars telecast.

The NFL and Time Warner agreed to settle their dispute over distribution fees through a neutral arbitrator. As the NFL Network gains prominence and the current series of NFL broadcast rights deals expire beginning in 2012, this minor skirmish will pale in comparison to future battles over how and under what terms fans see the big game.

Senator Specter, a one-time Philadelphia district attorney, was not finished with intervening in NFL issues. Days before Super Bowl XLII, he intensified appeals for further investigation into the Patriots' Spygate videotaping scandal. He even suggested that the history of Pats staff members who improperly recorded opposing team signals could have played a role in the Eagles' loss to New England in Super Bowl XXXIX. Few outside a rabid subset of Philly fans took Specter seriously on the notion.

While Mindy and I quaffed beers in Tempe on the eve of Super Bowl XLII at the Tavern on Mill, Goodell and Specter sparred publicly on Spygate. The commissioner defended his decision to destroy the infamous New England surveillance tapes, most notably those taken of the New York Jets prior to the season opener.

During Super Bowl week, Goodell contended the Patriots had already been stiffly fined and penalized for the conduct; there was no longer a need for the damning evidence to continue to exist.

"I do believe that it is a matter of importance," Specter said in a Capitol Hill news conference on February 2, 2008. "It's not going to displace the stimulus package or the Iraq war, but I think the integrity of football is very important, and I think the National Football League has a special duty to the American people and further the Congress because they have an antitrust exemption." *(Fish, ESPN.com)* There was Specter again playing the monopoly card. I polished off the remaining contents of my beer mug as the senator's statement dissolved from the screen.

"Well, I hope it's at least a close game." Mindy said as music blared in the crowded bar while classic Super Bowl highlights flashed in near synchronous motion from the screens overhead. "In fact, I'm making my prediction," she boldly continued. "I think the Giants are winning tomorrow".

"You and Jon Stewart are the only people I've heard say that all week," I said gathering myself up from the barstool.

On Monday, Comedy Central Daily Show host, and avid Giants fan, Jon Stewart, predicted a three-point New York win as he interviewed former quarterback Phil Simms. Simms must have been less conscious of Stewart and more aware the looming graphic of New England quarterback Tom Brady hovering over the set. In an absent-minded blunder at the end of the piece, Simms called Jon Stewart "Tom." It was similarly hard for me to pay much mind to the comic's predictions of a Giants upset.

"I think it's going to be close but I'm sticking with my prediction," Mindy playfully drew out her words and raised her finger for emphasis as we left the bar. I remained unconvinced she would be right.

"If it's a close score at the end and Tom Brady is out there, look out." I said. "The guy reminds me so much of Joe Montana. Do you remember those Niners games in the eighties?"

"That was before I met you. I wasn't going to games with my dad then."

"Well, I was watching. Fourth quarter. Niners behind. You just had that feeling Montana was unstoppable. He had a certain confidence. Brady has it too. If he has the ball with two minutes left, forget about it. Patriots win."

Our forecasting and liquid refreshment complete, we crossed Mill Avenue and I spied dinner. Corleone's Philly Steaks offered Tempe's rendition of the cheesesteak sandwich. Mindy knew when I got a cheesesteak urge there was no stopping me. I fit right into the place since I was wearing my McNabb Eagles replica jersey. A Pennsylvania Senator aside, no act of congress could get the Eagles to the Super Bowl this weekend. However, I could still find a bit of Philly right here in Tempe Town even amongst the Boston and New York faithful.

Our next stop was a couple of short blocks away in Tempe Beach Park for *NFL Super Bowl Saturday Night*, a free fireworks show and concert.

The big game has become as much a showcase for pop music stars as for the two best football teams in the league every year. This year was no exception. At least ten chart-topping artists played various venues throughout the week. Musicians now hold court in yet another ring of the Super Bowl circus joining the mind-numbing parade of general celebrity preening, media gawking, advertising, power-brokering, and deal-making.

Going to a Super Bowl and not participating in at least some star-studded, off-field event just would not do.

For many, the football game is simply a pretext for other agendas, whether getting into Paris Hilton's private party or chasing the endorsement of a political party. The latter would happen on Sunday across the Arizona state line in Santa Fe, New Mexico. It was there that former President Bill Clinton planned to watch the game at the governor's mansion. Bill's game plan was to woo former Democratic presidential candidate and sitting New Mexico Governor Bill Richardson to support Hillary Clinton for the nomination.

A photo of the meeting published later in the *Santa Fe New Mexican* shows the two politicians sitting on a couch on game day. Richardson, a man recently removed from the rigorous campaign trail, sports a new beard. He is clearly relaxed and enjoying the game. Next to the governor is Clinton, who is slumped and propping his head in one hand looking weary. I had done my share of time in VIP seats and luxury boxes during various sporting events of less magnitude. Whether advancing a sale, servicing a client, networking, or otherwise schmoozing, it can be hard to enjoy an event for the event's sake when burdened with other details and desires involving your fellow spectators. Clinton was grinding away at work. Richardson had the better Sunday.

Mindy understood the occasionally draining interplay of business and pleasure as well. Before becoming an attorney, she spent several years in the record business. We even worked together on some projects at the busy intersection of the radio and music industries. As a regional sales representative, she often enjoyed the perquisites of free CDs and concerts. She also at times found herself in settings where she envied those who could just enjoy the show.

On one such occasion, Mindy's brother, Tony, a big Grateful Dead fan, tagged along with her to a Northern California concert featuring the band's long-time drummer, Mickey Hart. The band for years encouraged and endorsed fans making bootleg recordings at Grateful Dead shows. Most musicians, and certainly every record label, frowned on the practice believing it denied fair compensation for artists and hurt music sales and revenues.

While advancing technology seems to be leading to shifting attitudes and looser restrictions on today's amateur concert recordings, the Grateful Dead were perhaps the first to adopt a laissez-faire stance.

For Mindy, the Mickey Hart concert at Shoreline Amphitheater in San Jose was a required workday event. Her employer at the time, Rykodisc Distribution, carried noteworthy catalogs of many artists including Jimi Hendrix, Elvis Costello, and Frank Zappa. For Mindy's brother Tony, an attendee at dozens of Dead shows and a collector of the homemade recordings exchanged among fans, the event was a greatly anticipated opportunity. He looked forward to a brief backstage meet-and-greet with Hart who was on tour to promote a solo album.

After the concert, Mindy and Tony milled about offstage with various retail buyers and record industry executives waiting for Mickey and the other performers to file into a cramped room. When Hart entered, an obligatory round of handshakes, greetings, and shallow banter ensued.

"Hi, I'm Sam with Tower Records."

"Nice to meet you, Sam."

"Really like the new record"

"Thanks."

"Mickey, I'm Joe with BMG Distribution. We met at the store appearance last month."

"Sure. Good to see you again, Joe."

Eventually, the artist worked his way over near Mindy.

"I'm Mindy with Rykodisc. Great show."

"Thank you, Mindy."

Tony extended his hand, smiled, then deadpanned.

"Hi, Mickey, I'm Tony. I'm representing my tape collection."

Hart broke up laughing. Finally, just a regular fan was in his midst.

On Super Bowl Eve as Mindy and I made our way through the gates at Tempe Beach Park, we were equally grateful to be just regular fans with no clients, no meetings, and no agenda other than completely immersing ourselves in the celebration. Many of the nearly thirty thousand concertgoers around us were ASU students and locals with and without game tickets who were at that moment thoroughly enjoying the spoils of living in a Super Bowl host city.

On the bill that evening was Counting Crows, a rock ensemble with five studio recordings and numerous film credits, along with Boys Like Girls, a rising new act hailing from the Boston area.

Shrewdly marketing to a young demographic, the slick NFL

production featured a massive screen behind the bands with smartly edited color highlights of the regular season and play-offs, thus providing total sensory overload. Cell phone cameras sprang up like illuminated weeds across the wide, rolling lawn as we moved in towards the stage for a closer look.

Jason's inbound flight was descending over Phoenix around ten at night, as a spectacular and deafening post-concert fireworks display turned night into day over the man-made lake bordering the park. I wished my cousin had been able to arrive in time to see the concert, but in the fashion of the new millennium, he would see much of it anyway. Within days, concertgoers posted no fewer than a dozen handheld video recordings of the show's songs on YouTube. Some enthusiastic fan even recorded a Counting Crows sound check earlier in the day and posted it. Clearly, the age of getting a camera confiscated at the gate was ancient history. Artists and labels now fully embrace, and fans fully enable, the kind of grass roots viral marketing opportunity such an event presents.

The last wisps of fireworks' smoke hung over the park. Along with the masses, we shuffled back to Mill Avenue. The woefully inadequate and overtaxed transit system offered no obvious means to cover the three miles back to our inn. Cabs rides were a two-hour wait. In that time, we could walk a long flat stretch of University Drive back to our room. We did just that.

Earlier, we had left a room key at the front desk for Jason. When we completed our late-night hike from Tempe Town, he was sprawled out on one of the double beds, munching on airplane snacks and watching Sports Center. He had successfully passed through a long and narrow travel window with little margin for error and without unexpected delays. He was lucky and glad to be there.

"Great to see you, finally!" I gripped my cousin's arm and gave him a little shake and hug.

"You too, man. Hey, Mindy!"

"Long flight?" Mindy asked as she greeted Jay.

"Hell, yes. But I made it."

I reached into my bag and handed Jason the ticket we had secured earlier in the day. Remarkably, the accounting worked out exactly as I had projected it would a week earlier. It was both a pleasure and relief to have three tickets and three people in Arizona. Tomorrow, Mindy and I would be in a Giants' season ticket holder section. Jason would be a few sections over sitting among Patriot fans.

The three of us caught up a bit until about midnight. We informally planned to get to the stadium as early as possible to take in the full game day experience.

Although I had newfound peace of mind with ticket and travel hurdles cleared, for the eleventh consecutive night, I slept erratically and fitfully, when I slept at all.

VIII. Phoenix Rising

CNN talking heads droned on from the television monitor mounted high in an upper corner of the lobby inside the Red Roof Inn. Commentators dissected every angle and nuance of the fast approaching Super Tuesday presidential primaries for consumption by an over-stimulated electorate. The volumes of campaign coverage generated in an endless news cycle over the previous months made the two-week sum of professional Super Bowl prognostication succinct by comparison.

In the distilled version of the political horse race, Mitt Romney clung to fading hopes buoyed by a Saturday win in the Maine republican caucus. Romney tried with little success to coax remaining Mike Huckabee supporters. He suggested a vote for the former Arkansas governor Huckabee was effectively a vote for front-runner John McCain. The campaign grind also whittled down a once crowded Democratic field to Hillary Clinton and a surging wild card. Freshman Illinois Senator Barack Obama chipped away at the Clinton lead as the race dragged on. Nearly two years of political play-off season leaves little time for regular season governing.

Super Tuesday could wait. Today was Super Sunday.

Exhaustion blended with anticipation again robbed me of anything resembling quality sleep on Saturday night. Our Sunday morning eight o'clock wake-up call, best described as a self-imposed *get*-up call, broke the sweet silence in our temporary quarters. From this point forward, adrenaline and caffeine would serve as primary energy sources. In a few hours, a pitched roar of 71,101 fans under a massive, bubble roof would replace the calm of dawn in the desert.

Our traveling duo had grown to a trio. Before seriously contemplating transportation options, Jason, Mindy, and I had a little time to collect our faculties while we downed pastries, tea, and cold juice. Twenty-five miles separated us from our lodging in Tempe and the stadium in Glendale. We had no fixed plan for making this essential leg of the trip.

Like much of the West, Phoenix is a home to an automobile culture. Parking passes at University of Phoenix stadium commanded a hefty resale premium just like game tickets. Securing a rental car on a few days' notice had proved impossible. Multiplying the demand the Super Bowl exerted on transportation infrastructure, the PGA had descended on nearby Scottsdale on this same weekend for the FBR Open, formerly the Phoenix Open.

The golf tournament drew record galleries and expanded the hordes of media, visitors, celebrities, and assorted hangers-on scooping up all available vehicles.

Hundreds of taxis continued to chase too many calls. Over twelve hundreds limos ferried the elite, the privileged, and the connected. Hundreds more privately leased charter buses carried other groups to the game. As part of the transit-challenged or simply the able-bodied impatient, Mindy and I had walked the three miles back to our motor lodge from the previous evening's concert in Tempe Town. On Sunday morning, the desk clerk would hazard only a vague guess at taxi wait times. A handful of fellow fans loitered in the lobby and speculated that a couple of hours might pass before a cab driver responded. The whole business was imprecise and unpredictable. The fare would likely push a hundred bucks. The idea of idling here in wait had little appeal.

While Mindy finished readying herself back in the room, Jason collected an orange juice and sticky bun and dropped into a comfortable lobby chair draping a complimentary *USA Today* over his lap.

I squinted at the text crawling above me on the television screen and printed across from me on the front page of The Nation's Newspaper. I was impervious to any unlikely new insight the Sunday morning commentators might offer on the narrowing race for the White House. Paid commentators had revealed themselves as no better forecasters of presidential politics than the average Joe or Jason.

"So, Rudy dropped out last week. Guess that leaves just one New Yorker still in it," I remarked to my cousin. The exit of former New York mayor Rudy Giuliani had drawn wide coverage this week.

"Yeah, a lot of people made a big fuss over him." Jason yawned. The whole America's Mayor thing, 9/11, blah, blah, blah. I know my firefighters' union wasn't too wild about the guy."

Jason was being kind. Rudy made the pictures of his reassuring, calm stride through Lower Manhattan on September 11, 2001 a personal calling card for his presidential bid. Many New York firefighters still seethed over what they perceived to be the mayor's failure to provide them with reliable communications equipment. The City acquired handheld digital radios through a thirty-three-million-dollar, no-bid contract. Six months before the catastrophe, the New York Fire Department recalled the new radios. They were defective and replaced by older models apparently not up to the task.

"I heard about the radios," I said sympathetically. "Guess the campaign revived some of those old news reports. I wondered about your take on it."

Unlike national political pundits, a few of whom I had met at various media functions, Jason required no shouting to speak loud and clear.

"I know a lot of people who won't miss Rudy much," he said as he tossed aside the news section and escaped into the sports page.

The premature coronation of Giuliani as a certain Republican nominee in the news media now read like one of the NFL Network's hysterical *Get Your Story Straight* promotional commercials. The popular spots lampooned armchair quarterbacks everywhere with true-to-life imaginary flashbacks. Satirical depictions of Everyman predictions echoed the early season conventional wisdom about teams and players. The spoofs held up for ridicule fans' bold preseason assertions and amateur analysis that in hindsight was faulty. In one of the vignettes, a man in a hotel room yaks away to an associate, "Eli? The closest Eli Manning comes to a Super Bowl ring is when he gives Peyton a manicure." Behind the man, a hotel housekeeper stumbles and drops a pile of dirty linens.

Cracked crystal balls were in ample supply this week.

I wandered across the lobby to the drink dispenser, rubbed my eyes, and noticed a man that had been a fixture here. A scalper ticket-runner had adopted the lobby area as temporary office space all weekend. He was a thin, leathery-skinned fellow dressed in a plain navy jacket, dark slacks, and casual brown shoes. Except for the lack of a uniform accessory, he looked the part of a valet, porter, or other ready-to-assist service attendant. He required no nametag or logo that would mark him for easy identification. His clientele tracked him down for quotes, deliveries, and pickups of the week's most prized commodity. His was not a futures market but an exchange of the here and now. He was part of an essential, loosely-structured human network scattered throughout the region consummating transactions between Super Bowl ticket buyers and sellers. Even in the age of the faceless Internet, his kind had not faded away.

Scalping was legal in Phoenix but retained an illicit air similar to state-sanctioned gambling or prostitution in Nevada. After my week on the open range of mostly lawless cyberspace, a physical presence at this way station gave legitimacy to the ticket man even though offline frauds and counterfeiters also ran free in Phoenix. I felt a tinge of guilt for having casually eavesdropped on fragments of his frequent and concise phone conversations and brief in-person cash-and-carry exchanges. A friendly overture now that I was out of the ticket market would be a polite, no-obligation gesture of acknowledgement. It might even produce some insight into his trade.

"Pretty brisk business still, eh?" I remarked as I reached over for a less than fresh donut. As expected, nothing eluded the discerning attentiveness of a man who could make Super Bowl dreams a reality with a timely call to run down a lead, connection, or situation wanted.

"Yeah, it's slowed down now though. You got a ticket?"

"I do. Finally picked up a third I needed yesterday for sixteen hundred." I replied with some measure of pride.

"That's pretty good. It may come down a little more before kickoff but who knows for sure how many are still out there."

I briefly recapped for him the story of my unpleasant Friday experience with the online broker. He had an opinion and did not hesitate to offer it.

"That's such bullshit," he said of the mid-transaction price jump. "We all work off the same big board. They had that price locked up and could have sold you the ticket. They just tried to jack you up. You should sue the bastards."

Since I measured the loss only in time and aggravation, I knew such action was hardly necessary or practical. However, this man clearly knew his industry. His vitriolic reaction to the moving target price intrigued me. Before he might elaborate, the ticket man nodded, and then disappeared into the lobby elevator with his coffee.

My attention returned to the matter of getting to the game. Getting in was no longer an issue.

The day before, Mindy located the Phoenix area Valley Metro public transit map online. She emerged from our room this morning to join Jason and me in the lobby. The bus was our transit plan B. We needed it.

In the time it would likely take to wait for a cab here, we figured we could ride the bus from Tempe on Phoenix's eastern flank to Glendale over on the west side. We collectively agreed to set out from the motel on foot to the nearest transit stop about a half mile away. The stroll would help us all wake up and catch up on both the East and West Coast editions of family news.

We walked along the near empty expanse of South Fifty-second Avenue towards a transit shelter at University Drive, another long, desolate artery connecting the eastern edge of Tempe with its central core. Here we planned to board the Red Line, the first of two bus links in what would prove a colorful, two-hour ride to the stadium. The Valley Metro system offered unglamorous conveyance to arguably the planet's most glamorous sporting event.

On the way to the bus stop, I pulled out my cell phone and called my mother in Pennsylvania to give her the abridged version of our partially completed Super Bowl saga. She still had no idea her son, nephew, and daughter-in-law had undertaken any of this grand adventure. In the past ten days, just getting to this point had consumed me. There had been no time to update anyone, including my mother, regarding the fluid, changing situation over the past few days. Like Mindy, I also was a bit superstitious and did not want to jinx anything by calling family until we had three game tickets in our possession.

It was early afternoon in the East. My mom answered the phone at home at her quiet retreat in rural Berks County, Pennsylvania. She delighted in our unexpected tale. Then she revealed something very odd.

"You won't believe this son, but Fox 29 is coming in clear as a bell."

My mother's television was not wired for cable or satellite. She resided nearly fifty miles away from the WXTF Philadelphia broadcast center located adjacent to Independence Hall. At her home, I had watched a couple of Eagles games through snowy static. In 2009, a long-awaited industry conversion to a digital TV standard would assure a clean picture even for antenna holdouts like my mother. Until then, the relatively weak UHF signal from her nearest Super Bowl television affiliate ranged from unreliable to barely watchable, except on this Super Sunday in February 2008 when either an engineering tweak at WXTF or some higher force delivered a brilliant reception to her.

I passed the phone on for Jason and Mindy to exchange greetings and pleasantries with my mom while I rummaged under the heat lamp inside the aptly named Quick Trip convenience mart. I plucked out a foil-wrapped breakfast sandwich and tucked my phone away as we exited the store. We had neither time nor equipment for festive tailgate feasting.

The three of us fixed our gazes on two transit shelters perched on either side of the four-lane boulevard.

"Which side of the street do we catch the bus on?" Mindy inquired. She had been a highly capable navigator to this point but did not possess much of an innate global positioning system. I reluctantly refocused my own sense of direction.

"We need to go west," I said wearily.

I already knew that observation would be useless. With a map or printed set of directions, Mindy was fine. However, like many couples, we had our share of tiffs on the way from point A to B, particularly in less-than-familiar surroundings. As a past traveling companion, Jason had seen this uneasy dynamic in action before.

My theory on the modern-day tension between men and women regarding directions has primal roots. I presume the traditional role of prehistoric men had been to venture from the cave and hunt prey while the slighter female huddled with children and tended to the dwelling. Given no access to directional signage, auto clubs, or convenience marts for guidance from rocky bluffs to tar pits and hunting grounds, ancient man developed an internal compass, perhaps referencing the positions of stars and sun, to survive. Modern man is reluctant to relinquish that genetic compass lest he reveal fatal weakness to a woman or a gas station attendant.

"West is the direction you and I walked from last night. That way," I said pointing down University Drive towards central Tempe.

"OK, that still doesn't tell me which side of this street we get the bus on."

She had me there. In the absence of any visible, moving traffic on the deserted avenue, I had lost any sense of which side of the street we needed to be on. I was too foggy-brained to know for sure until a car drove past the shelter opposite us, heading west.

Jason quietly observed and maintained respectful distance from maritally entwined, frayed nerves as we all stood at the intersection. With the navigation crisis over for now, Mindy and I stared ahead blankly at the crossing signal waiting for an illuminated red hand to transform into a strolling white silhouette. I fancied the stubborn, mocking red hand enjoyed presenting one more obstacle, delay, and pointless roadblock on the road to the Super Bowl.

Engineers obviously design wide, four-lane roads for fast and heavy traffic. Yet, on this Sunday morning, still well removed from the Big Game, you could gaze eternally into the horizon in either direction and not see a vehicle.

The red hand of the crossing light continued to glare at us from the other side. Jason looked down the vast stretch of vacant asphalt. A single car appeared as a distant speck a long block and a half away in the hazy distance. I lingered in my own sleep-deprived haze. My cousin had maintained diplomatic silence over the past couple of uneasy minutes. Now was his time to free us from the tyranny of the suspended moment.

"F--- it, I'm from New York," he declared and stepped out in defiance of the *Don't Walk* signal. Mindy and I promptly and dutifully jaywalked behind him to the bus stop.

Valley Metro scheduled buses that Sunday only through seventy-thirty in the evening. With a four-fifteen kickoff, extended halftime, and anticipated slow exit from the stadium, we had no clue exactly how we would return to Tempe that night.

After about a fifteen-minute wait, our bus approached and groaned to a halt. As we stepped on board, my gut sank. I realized Mindy had about five thousand dollars street value in game tickets tucked in her purse. I had forgotten to take physical possession of our most valuable current paper asset as we originally planned. Under the circumstances, cautious street sense guided me more than irrational paranoia. Crime was a distant concern, but unwise to ignore completely. I whispered to my traveling companions as we took our seats among an eclectic cast that included bus dependent Phoenicians.

"Let's not be too obvious about where we're heading considering what is in that purse."

"Oh … right." Mindy said and drew her arm a bit more securely around her satchel. "Guess they should stay there now. I know you wanted to carry them. I forgot to remind you."

"I know. I did too." I answered apologetically.

"We're good. We'll just pay attention," Jason added. "I don't think anyone will mess with us."

We knew how to cast watchful eyes in an urban environment. The three of us had walked the streets of New York together at night. We were not particularly intimidated here on a Phoenix public bus, just a bit anxious with a long ride ahead of us. We knew advertising our destination and the three oversized glossy documents on Mindy's person would be ill-advised for the next hour and fifty-four minutes. I suggested Mindy sit to my immediate right next to the center exit as my cousin took up an opposite side standing post.

Our seats faced out to center aisle allowing us to scan fellow passengers from the front to the back of the bus. This orientation also unfortunately made small talk among strangers unavoidable. Chitchat among passengers on either of the two long legs of the ride ahead might touch on the big event in town that day. It was highly unlikely any other present company on the Red Line would be in the stadium this afternoon.

A grey haired and free-spirited cowboy type strummed a beat-up guitar from one of the seats facing the aisle. His country-bluesy serenading was better than most I had heard at in my travels through various airports and rail stations.

"Oh, lordy! The big shots are all here today," the guitar-strumming cowboy announced to no one in particular. He wrapped up his tune and gave the body of the instrument a satisfied tap. He adjusted his wide rimmed brown felt hat then looked again over his shoulder out the window towards the distant terminals of Sky Harbor International. Clearly visible in profile over a cargo building was the parked corporate jet of Indianapolis Colts' owner Jim Irsay. Irsay brought some of his employees from last year's Super Bowl to Phoenix, including Colts' star quarterback, Peyton Manning, who was there to watch little brother Eli try to match his feat of the previous year.

"Saw that plane drop in here a couple days ago. Look at that big old blue horseshoe on the side," the scruffy cowboy-poet quipped. Our Super Bowl-bound crew remained silent. Jason threw me a sidelong smile I promptly returned.

"Come on y'all. Who's gonna win today?" The cowboy tossed the question to an open but unresponsive floor before he looked over at me. I chose brevity over rude silence.

"Don't know. Those Pats look good," I replied as I rolled my neck casually to avoid sustained eye contact. Of course, even the slightest reply provided fodder for his unsolicited game day analysis.

"Yep, they're tough all right. I hope it's close though, and those New Jersey boys stay in it to the end. Yes, sir," he replied without giving in to rambling further.

Just as I silently nodded in agreement, a startling voice rose from high on my left side over a chrome metal divider and elevated seat behind me.

"Jersey? Did somebody say NEW JERSEY? I'm from Jersey, man!"

I glanced up in the direction of the booming, partially coherent voice. It came from a man of the street, or maybe the freeway, since he might have lived under one. His head bobbed, shoulders swayed, and eyes rolled. He wore a greasy, red, hip-hop style cap covered with fifty or so tiny white New York Yankees logos arranged in lines across the bill.

In recent years, youth clothing and culture has creatively adopted and reinterpreted pro sports insignias. Some designs pay homage to teams of yesteryear like the Brooklyn Dodgers. Others revive retired, old school logos of the seventies. Some adaptations are more chilling. For example, in Southern California, logo-dotted apparel of the NHL L.A. Kings doubles as identification for the violent Latin Kings street gang. Dozens of other pro and college team symbols and mascots serve notice of various gang affiliations. The line where fan fashion statement ends and criminal code begins can be fuzzy and potentially dangerous.

I guessed this character was probably more hazardous to himself than any one in his vicinity. Still, his eventual departure from the bus would be welcome. Our traveling group also welcomed unexpected directional aid from a fellow rider we would know only as Rod. He carried a beat-up old briefcase. It looked as if it had been through a war zone.

Rod was an off-duty Phoenix taxi driver. Like many cabbies, he could not afford to use his leased rig for strictly personal transportation. He commuted by bus from a main taxi garage in Phoenix to his home in Glendale. A chatty, rail-thin, fifty-something gent with wire rimmed glasses and few days of gray stubble, Rod looked a bit worn down, but not worn out, by life. We struck up a conversation to divert ourselves from the half-crazed musings of the New Jersey transplant.

Cabbies often have great stories of brushes with celebrity. Another driver we engaged the day before on the topic had ferried Boston Red Sox star Manny Ramirez around Phoenix. The closest Rod had come to any Super Bowl stardom was earlier in the week. He had given a ride to an Arizona Cardinals equipment manager who was giddy about being on loan to work the Giants sideline for the game. As we chatted, Rod became our informal tour guide while the Red Line rumbled towards Phoenix's Metro Center terminal.

"That's the Arizona Diamondbacks' ballpark over there," he pointed to the impressive stadium built in 1998. A half-cent Maricopa County sales tax financed much of the two-hundred-thirty-eight-million-dollar project cost.

"They used to call it 'The Bob' for Bank One Ballpark," Rod explained. "I kind of liked that name. They don't call it that anymore. I guess somebody bought out somebody so now it's Chase Field. Wish they would just stick with a name. Anyway, Chase Field has a nice ring to it. You think?"

"Sounds good to me," I answered agreeably instead of offering Rod a tutorial on the evolution of naming rights agreements. I tried consciously exercising good listening skills even though my own familiarity with this subject invited otherwise.

Almost three decades had passed since I entered freshman studies at Syracuse University and the Carrier Corporation opened a new chapter in the history of American sports. By today's standard, the Carrier Dome was a steal in 1980 as a corporate brand building investment. The $2.75 million Carrier gift to the University predated by several years the naming sales practices for pro stadiums. The Carrier contribution covered only about ten percent of the actual construction costs but closed the deal to name the structure.

During my early college days, I worked at the Dome for student security services. One idle night, nearly alone inside the stadium, I set my two-way radio down in the end zone and ran the length of the field in the empty darkness under the huge inflatable roof.

On campus, I listened to a few fellow students rail indignantly over what they viewed as the administration's callous sale of the school's new sports shrine. Personally, it made no difference to me. Maybe selling the name to a Syracuse air conditioning firm in some way kept my tuition in check. Selling the naming rights was no more scandalous than supplying student athletes with special tutors. Other booster-driven privileges for star players pushed the letter of NCAA rules to the limit. The college game is big business, pure and simple, especially at high-profile institutions. Allowing big business to finance the game might encourage fans to leave their illusions of amateur athletics at the turnstile.

The Carrier deal and the debate over its merits and faults provided me with an early business orientation that would later prove useful in my negotiations with a variety of companies for nontraditional advertising exposure. Marketers have discovered countless variations on the naming-rights theme. Everything from stadiums, tournaments, and festivals to event media centers and diaper-changing areas invite titled sponsorship.

Some naming arrangements work well and please the ear like Chase Field or Monster Park. When stars align, namely a brand, a marketing budget, a venue, and a concept, the result can be a powerful, long-term association that is readily accepted by fans and the media alike.

When rushed through with the wrong partners, naming-rights value can diminish for all parties involved. Step right up with a high bid to rename the former Enron Field after accounting scandals brought the company down. Name the title sponsor's successor correctly and score bonus points. Consider as well the misfortunate naming of the former First Union Center, home of the NHL Flyers and NBA Sixers. Fans in Philadelphia promptly and unofficially titled the building the F. U. Center.

Each naming deal translates to monetary value calculated by the estimated number of times attendees, readers, viewers, and listeners see and hear the name of the sponsor. Only long-term, if not lifetime, naming agreements maximize the potential for transferring a large share of the rising facilities costs to the private sector.

Once upon a time, a university invited a corporation to brand a campus stadium in upstate New York. In 2006, a different set of players turned the transaction inside out in the Valley of the Sun. A municipal corporation, the Arizona Sports and Tourism Authority, invited a university without a sports program to paste its brand onto a stadium without a campus. Just over one hundred fifty million dollars locked up twenty years of naming rights, more than fifty times the price tag for the lifetime Carrier deal. Construction costs for the Arizona Cardinals' new home pulled up just short of half a billion. The stadium in Glendale connects to a place of higher learning in name only.

Unlike the ASU Sun Devil stadium in Tempe, the host venue for Super Bowl XXX in 1996, the University of Phoenix Stadium does not straddle classroom buildings and dormitories. Instead, the stadium sits next to Jobbing.com Arena, home of the Phoenix Suns and Coyotes, and a shiny new retail village.

The actual university is the subject of some controversy and criticism in traditional academic circles. Accreditation issues prompt some employers, among them Intel Corporation, to deny employee tuition assistance to would-be University of Phoenix attendees. As the largest private university in the North America, the school caters to working adults seeking an efficient degree track to improve their careers. According to the university's Web site, the average student age is thirty-five.

The stadium name association lends instant institutional credibility, or it at least creates curiosity, for a school lacking ivy covered walls or storied tradition. In addition to online and correspondence classes, decentralized in-person learning occurs at over two hundred satellite instruction centers inside leased corporate office spaces. A traditional campus alone does not make a credible school, but a quick blimp shot that was broadcast to millions and tagged "University of Phoenix Stadium, Glendale AZ" subtly defies critics who consider the school a diploma mill. Friends watching Super Bowl XLII on television asked me later if I had seen much of the campus.

Early Sunday afternoon, our bus was still several miles from both the stadium and any illusion of a University of Phoenix campus. Around noon, the Red Line reached Phoenix Metro Center. The coach idled at the curbside for a several minutes. Sensing our hesitation to remain in place, our impromptu tour guide Rod confirmed that Mindy had accurately deconstructed the perplexing Valley Metro system. We needed to stay on this bus for a bit longer before transferring. Finally, the bus got moving again.

Coincidentally, Rod's Glendale stop was along the route we needed to take. The Red Line rolled out of Metro Center. A few stops later, we spilled out through the center doors. Jason, Mindy, and I followed our cabbie without a cab to another transit stop along a gritty industrial stretch of Glendale Avenue. We were still a good sixty blocks east of the stadium. The four of us spent about fifteen minutes clustered together with other riders waiting on a narrow, eroded sidewalk next to a graffiti-scarred Valley Metro shelter. This structure looked much worse for the wear than the one at our origination point in Tempe. We were on the dreary western edge of Phoenix. The Super Bowl may as well have been a universe away.

We had been reluctant to tell Rod we were already carrying our tickets. Instead, we referenced the free public pregame venues and vague hopes of landing stray, last-minute seats. He never pressed for more details. He might also have sensed and respected our desire to keep the prying eyes of relative strangers away from our tickets, at least in this part of town.

As Mindy leaned and shifted uncomfortably against the side of the bus shelter, Rod offered to share a cab with the three of us if one approached before the next bus arrived.

"That's cool. We could do that." Jason said as he surveyed the young, old, and generally ragged assemblage sharing the street corner with us.

Rod had only a single condition for sharing a ride. He would not patronize one particular cab company. For a variety of reasons, the offending firm had fallen out of his favor.

"Anybody else is fine but I won't ride with them. It's OK by me if you do. I just won't give them my business, that's all," Rod explained.
Not all taxi companies treat contract drivers equally. I did not delve into the particular issues with Rod though it was clear his one-man boycott in some way involved labor. Rod did volunteer one company fact and an astute observation about marketing and ethics.

"You'll know the cabs I don't ride from the slogan on their doors," he said. "They put it on all their business cards and in their yellow page ads too."

"What is the slogan?" I asked Rod never missing an opportunity to study product positioning.

"You won't find a lower fare."

I turned the phrase over in my mind. This was part of what I did for a living. Something did not sit right with the wording. Then Rod put his finger on it for me.

"I guess it's not false advertising to say you won't find a lower fare but that don't mean they're the cheapest. They aren't. I know."

"Now I get it." I said. "Since it's not a fact they're the lowest fare, they aren't really lying. They're just betting the customer is ignorant. Instead of 'You won't find a lower fare', they might as well say ..."

"You *can't* find a lower fare because you're a dummy."

As Rod finished my sentence, we had a good laugh.

He stood up on his toes, cupping a hand to his brow, and looked down Glendale Avenue.

"See? There's one of their cabs now. I can tell by their colors."

Jason, Mindy, and I reached quick consensus and let the empty cab whiz past. The act supported of our temporary wingman and the elusive cause of deception free advertising. Minutes later, our connecting bus arrived to carry us over the long straightaway to football nirvana.

As numbered avenues crossing Glendale edged closer towards our final stop at Eighty-first Street, the Route 70 bus slowly filled with other fans bound for the game. They mingled among the ticketless ranks of the working-class as well as a few destitute Phoenicians. We bid farewell to our accidental guide when he stepped off about twenty blocks shy of the stadium stop. Though Rod planned for a relaxed evening off work, he gave us his home phone number just in case we had trouble getting a cab after the game. We appreciated his selfless help at least as much as that of any officially licensed host of Super Bowl XLII.

Our bus chugged closer to the stadium. This public motor coach certainly lacked the amenities and ornate trappings of NFL color analyst John Madden's Madden Cruiser. It did not matter. We still felt like fairytale peasants arriving in Cinderella's coach for the royal ball. The bus deposited our trio across from the palace, the University of Phoenix Stadium.

Mindy and I had so far only seen the stadium from the aircraft window on Saturday. From the sky, it resembled a giant toaster oven. This morning, low-hanging clouds had rolled in. As we gazed upward, overcast skies blended into the roofline of the gargantuan mass of gray at the south edge of the Glendale Sports and Entertainment Complex. Getting here was a marathon. With the stadium in sight, we got our second wind.

Before entering the dome, the three of us circulated through the tent village lining the outdoor mall of Westgate City Center. I took a professional interest in the merchandising frenzy.

"Is every other booth here a sports drink sponsor or what?" Jason remarked as he downed yet another free sample.

Certainly, sports beverages were hot, unrestricted prospects for this real estate. "You pay you play." I answered my cousin.

Mindy spotted an *Arizona Republic* newspaper promotional table.

Fans picked up complimentary, mock souvenir front pages from large stacks the *Republic* had printed for the day. The special section attracted advertising funding primarily from Verizon Wireless, a company with a retrievable online news platform likely aiding the demise of the traditional newspaper.

Separate, splashy, bold headlines accounted for either possible outcome. One shouted, "Perfect! Patriots Beat Giants, Claim Place in Football History" and featured a photo of an exultant Tom Brady. The large-font headline on the alternate edition read, "Champs! Giants Defeat Patriots for Super Bowl XLII Title" over the embracing figures of Giants' defenders Michael Strahan and Osi Umenyiora.

We picked up copies of both versions. I then made one of my only two accurate game predictions all weekend.

"I get 'Perfect!' but 'Champs!' is too generic a headline if the Giants pull this thing out." I scoffed.

Contemplating the headline writing art form I practiced in my journalism school exercises years ago, I added, "There's only one perfect headline the *Republic* can publish if New York wins: 'A Giant Upset'".

In a few hours, that very headline would roll off the presses for real.

Immediately across from the *Arizona Republic* table, a cluster of the curious gathered around a tent manned by Tickets Now. Tickets Now had been one of the large broker sites I checked up on throughout the week. According to the industry publication, *Ticket News*, they were the second-largest secondary ticket reseller in the nation behind Stubhub.

Big things were in store for Tickets Now whose slogan was The Power of In.

In a matter of days, Ticketmaster, at the time still a division of IAC/InterActive Corp, would acquire Tickets Now for an estimated $265 million. Until now, Ticketmaster profited mostly from service fees charged on face-value sales. Promoters, teams, and entertainment venues paid Ticketmaster for use of the company's online storefront and retail purchase points in malls, music stores, and other locations linked to Ticketmaster's central hub. This expansive network extended and complemented walk-up purchases at local box offices, stadiums, theaters, and arenas. Once any single event sold out, Ticketmaster moved on to the next unsold game, concert, play, or performance.

In 2007, on behalf of its clients, the company sold more than 141 million tickets valued at over $8.3 billion.

In recent years, Ticketmaster had begun to seek entry into the lucrative secondary market for sold-out events. Ticketmaster initially attempted to create from within a ticket resale entity called *Ticket Exchange*. The existence of Ticket Exchange has prompted at least one major national concert promoter, Live Nation, to allow its box office contract with Ticketmaster to expire in 2009. Live Nation plans to take direct control over all the events it owns.

A few weeks before Super Bowl XLII, Ticketmaster, and the National Football League inked a deal. Ticketmaster became the Official Ticket Exchange Provider of the NFL. Not all thirty-two teams are bound to enlist Ticketmaster as their exclusive resale agent. Still, some sports business analysts see the move as an effort by the league to control a bigger slice of ticket resale profits and perhaps even pressure season ticket holders into limited resale options. Just two weeks after Super Bowl XLII, the New England Patriots, hoping to enforce their own exclusive resale arrangement with Stubhub, subpoenaed numerous independent Boston area ticket brokers for six years worth of purchase and sale records.

The Ticketmaster acquisition of Tickets Now would give the world's biggest primary ticketing company and the NFL's official resale partner a second operational arm to buy and sell the same tickets multiple times.

I peered through the opaque, mesh screens along one side of the Tickets Now tent. Fans lined up to sit at a bank of computer terminals. If we had not found a third seat the day before, this tent could well have been our destination of last resort. With about two hours to kickoff, Tickets Now was one of the most popular destinations on the sprawling outdoor mall. I wondered what the Super Bowl ticket market I had tracked for days looked like now. Had prices surged again or collapsed? I briefly caught the attention of one of the workers posted near the head of a line snaking into the tent's entrance.

"So, how much does an upper-level ticket set me back?" I asked casually.

The busy line attendant was a stout fellow. He could have easily moonlighted as a vigilant bouncer behind velvet-roped nightclub lines.

He looked past me, scanned around the crowd, peered into the tent, and finally said, "I can't tell you. You won't find out until you get on one of the terminals. It looks like about a half hour wait right now."

I did not see any of the other big online brokers like Razor Gator or Stubhub with a booth in the merchandising village. Tickets Now had effectively secured what event sponsors commonly refer to as a *category exclusive*. They operated in an enviable selling environment.

The stadium loomed large over the scene. The clock to kickoff wound down. Fans lined up to point and click. The market and the cyber auctioneer churned on in real time, ruthlessly assessing the last potential dollar in profit. Frankly, I was a bit surprised to find a computer-assisted sales infrastructure still active so close to game time. How many milliseconds before game time would the last fan click the final Buy icon? How much would the seller ask? Would the prospective buyer pay the sum, negotiate, or step aside for someone waiting behind in line?

The economic, electronic, and human behavior fascinated me as a person who also represents a perishable commodity. Even in radio, renowned for taking last minute advertising contracts, commercial inventory sales shut down at a reasonable point before airing. This deadline is generally the morning of the business day before broadcast. At that point, advertisers who've procrastinated might pay a steep premium or more likely wait until the next day. The Super Bowl has no next-day, only next year.

Thanks to a progressive local ordinance protecting the activity, a scattering of private-party sellers and old-fashioned scalpers freely trolled the outer parking lots. The presence of these entrepreneurs reassured me that the free marketplace still operated outside cyberspace. I no longer dismissed these free agents as purely parking lot predators. They were a necessary safeguard against the monopolization and manipulation of the marketplace.

With a bit less than two hours to kickoff, Jason, Mindy, and I snapped some photos in front of the University of Phoenix stadium. The building resembled a spaceship ready take us into another world.

We shuffled through a long, winding set of barriers and gates. We passed through the metal detectors and electronic wands that have become ubiquitous at every large American sporting event since 2001. Finally, a gate usher passed an optical reader over the bar codes printed near the top of the gold-framed commemorative tickets. A digital beep verified authenticity. We were finally inside the belly of the Super Bowl beast. We had truly made the Big Game.

As part of our spectator game plan, we walked the entire concourse and immersed ourselves in the moment. A concrete canyon dotted with concession stands teemed with fans and alternated between dim and bright light. Every hundred feet or so, natural daylight passed through the specially designed, domed roof and poured between yawning section entrances into the concourse.

I knew we were at more than just another game when I pulled up at a refreshment stand. With wallet in one hand and game ticket in the other, I waited at the counter. One server took a fresh twenty from my hand. A second drew a cold draft beer from the tap. A third server hovered immediately across from me. He gestured for my attention. He was eying my game ticket.

"Excuse me, sir. Could I ask you a favor?"

"Sure, what is it?" I asked.

"Would you mind if I took a picture of your ticket?"

The question caught me off guard until I realized this concession vendor was as thrilled to be here as I was.

I imagined at some point in his busy shift, he might get a short break, walk out from his station, glance through an entryway, and tell friends and family he too saw a Super Bowl. He lacked only a seat and a souvenir ticket. A photograph of my ticket would do nicely for his game day scrapbook. Since I was already inside the stadium, I happily obliged. He produced a digital camera from his uniform vest pocket. The camera flashed as the piece of paper in my hand succumbed for a moment to paparazzi.

After collecting our own souvenirs, our game day threesome prepared to split up. Jason's seat was near the northwest end zone corner over the Patriots sideline. New England faithful would surround him. The reigning AFC Champions were making their fourth appearance since 2002. My cousin's neighbors in the stands would include many veteran Super Bowl fans. They brought with them the expectation of perfection given the Patriots' historic, unbeaten jaunt through the current season schedule. Although the Pats' recent big game history had jaded some supporters, this game was different. This was for 19–0.

Mindy and I had tickets facing the north end zone. We were West Coast anomalies in the sea of Giants' season ticket holders. The accented buzz around us claimed New York, New Jersey, and Long Island origins.

We arrived at our seats in time to watch the Arizona State University marching band. They formed precise patterns across the two-acre, retractable field of natural grass. My thoughts wandered to my late grandfather and his own marching band director days. He would have marveled over this stage, a nineteen million pound playing surface, literally a sod tray that rolls in or out of the stadium on thirteen tracks in the concrete floor.

The ASU band filed out and another smaller one filed in to take their place on a raised platform. As Grammy-winning songstress Alicia Keys belted out an entertaining set, I gazed down onto the field and spotted familiar faces from the 49ers Super Bowl glory days. Ronnie Lott, Steve Young, and Jerry Rice would preside over a coin toss honoring former San Francisco head coach Bill Walsh. The previous summer Walsh died after an extended fight with leukemia. At San Francisco's home opener in September 2007, I had held aloft a framed portrait of Walsh from the stands behind the Niner bench during a halftime commemoration.

Above us, the translucent, retractable stadium roof remained closed. A game day decision by the league sheltered the crowd from the slightest possibility of rain that had been forecast earlier. Two panels, each weighing over a million pounds, allowed ambient daylight to penetrate the roof while sealing us in at a climate-controlled seventy-five degrees.

Barely a mile away at Luke Air Force Base, a group of Navy Blue Angels jets lifted off the runway for a pass over the stadium. The public address announcer acknowledged several special guest service members on leave from duties in Iraq and Afghanistan. The combined American deployment in those two nations would have filled the stadium roughly two and a half times over.

The Blue Angels thundered overhead following the national anthem. The assembled civilian masses largely saw the jets only as streaking tracks across the scoreboard video screen. An insulated bubble separated the stadium occupants from the pilots and their reality, a reality that was anything but a game.

IX. True Giants and Patriots

More than twenty years prior to Super Bowl XLII, I sat with a quiet, deferential man inside his county jail cell. I tried to forget that the previous morning, this Marine reservist had committed murder. In a fit of marital rage, he shot dead his wife, an Air Force enlistee, in the middle of the street just outside Castle Air Force Base in rural, central California. There had been multiple, terrified witnesses. There was no question he would never take custody of his two-year-old, now motherless, son.

I was duty-bound to treat the prisoner sitting in front of me just as the whole of the judicial system was treating him: innocent until proven guilty. He was currently entitled to sign, and I was obligated to present, insurance and survivor's benefits documents as well as an authorization to release a death benefit payment to the temporary guardians of his child. Inside the cell, the two of us stayed focused on the welfare of his infant boy. I managed to earn enough of his trust for some essential preliminary signatures before he deferred the rest to an attorney.

Highly charged moments such as these punctuated my otherwise unremarkable military career. My enlistment in the U.S. Air Force was a temporary vocational choice with permanent ramifications.

Unhappy, uneasy, and three years deep into a newspaper journalism degree program at Syracuse University in the early eighties, I took what would become a permanent leave of absence before taking an oath. I walked away from a partial scholarship, a solid grade point average, and a communications school that produced such notable journalists as Ted Koppel, Marv Albert, Bob Costas, and Mike Tirico among others.

My mother had attended the school a generation earlier. She had been active in the drama department as a costume designer working with talented alumni of her era including Peter Falk and Suzanne Pleshette. She designed the first Dracula costume worn by actor Frank Langella, who later won three Tony Awards and reprised the Dracula role on stage and film. During her college years, the Orangemen of Syracuse enjoyed their greatest gridiron success, winning a national title in 1959. She knew the late Heisman trophy winner Ernie Davis and met the legendary Jim Brown. Brown once held and bounced me playfully on his knee when I was an infant. She babysat the son of Dolph Schayes. Schayes, an NYU graduate, was the hero of the 1955 Syracuse Nationals NBA championship team. Dolph's son, Danny

Schayes, went on to play basketball for Syracuse University during my own enrollment there.

Unlike my mother who graduated Orange, I did not stay at SU to complete my four-year journalism degree. However, I still learned much in my days there. I even reestablished ties with my father for a period of time. Nevertheless, I came to doubt my chosen academic path and eventually myself. I no longer knew if I was building a future at Syracuse or merely chasing the past in a locale not far from my childhood home. Though she understood and helped me, my decision to withdraw crushed and disappointed my mother. She was once again alone and scraping by apprehensively on a single income.

I returned to Philadelphia in the midst of a deep recession. Shortly thereafter, I enlisted in the Air Force to buy time, finish college, climb out of debt, and find an identity beyond both Philly and the winter chill of upstate New York. After basic and technical training, I would be off to the sunny central valley of California, a setting that masked the nature of a commitment to the armed forces. Beginning in basic training in San Antonio, Texas, stark and jolting reminders of what a military oath entailed surfaced every so often.

To keep recruits focused on training, our drill instructors imposed a news blackout. This shield from distracting headlines was lifted only once during six weeks of basic training. The lead drill sergeant gathered us in our dormitory briefing room and asked the squad if we wanted good news or bad news first. A majority asked for the bad news. We then learned the Palestinian group Hezbollah had carried out a suicide bombing on a Beirut barracks that had claimed the lives of 241 Marines deployed as U.N. peacekeepers. The good, but unsettling, news was the success of Operation Urgent Fury, a U.S. invasion to overthrow a short-lived military dictatorship on the small island nation of Grenada.

The reality of war suddenly became a degree more tangible to me just two weeks after first putting on the uniform. I remained fortunate enough to serve outside of direct, open hostilities. However, the tangible consequence of the ultimate sacrifices made by others would follow me closely into my assignments.

At Castle Air Force Base, the only thing I flew was a desk in the personnel office. My first duty was as an administrative assistant processing military awards and decorations. I hated the job. Senior officers and enlisted personnel active during Vietnam confided to me that in relative peacetime, military office politics resemble those of major corporations.

Chasing promotions, pleasing superiors, and posturing for the next written performance report frequently took priority absent an immediately visible enemy. Serving at a stateside Strategic Air Command base in the waning days of the Cold War sometimes made the mission an abstraction. The Soviet nuclear missile force was massive but largely buried in underground silos. The threat had less effect in curbing career posturing among American military members than the Viet Cong of a generation earlier, at least according to many older service members who quietly shared their thoughts. This fact made my own work important for all the wrong reasons.

I processed nominations for medals, cross-checked official photos of captains and majors for promotions boards, and researched questions on Air Force Regulation 35-10, Dress and Appearance of Air Force Personnel. With no word processor or permission to use correction tape, I painstakingly prepared error-free award certificates on my IBM Selectric typewriter.

After about a year of this mind-numbing duty, another opportunity in the same office opened up. My supervisor sensed my misery in "awards and decs" and recommended me for the more challenging position of Casualty Assistance Representative. When first assigned, I was the lowest ranking individual of roughly one hundred and thirty civilian and military Air Force casualty representatives worldwide.

In many respects, the new task was comparable to a civilian human resources position. I administered military retiree annuity and insurance programs. Paperwork was still voluminous, but helping assure a smooth flow of family oriented benefits, many for World War II and Vietnam era retirees, satisfied me more than processing another Meritorious Service Medal certificate with Oak Leaf Cluster. I worked with the local Veterans Administration, the base's Family Services volunteers, civil servants, and California transitional veteran employment programs for recently retired Air Force members.

About once a week, I would check a vehicle out of the motor pool and drive to California cities and small towns like Fresno, San Jose, Modesto, and Monterey. Typically, these trips were to collect documents and personally brief surviving wives after their aging veteran husbands died. They needed to file claims with the VA, Social Security, and the Air Force. I visited homes ranging from trailer parks in small farming communities to mansions at Pebble Beach. While completing forms with these mostly elderly and sometimes distraught women, I would listen to the stories of their late spouses. Some of the men took up second careers in civil service or landed lucrative defense contracts. Others lost their way after military retirement and died of idle hands and minds.

I had other, less frequent but far more intense duties. The absence of bombing and live enemy fire did not preclude active duty deaths in the military. Training accidents, heart attacks, car wrecks, suicides, and homicides need no declaration of war.

When those events happened every so often, I would be one of a small group of people working directly and promptly with the affected active duty families living on or near the base. Within twenty-hours hours following notification, regulations required me to meet with the next of kin of active duty causalities. My job included advising family dependents regarding transitional financial matters and access to personal medical, dental, and commissary services. In a small way, these initial meetings reassured shaken families. The nation for which their loved one had given his or her life would continue to be there for them.

On a brilliantly clear August morning in 1985, a KC-135 tanker assigned to Castle practiced "touch and go" landings at Beale Air Force Base north of Sacramento. In a designated maneuver, the aircraft landing gear briefly grazed the runway then quickly lifted airborne again. Investigators later attributed pilot error as the official cause of what transpired after the third runway pass during this particular training exercise.

An overly steep pull up, or "go," following a rocky "touch" phase led to a mechanical failure and subsequent dive. Several weeks later, I read an uncensored black box recorder transcript. For maybe half a minute, the crew of seven knew they were in a dire, fatal situation. The Boeing KC-135 is literally a huge flying gas tank designed to refuel long-range bombers in midair. The violent combustion at impact essentially disintegrated the aircraft.

That afternoon, I would drive a casualty notification officer, a chaplain, and an attending nurse to the front door of the home where the wife one of the crewmembers lived. Like every military spouse or parent, she knew exactly why our vehicle was there the moment I stopped the car at the curb and the team opened the doors.

The next day, I would meet with her and two other widows in consecutive private briefings. The commanding officer in the base's personnel building turned his office over to me for most of the workday. "You'll need the private space for your job more than me today, airman," the major told me. "Take all the time you think these families need."

I was a twenty-five-year-old junior enlistee with a clean starched shirt, a government-issued pen and a set of forms and pamphlets. Procedurally speaking, the task before me was defined and precise like an honor guard lowering a military casket into the earth, folding a flag into a neat, triangular shape, and presenting it graveside to a stoic widow. Except unlike those silent soldiers, many also untested by real combat situations, my involvement with the surviving family occurred before and beyond the ceremony.

A couple of weeks after the Beale crash, another sergeant in the personnel office delivered an item recovered from the crash site. Joe Gilchrist was a lanky, relaxed country boy from South Carolina. He was also my Air Force roommate. Joe worked in the Operational Readiness office pushing paper like me and issuing metal identification, or "dog" tags. The tags listed name, rank, serial number, and blood type.

"They're pretty bad, man," Joe drawled as he handed me a small brown envelope. Joe usually wore an easy smile but not while performing this particular duty.

Inside the envelope was a set of dog tags belonging to one of the deceased crewmembers.

I turned up the envelope flap and uncoiled the charred chain.

"What do I do with these, Joe?" I asked him, slightly annoyed.

"I dunno. The regulations say I gotta give them to you. So here they are. This is your problem now."

Regulations also called for my office to return to the next of kin any effects deemed to be in acceptable, serviceable condition. Whether these specific tags met this standard was a subjective, borderline call. They had belonged to the same crewmember whose doorstep I had driven to. I had seen his wife's shock and hysteria upon notification the day of the crash. Through our Family Services division, I knew from other military spouses that of all the surviving family, she was having the most visibly difficult time. How much more emotional damage might this badly burned crash remnant inflict?

The inscription was still legible but the once silver tags had been partially melted and severely blackened from the fuel explosion, even after cleanup in the mortuary. Was this a serviceable, personal effect? I brought the applicable regulation binder to my immediate supervisor in the office next door.

George Kilburn was a crusty, chain-smoking Technical Sergeant. I liked and respected him. I opened the regulation book, laid the charred tags on top of the vaguely worded clause, and set both on his desk. I tilted my head, raised an eyebrow, and tightened my facial muscles in a quizzical manner.

"What the hell is this?" he growled through a Marlboro cloud.

"Read it. What would you do?" In my own way, I was simultaneously issuing a request, a plea, and an order I could not give as his subordinate.

He picked up the burnt tags with one hand and rubbed them between his fingers. With his other hand, he reached for his coffee cup, took a slurp, and hovered over the language of the regulation.

"Goddamit," he huffed.

Now we both knew the regulation offered no definitive directive for the situation.

"I'd lose them," he finally said.

I would have welcomed an order but this was advice. George knew I was capable of good judgment. Technically, the disposition of the tags was my decision. He was not going to dictate or even escalate the question up the chain of command. It would not have been consistent with our mutual respect for one another.

I picked up the tags, walked six or seven feet around a corner and dropped them in the battleship gray metal wastebasket on the floor next to my lower desk drawer. They made an audible clanging sound I knew George could hear through the open door of his adjacent office.

"Come back and take the regulation book with you too, Fekete," he said. We said nothing more.

The regulation gave me more latitude than I gave myself.

Had I denied a grieving family a keepsake or saved them from a painful visible reminder of the fiery runway inferno? Just a piece of badly charred metal I told myself. It would only cause additional grief.

I continued to have mixed feelings about disposing those tags for two years until just weeks before the end of my enlistment. Something bittersweet and slightly magical happened involving another metal object inches from the same drab spot where I discarded those burnt identification tags.

In 1987, a sergeant serving on a flight crew in Spain, died in a similar training crash. His only surviving next of kin was his mother. She lived in California, just a few miles from my base. The dreaded staff car rolled up to her home and a notification officer delivered the news.

Paperwork was slow to move from the deceased sergeant's overseas post. Entitlements were minimal. The mother was not a military dependent. There were still a few loose ends to address. I called her and asked if she wanted me to stop by her home to complete some required forms with her. She said a personal home visit would not be necessary. She did agree to come to my office the next week.

A couple of days before her appointment, an unexpected delivery came to my desk. It was an approved military decoration, but not any run-of-the-mill commendation like many I had once processed. This was a Bronze Star, a prestigious combat award for valor superseded only by three higher decorations, including the Congressional Medal of Honor. I read the citation that some airman in Europe had typed out to letter perfection.

Four years before the sergeant's death in Spain, he had been part of the Grenada incident. In the face of Cuban and local pro-Marxist resistance, he helped support the evacuation of a small group of American medical students from the island nation. His actions during Operation Urgent Fury, the same event I first learned of nearly four years earlier while in basic training, earned him the Bronze Star nomination and award.

The bureaucratic wheels of the military turned with agonizing slowness. It had taken almost four years for the Air Force to approve the medal. The date on the final authorization was days before his death in the training flight accident. Since the award was not posthumous, or conferred after death, the certificate came to my office as a serviceable personal effect never formally presented to the original owner. The sergeant was unmarried, therefore his mother was the person entitled to receive the medal.

Regulations dictated the Air Force offer the nearest family member a formal presentation ceremony presided over by a senior ranking officer of major or above. I could easily arrange that for the mother if she wished. I would inform her when she came into my office.

Immediately behind my desk, a tall, gray metal storage locker stood. It contained nearly every current Air Force ribbon and medal along with presentation cases inside brown cardboard packing boxes. Basic Training ribbons, Good Conduct Medals, the award for shooting range marksmanship, even the small uniform ribbon denoting the Medal of Honor were all inside this ugly piece of office furniture.

Sometimes I reached into the locker to give an elderly, retired, surviving spouse an appropriate ribbon to replace one worn, lost, or damaged in storage. In this way, families could complete a keepsake ceremonial set of awards earned by a deceased service member.

Occasionally, I respectfully rummaged around the locker out of curiosity. I found it odd that a stockpile of medals both routine and coveted were unceremoniously stored behind my desk. Then again, where else would they be except here, where we pushed through award paperwork?

I found a box containing a Bronze Star and tucked it along with the citation in my desk drawer. When the mother of the late sergeant came in,

I welcomed her, offered coffee, and took care of a few routine documents for her signature. When I finished the last form and rolled it out of the typewriter, I turned to her.

"Ma'am, there is just one more item."

"What's that?" she asked somewhat wearily.

"Well, I know your son served in Grenada in 1983. Like a lot of things in this business, it took quite a while to get done, but the Air Force recognized your son for his service there with the Bronze Star. He was due to receive the award a few days after the accident."

She had not lived in a military household. She looked puzzled and slightly uncertain of the significance of the award.

"It's quite an important medal, ma'am," I offered. "The Bronze Star is only given for service during combat operations."

"I see," she said.

She was numb. She may have been regretful or even angry her son ever enlisted. That happened sometimes with surviving parents but it was not my place to go there. It was also not for me to exude any visible enthusiasm for a significant honor in a circumstance calling for somber acknowledgment. The official recognition was for a battlefield encounter her son handily survived. No award or citation could ever console her for his subsequent accidental death in the line of duty. I went forward with her tentatively.

"Ma'am, the medal now belongs to you. Your son knew he earned it but his commander in Spain did not have a chance to present it to him. Air Force regulations allow an officer here to present it to you in a formal ceremony. I can make those arrangements if you choose."

She nodded silently with a distant, detached gaze. I could not tell whether she nodded just to acknowledge my statement or if she was accepting my offer to arrange a presentation. As she processed the information, I filled an ensuing gap in the conversation.

"I just found out about this a couple of days ago after we already scheduled our appointment. I'm sorry to bring it up this way, but it seemed better to tell you here than on the phone. The notification came here to the Personal Affairs office since we also process Awards and Decorations."

She had no idea both the citation and the medal were at that moment sitting in my desk drawer. I could tell from her demeanor she wanted to put the whole ordeal behind her. Driving to the base probably created less anguish for her than the sight of yet another staff car arriving at her doorstep. Now she weighed just how much more protocol she could take.

"Is it possible I can pick it up somewhere? Can they just mail it out to me? You've got my address," she finally said.

The regulation did not precisely address who "they" were if she declined a presentation ceremony. I knew I could not in good conscience initiate postal delivery of a Bronze Star for receipt alongside bills and junk mail.

"Ma'am, are you saying you would prefer not to have a formal presentation?" I asked.

It was her decision. I took care not to lead her. Her eyes watered.

"I just don't think I'm up to that. Besides, all of his buddies it might mean something to are still over in Spain anyway."

She was right. A presiding officer here in California would place the presentation as a five-minute agenda item in a regular unit meeting. The commander would read the citation. The subordinates there for other unrelated business would stand at attention. It would be like attending a memorial among strangers unknown to the deceased.

"I understand, ma'am," I said quietly.

It was lunch hour. There was no one else in my office. Our one major assigned to the building was off-site. The mother's boy was a staff sergeant when he died and a Senior Airman while in Grenada. At least in terms of rank, he had been my peer. I made my one of my largest decisions while in the Air Force, as big as dropping those haunting, charred identification tags in the trash two years earlier.

"Well, as I said, we do handle Awards and Decorations here, ma'am. You don't need to go to another office today or wait for a package in the mail. I can send you home with your son's award now, if you're OK with that."

"I think that would be much better," she said wiping away a small tear.

I slid the drawer below me open.

"The citation arrived here this week. I hope you don't mind that I read it before you came in today. I wanted to know something about your son."

"Not at all," she said as I nudged the citation, contained in a neatly bound closed cover, slowly across my desk to her. The citation summarized the actions of her son during the Grenada operation. She could read it herself in private later. After a moment, I reached in the drawer again.

"I didn't quite expect to be doing this, but I do understand your wish to not make it a public event. I just wouldn't feel right mailing this to you."

From the drawer, I picked out a small blue case with an embossed Air Force insignia and handed it to her. It contained the medal. Her hands trembled as she opened up the case to look at her son's Bronze Star. I bit my lip knowing that this rather informal moment was the extent of any presentation that would occur.

"I just want you to know everyone who wears this uniform appreciates your son's service, ma'am. If there's anything else you need, you have my number here."

"I do. Thank you, Sergeant Fekete." She rose, grasped my hand briefly, and returned to the civilian world.

In a matter of weeks, I would return to the civilian world also, now with a marketing degree in hand and eyes on the business end of commercial media. My mostly predictable office hours while enlisted had allowed me to take full advantage of evening undergraduate classes and military tuition assistance.

Twelve years passed before I set foot in an Air Force office again.

After an exit from journalism studies at Syracuse and an unintended but meaningful detour in the service, I eventually found more financial security selling advertising time in the news than I could realistically expect to earn from reporting the news.

In 1999, I visited the 364th Recruiting Squadron in Sacramento as a news talk-radio advertising representative with a proposition. The Defense Department endows all branches of the armed forces with substantial marketing budgets to field new recruits. Most locally sponsored recruiting outreach occurs at large-scale gatherings ranging from concerts, fairs, and festivals to major sporting events. This particular squadron's regional territory covered over 90,000 square miles of the West. Over the course of the next five years, the United States Air Force would be one of several advertising clients I developed as event sponsors.

The Sacramento Sports Commission had successfully persuaded the United States Olympic Committee (USOC) and USA Track and Field (USATF) to hold the 2000 U.S. Olympic Track and Field Team Trials in California's capital. Through a complex, overlapping series of agreements between various parties, our local radio properties secured the opportunity to broker space in a Fan Expo area adjacent to the stadium's entrance.

In effect, I became a sponsorship agent for the largest track and field event ever held on American soil excluding the actual Olympic Games. The Trials offered a unique selling proposition to attendees and sponsors.

No other nation selects Olympic athletes in quite the same manner.

Outside the United States, past performance standards are generally the primary criteria. When qualified athletes outnumber the spots allocated on a national Olympic team, complicated formulas, point systems, and more intangible factors such as recommendations of coaches, and even political patronage, enter the equation.

Here is one illustrative example of the shades of gray pervasive in national team selection. The selection criteria document for the Canadian Biathlon team for the 2006 Winter Games in Torino is ten pages long. It includes standards of both demonstrated and perceived excellence across a broad spectrum of competitive events. There is also an extensive injury provision in the document in the event a potential candidate for the team has a medical issue that might affect the athlete's ability to compete. The provision requires a medical certificate indicating the date and nature of the prescribed rehabilitation program and an estimated recovery period.

To understand the complexities of the Olympic athlete selection process, consider the convoluted Bowl Championship Series (BCS) power rankings in American college football. In this system, computers produce a national championship matchup by crunching arcane factors that include coaches' polls, media polls, and won-loss records of opponents. Multiply this imperfect system by dozens of sports across nearly all the nations on the planet. Add in the variable factors such as national citizenship standards, immigration waivers, politics, and the burning desire of many athletes to compete in the games under any flag that will accept them. All these circumstances often make athlete qualification for the Olympic Games any thing but a black and white decision.

By contrast, U.S. Olympic Track and Field team selection is elegantly simple. The qualifying meet lives up to the marketing as a trial by fire mainly because the process is a brutal winner-take-all affair.

Before the trials, any athlete who meets the qualifying standard in time, height, or distance has a shot to represent the U.S. team in his or her respective event. The only consequential result for American athletes who are selected to step onto the global stage of the Olympics is the finishing order at this single meet, the Trials. There is no regard for reputation, past performance, injury recovery time, or any factor other than the marks recorded in the event finals. Preliminary qualification narrows the competition to one race or one set of throws and jumps. Some call it unfair. For track fans, it is an electrifying format: preseason, play-offs, and championship crammed into eight days across every event from sprints to distance, hurdles to high jump, pole vault to pentathlon.

On July 23, 2000, Maurice Greene and Michael Johnson, America's two top sprinters, squared off in Sacramento for the final event of the eight-day Trials, the highly anticipated final heat of the 200 meter. This clash was to be a preview of an inevitable showdown between the two U.S. rivals in Australia for Olympic gold. Greene had clocked the year's best time and Johnson sought to repeat his gold medal performance from the 1996 Atlanta Games again in Sydney in a few weeks. After the gun sounded to open the qualifying final, Johnson and Greene flew out of the blocks. A capacity crowd rocked Sacramento State University's Hornet Stadium, a facility extensively upgraded specifically for this event.

Within seconds, both Greene and Johnson pulled muscles in mid-stride and jogged off the track. Lesser-known competitors blew past the prerace favorites to claim the top three positions on the Olympic squad. The race had produced a shocking and unexpected result in the most hyped race of the entire track meet and vividly demonstrated the winner-take-all aspect of the Trials.

While the crowd filed out, I cornered Craig Masback, the director of USA Track and Field, in the VIP area. I thanked him for his role in selecting Sacramento as host city for the meet. The 2000 Trials in Sacramento had been a stunning logistical success and elevated expectations for future meets to unprecedented proportions. Over one hundred eighty-seven thousand spectators attended the eight-day event. I had a relatively small role among literally thousands of area residents engaged in the effort to host the most successful U.S. Olympic Trials ever.

"I know you've heard this from plenty of people here all week, Craig, but I hope you see this town really stepped up and embraced the opportunity," I said. "We've got a lot of track fans and a lot of people who want to bring the Trials back here and make them even better in four years."

"Thank you. We've been impressed by what we saw here," Masback replied diplomatically. "I'm sure we'll take a close look at it for the next time around."

The selection bidding process for 2004 was a long way off. My brief encounter with Masback was but a tiny fragment of Sacramento's intense, and ultimately successful, lobbying campaign for a 2004 encore hosting of the Trials. To be sure, I would likely have a financial interest in the trials returning four years later, but that moment with the governing national executive of the sport was all about emotion, local pride, and unfinished collaboration with my new Air Force partners. With the aid of my client sponsor, I knew we could add to the Trials spectacle in 2004.

The U.S. Olympic Track and Field Trials had moved around the country to Los Angeles, New Orleans, Atlanta, and Indianapolis. The last time the meet came to Northern California, in 1968, athletes competed in relative obscurity near Lake Tahoe. The USOC and USATF had held the trials in the same venue consecutively only in one other location: Eugene, Oregon, also known as Track Town USA, hosted at Hayward Field in 1972, 1976, and 1980.

Competition among cities seeking to host a roving, high-profile event demands community-wide collaboration involving local elected officials, business, and media. Securing the Trials in Sacramento, not just once, but for consecutive Summer Olympics, was a victory for the entire region.

In late 2003, I returned to the 364th Recruiting Squadron with an Olympic Trials sponsorship renewal proposal that easily won the support and requested budget allocation from the unit commander, Major Tom Fredericks. Since September 11, 2001, the armed forces had refocused and intensified recruiting efforts across all branches. I knew the local recruiting team would again want to return to the Olympic Trials Fan Expo to engage the crowds upon entry, exit, and during the frequent breaks in event competition during the eight days in July. Several Air Force athletes were even U.S. Olympic hopefuls participating in the meet.

A display area inside the Fan Expo would again serve in 2004 as an ideal venue for an Air Force recruiter team. The business relationship I had developed with the recruiters had a personal dimension as well. I wanted to facilitate a greater presence for the Air Force this time around than the basic terms of the sponsorship included. I asked my primary enlisted contact at the squadron, Technical Sergeant Monte Mitchell, about something we might initiate together to make a lasting impression on the second Olympic Trials in Sacramento. It was something that I couldn't pull off in 2000 given limited advance time to clear bureaucratic hurdles. I shared the idea with Monte. His eyes widened.

"I think we can get that done," he said enthusiastically.

Two days later, I was back in Sergeant Mitchell's office with the thick stack of forms required to reserve the squadron's space in the Fan Expo as well as assure a few additional in-stadium promotional entitlements I had built into the sponsor's package. Between the local Sacramento Sports Commission, USA Track and Field, the U.S. Olympic Committee, multiple outside contractors, and my own corporation's parent company, just navigating the basics of a simple sponsorship could be an exhausting exercise. Some of the checks and balances existed to protect standing contracts right up to multimillion-dollar, worldwide partnerships with the International Olympic Committee. Various organizational foot soldiers tied to the Sacramento event did not always comprehend overlapping concessionaire interests, onsite product sampling rights, and athlete endorsement ties. This meant many individuals vetted and scrutinized everything related to the event, a process that could take weeks.

When we finished with the hefty paperwork for the Fan Expo, I asked Sergeant Mitchell about our other idea.

"Oh, yeah, I almost forgot," Mitchell said excitedly as he reached into a file folder. "We don't need very much paper for *that* deal." He produced a single-page Department of Defense form, DD 2535. The completed form would need to run through multiple approval authorities and eventually would require final clearance from the Pentagon.

I scanned the sheet Monte handed me. "This is great. When are you sending this out?" I asked. The Trials were a few months away, but given the slow, grinding wheels of the military command structure, I did not want to wait a single day.

"All I need is the signature of a Civilian Requesting Official," the sergeant said as he pointed to an empty box at the bottom of the document.

"That's it?" I asked. I expected more obstacles.

"That's all. But without a civilian, I can't send it anywhere. If I could, the Air Force might just do this whenever we felt like it, just like in Russia or China."

I thought of all the people involved with the Olympic Trials, the process, the protocols, and the politics. Securing further permission at this point would be a redundant formality and prompt an unnecessary delay. The production logistics could be worked out later. The United States Air Force was bigger than anything the United States Olympic Committee could conceive of to slow the progress of our plan.

"Monte, is there anyone in particular associated with the Trials you think should sign this?"

"It doesn't much matter as long as they're a civilian and an American citizen. I'm guessing you're associated with the Olympic Trials. If not, I'll be in a world of hurt when my team shows up to work a space out there in July," Mitchell kidded.

"You got that right," I replied and again reminded myself I really was involved in something much bigger than just prospecting for advertisers.

"I guess this means I can be a Civilian Requesting Official," I concluded.

"That gets it done for me," Sergeant Mitchell replied as he handed me a pen to sign DD Form 2535, Request for Military Flyover.

Five months later, on July 9, 2004, a squad of jets from Beale Air Force Base soared over Hornet Stadium to open the U.S. Olympic Track and Field Trials as they had never been opened before.

My most-coveted keepsake from a sporting event is not an autographed jersey or ball. It is not a program, ticket stub, or photo taken with a star athlete. On that opening day of the 2004 Trials, Tom Fredericks handed me a squadron coin unique to his unit. In a private moment trackside, the major gave me the silver-dollar-sized disc, deliberately, and with measured consideration. The coin displayed the squadron's coat of arms, a Phoenix rising from the ashes, encircled by the words, *Service Before Self … Excellence In All We Do … Integrity First.* These universal, guiding tenants applied to both the unit and the entire military branch of which it was a part.

"We don't give these to just anyone," the major said to me. "Everyone in our unit carries one of these as a reminder of our mission. Thanks for everything you've done for us here."

I slipped the coin into the pocket of my dark blue, civilian suit jacket. It had been seventeen years since I had last worn an Air Force uniform. At that moment, it felt like no time had passed at all.

X. Living up to the Billing

Jeff Feagles glanced down at the Roman numeral XLII. The engraved imprint shined from the reverse of a gold commemorative coin laying at midfield. Seconds earlier, the senior captain of the New York Giants had called *tails*. The Giants would receive the ball first in Feagles' three hundred and twentieth consecutive start in an NFL uniform. The largely unheralded specialist is the Cal Ripken, Jr. of pro football. After twenty seasons in the league, the Phoenix native and journeyman punter was playing in his first Super Bowl.

"Jeff Feagles is so old. Every time he punts, he farts dust," Michael Strahan had joked earlier in the week to reporters during Super Bowl media day.

The forty-one-year-old Feagles spent almost half his life as a member of the National Football League. He had waited the longest of anyone else suited up to reach the title game. While Feagles would play his part in keeping the New England Patriots bottled up deep in their own territory, youth would carry much of the day for the New York Giants.

Youth and passion for a team he had followed since childhood may have been all that kept Jay Himmelstein standing upright in section 430 as the Patriots' Steven Gostkowski kicked off Super Bowl XLII. Ten hours earlier at six in the morning on Sunday, Himmelstein, a young financial planner living in Manhattan's Upper East Side, boarded a plane departing from New Orleans. He cut short a long-planned trip with three friends to go to Mardi Gras. He left them behind so he could let the good times roll in Phoenix. If Himmelstein's beloved Big Blue could pull off a monumental upset, the ensuing celebration would exceed any other as far as he was concerned, including the fete he was passing up in the Big Easy.

As Eli Manning guided the Giants downfield in the opening drive, Himmelstein was the section cheerleader. He wore Manning's number ten Giants' jersey. His sister, Bree, took up an adjacent seat. She selected a neutral red, number forty-two Super Bowl game day jersey, but like her brother, Bree also bled blue. On the opposite side of the stadium, the siblings' father and a cousin watched the Giants march sixteen plays towards them. New York chewed up nine minutes and fifty-nine seconds of the first quarter to open the game. Lawrence Tynes booted a thirty-two-yard field goal to close out the most time-consuming drive in Super Bowl history and put New York up 3–0.

The Himmelsteins and hundreds of longtime Giants' season ticket holders surrounded Mindy and I. Fate had dropped us into the beating heart of the Giants' fan base where families had followed the franchise for generations. As the game got underway, we could only imagine how spectators like Jay Himmelstein hung on every tick of the clock. He intentionally wore Manning's standard white road jersey that day. The Giants' nomadic road through the play-offs ran entirely away from New Jersey through Tampa, Dallas, and Green Bay. Until our formal introduction after the last second of the game clock ran off, I knew and thought of Jay Himmelstein only as "Manning Jersey."

A Giants' victory relied on shortening the game and keeping the ball out of the hands of New England's potent offensive machine. The opening drive followed the blueprint of Tom Coughlin's game plan almost perfectly. Hold the ball. Roll the clock. Deny New England offensive chances. Wear out their defense. New York converted on four, third-down plays. Rookie wide receiver Steve Smith made two key catches while the Giants' offensive line protected Eli Manning. The line also plowed a path for an effective ground attack.

"Keep pounding!" I heard over my left shoulder. "Keep sending Jacobs and Bradshaw right up the gut!"

Brandon Jacobs, a six-foot-four-inch, two-hundred-sixty-four-pound, third-year man out of Southern Illinois, outsized all but one of the Patriots' linebackers. He had eclipsed a thousand yards rushing during the 2007 campaign despite missing nearly six games due to injury. Ahmad Bradshaw joined Jacobs in the New York backfield. Bradshaw ran bigger than his comparatively slighter frame. Together, the pair tired the veteran New England defense by keeping them on the field.

I sensed that the voice behind me urging on Jacobs and Bradshaw belonged to a knowledgeable fan. At every game, there are always those who watch with a keener, sharper eye than the casual partisan. This fan did not watch the game like most casual fans, and certainly not like someone at Super Bowl XLII present merely for parties and celebrity watching.

Unlike the raw, exuberant Manning Jersey in front of me, the man behind me emoted more cerebrally. With the game unfolding at a pace favoring the Giants, he rooted with a cautious optimism. He became the voice over my ear, talking to mostly himself, thinking aloud, analyzing like a coach patrolling the sideline.

The modern dialogue between head coaches, assistants, and players on game day includes sophisticated communications connections between field, sideline, and upper level stadium boxes. In 2007, the NFL mandated for the first time that players wired with radio receivers for sideline instructions display green dots on their helmets. I added a small wraparound microphone to the twenty-first century head coach alter ego I imaginatively assigned to the spectator behind me. With the picture in my mind's eye completed, this anonymous fan to me became Headset Guy, a fellow with special insight who continually absorbed and relayed information.

I would eventually learn that Headset Guy was Bill Sharples, a professional chef from Hazlet, New Jersey. After accumulating enough seniority, he managed to arrange his work schedule to finish a typical day at three. The mid-afternoon exit gave him time to coach his two sons through their years of Pop Warner Little Scholars football. Headset Guy was a coach all right, but decidedly low-tech.

"There's no film allowed in Pop Warner football," Sharples would later tell me. "It helps you generate your thoughts. There are fewer things to process. It trains your mind to think ahead. When you have a twenty-five second play clock and someone is talking to you from upstairs, you can start to second-guess. Usually, your first instinct is right. If it's not, you can only blame yourself."

Tom Brady's first instinct, when he finally touched the ball with just less than five minutes to play in the first quarter, was to take advantage of good field position. Laurence Maroney scooted forty-three yards with the Giants' kickoff to set up his quarterback nicely on the Patriots' first possession of the game. Maroney, the Patriots' leading rusher in the regular season, added to his post-season totals as New England methodically worked the ball down the field. With under a half minute to play in the opening quarter, the Pats entered the red zone and faced a third and ten as they attempted to answer the Giants with an opening score of their own.

Brady spotted tight end Benjamin Watson streaking towards the back of the end zone and rifled a pass over the swarming Giants' defensive front. New York linebacker Antonio Pierce got up into Watson's face to knock the ball away. Yellow flags flew. Pierce was called for pass interference, placing the ball on the Giants' one-yard line as the first quarter wound down. On the opening play of the second quarter, Laurence Maroney finished the drive he had started with the kickoff return. He pushed forward over the right side for the final yard behind the block of tight end Kyle Brady. The Patriots snatched back the lead that so many believed they were destined to keep.

The New England touchdown deflated the Giants faithful around us including my immediate neighbor in the stands, Michael Hochman, a certified public accountant from Bergen County, New Jersey. He might have been on the other side of the country watching on television instead of sitting here if not for his seventeen-year-old son, Justin, in the next seat over.

The elder Hochman had attended his first Giants game with his father forty years earlier at Yankee Stadium. His most vivid memory from that contest was the impromptu chorus of disenchanted fans singing "Good Bye, Ally." After eight years as head coach, the Giants fired Ally Sherman at the end of the lackluster 1968 campaign.

By the time Michael Hochman started taking his own kids to Giants games, team fortunes had turned considerably. In January 2008, a coveted lottery selection letter landed in his mailbox. He hesitated before exercising his purchase rights.

"When I originally found out my number came up in the lottery, I wasn't definitely sure about going to the game," Hochman said. "It's a lot of expense and a long trip. Then there's the airfare, the hotel . . ."

Michael's reservations sounded familiar to me and then he continued.

"Early on, my son just said I would be crazy not to go. He said we have to do it. It's a once-in-a-lifetime thing. We gotta go he told me."

With that assessment from Justin, Michael got creative. He planned intensively over a narrow window of time. A brother-in-law who works on Wall Street connected Hochman with a friend who owned a private jet. Michael and Justin hitched a ride and flew in style from New York to Las Vegas. From there, they picked up a commercial flight to Phoenix. Now the two of them were seeing in their first Super Bowl live and their Giants were already giving the favored Patriots fits.

The Giants' defense manhandled the New England offensive line. Fifteen-year veteran defensive end Michael Strahan was playing in the final game of his career. He was exorcising the demons of a Super Bowl loss seven years earlier. Strahan and wide receiver Amani Toomer were the last active Giants remaining from the club's lopsided Super Bowl loss to the Baltimore Ravens in 2001. Toomer figured prominently during the Giants' second drive, pulling in a thirty-eight-yard catch on third and seven. The veteran receiver stretched over the painted sideline and dragged his toes over last few blades of green grass at the New England nineteen.

Judging by Eli Manning's deadpan expression alone, the New York quarterback looked almost disengaged from the magnitude of the moment. In fact, he was rising to the occasion. After coughing up the ball a league leading twenty-seven times during the regular season, the younger son of

Archie and younger sibling of Peyton, had shown nothing but maturity and control. He had yet to give up an interception in the post season. When a third and five pass bounced out of Steve Smith's hands into those of New England cornerback Ellis Hobbes, the promising second New York drive ended. It was the first pick Manning had thrown since the final week of the regular season. Coincidentally, Hobbes had grabbed that pass also.

"Come on, we don't play young like this!" Headset Guy barked.

An ominous shout from a Giants fan rolled down from several rows above me. "Eleven rookies and it's gonna haunt us!"

As the second quarter wore on, the Patriots' defense began to rattle the upstart underdog. Le Kevin Smith and Jarvis Green sacked Manning hard to the turf. On the same stalled drive, Ahmad Bradshaw fumbled a handoff. He recovered the loose ball before it could immediately fall into the enemy hands of Pierre Woods. In front of me, Manning Jersey shook his head and settled back into his seat while Jeff Feagles punted.

With the lead and the ball, New England went to work on offense and Michael Strahan eyed his prey. With seven minutes and fifty-five seconds remaining in the half, Tom Brady lined up in the shotgun at his own thirty-one with two receivers and tight end set wide on second and nine. Brady took the snap and Strahan maneuvered to his left around Patriots' right tackle Nick Kazur. Brady stood tall in the pocket and looked downfield. His feet straddled the *II* of the Super Bowl XLII logo. Linebacker Kawika Mitchell faked a drop back, then blitzed unimpeded straight at the Patriot quarterback. From the corner of his eye, Brady could also spot Strahan a few feet away, circling in for the kill. For a moment, it looked as if the tall, powerful defensive end might sail right past his target but the surging Mitchell pushed Brady back, allowing Strahan to reach a long arm out and collect the sack for an eight-yard loss.

The Giants fans came back to life.

"Something's wrong with Brady physically. Giants are going to win this game," Headset Guy said to no one in particular. Brady was nursing a tender ankle. He did not have the foot wrapped before the game. However, the injury was possibly reducing the mobility of a player already not known for scrambling.

On the following play, New England lined up in a similar passing set as in the previous down. Randy Moss, the big-play receiver who had been shut down by New York, went in motion to the right. The play clock rolled all the way to one second before Dan Koppen snapped the ball back to his signal caller.

Osi Umenyiora and Justin Tuck barreled forward shoulder-to-shoulder and caved in the Patriots' left side as Brady stepped back. Tuck pushed through left guard Logan Mankins and nearly tripped over Umenyiora who was working to get past Matt Light. Tuck steadied himself with his left hand. He lunged between Mankins and Light to face Brady as he brought the ball up with both hands and no time to throw. Tuck leaped and grabbed Brady from behind, collapsing the quarterback at the New England sixteen.

From well over a hundred yards away, Section 430 exploded in celebration. For the first time since kickoff, a Giants victory looked far more probable than the oddsmakers ever figured. New York was securing the psychological edge. They bullied over, around, and through Tom Brady's protective barrier, harassing the two-time Super Bowl MVP, repeatedly putting him on his back. When the Giants' defense was not sacking the quarterback, they were knocking him down and robbing him of time to connect with receivers downfield. A Patriots' offense that had led the league with an average of 411 yards a game produced just seven in the course of two possessions.

If New England were to emerge victorious on this day, it would have to be on the Giants' terms, namely, an all-out defensive slugfest. The aging Patriots' defense would have to reach deep. New York kept them running and chasing by sending their young backs rushing side to side. After a penalty pushed the Giants out of field-goal range, the Patriots got one more opportunity deep in their own territory before the first half expired. When New England lined up for third and thirteen at their own seven with one minute and thirty-five seconds remaining, their offensive production for the second quarter stood at negative ten yards to the Giants' seventy-six.

The Pats needed breathing space on the field, and if possible on the scoreboard, before intermission. They got the space on the field when Donte Stallworth snatched a short pass on the left side and weaved eighteen yards after the catch to the Patriots' twenty-six. New England relied on quick short passes to move the ball and keep Brady protected and vertical. Kevin Faulk came out of the backfield and came down with a drive-saving catch on third and four.

On the next play, Randy Moss hauled in an eighteen-yard reception to advance the ball to the Giants' forty-four with twenty-two ticks left in the opening half. The Patriots managed to drive eight plays for forty-five yards in about a minute and a half. A bit more real estate could possibly open the door to a Stephen Gostkowski field-goal attempt.

Brady dropped back on first and ten looking to cash in bigger.

He lingered in the pocket searching in vain for an open man while Tuck and Umenyiora closed in again. This time, Tuck reached from behind and grabbed Brady's throwing wrist. Umenyiora brought a right hand down over the quarterback's passing shoulder and pushed Brady to his knees. He then leaned back and alertly wrapped two hands around the ball Tuck had just sent to the ground before the center Dan Koppel could pull it back for the Patriots.

The half concluded with New England clinging to a 7–3 lead and New York clinging to hope.

At halftime, Tom Petty and the Heartbreakers performed four, chart-topping hits. One of the selections captured the Giants' mood perfectly as they prepared for the final thirty minutes against their 18–0 opposition. While Tom Coughlin reviewed the first half and planned the second with his squad, Petty sang "I Won't Back Down."

The extended halftime offered the crowd in the stadium uninterrupted entertainment for the first time since kickoff. A woman seated near me grumbled several times about longer than average timeouts prompted by television. After a while, I finally turned around to her and said, "Ma'am, at five million dollars a minute, the network has no problem with making us all wait."

She shrugged indifferently but that was the last I heard her complain.

A significant segment of the viewing audience actually is drawn as much by Super Bowl commercials as the game itself. I would want to watch the spots I was missing before colleagues at work spoiled my innocence with their own recap and commentary on Monday morning. I made a mental note to roll through my aging and almost quaint VCR unit back in Sacramento. In a Super Bowl first, FOX television promoted during the game the availability of all the ads on the My Space Web site. Tucked inside my seat cushion, an Apple card offered game highlight downloads at iTunes.com. With Super Bowl XLII, advertising continued to transcend the live-action viewing experience.

When they took the field for the second half, the Patriots initially performed as advertised prior to game day.

With Randy Moss largely contained as he had been throughout the postseason, New England turned to their most productive receiving weapon, Wes Welker. On the first play from scrimmage, Brady hit Welker over the middle for a sixteen-yard pickup. For the day, Welker amassed eleven catches for one-hundred–and-three yards.

The Patriots' reincarnated offense worked across midfield after the Giants sent too many men on the field with New England in punt formation. On a key third and thirteen, Kevin Faulk took a Brady pass at the forty and dodged the flying safety Michael Johnson to reach the Giant twenty-seven with just over nine minutes left in the third quarter. However, the drive would fizzle as Michael Strahan bagged his second sack to back New England up to the thirty-two and a fourth-and-thirteen situation.

In previous years, Patriot's coach Bill Belichick would likely have turned to his ace kicker Adam Vinatieri. However, Vinatieri, who iced two Super Bowls for the Pats with timely field goals, had taken a big contract with the Colts the season prior. Belichick elected not to send out the twenty-three-year-old Stephen Gostkowski to boot a forty-nine-yard field goal. Instead, he elected to go for broke and a potential two-possessions lead.

With Osi Umenyiora breathing down his neck, Brady overthrew Jabar Gaffney in the end zone. The Pats had controlled the ball for over eight minutes and came up empty. When the third quarter closed, two zeros went up on the board in one of the lowest scoring Super Bowls ever.

The Giants' youth movement continued with the opening of the final quarter. On New York's opening possession of the fourth quarter, Manning found rookie tight end Kevin Boss over the middle. The Giants' fifth round draft pick from Western Oregon shook off Rodney Harrison at the forty and trucked another twenty-six yards before Harrison finally made a shoestring tackle at the Patriots' thirty-four. For Boss, the forty-five-yard reception was the longest of his NFL debut season.

Once again, a first-year player stepped up for the Giants when Steve Smith fended off a tough hit from Brandon Merriweather and came down with a seventeen-yard catch. Smith kept the New York drive alive and set his Giants up at the twelve.

Headset Guy took satisfaction in Smith's redemption. He remembered that the first half interception deep in Patriots' territory had bounced off the receiver's open hands.

Manning Jersey, who had been the loudest voice in our section all game long, reached out over the row immediately in front of him. He vigorously shook a small boy wearing Smith's number twelve shirt as he had done each time the first-year receiver made a big play. So effective was Smith in the clutch that by the end of game, Manning Jersey wondered if he had traumatized pint-sized Smith Jersey.

On second and three from the five-yard line, the Giants lined up and sent David Tyree in motion on the right side. Manning took the snap and faked a hand-off to Bradshaw while Tyree streaked to the dead center of the end zone. Manning's strike hit squarely between the eight and the five on Tyree's chest. The Giants took a 10–7 lead, their first since the first quarter.

Rookies accounted for nearly all of the eighty yards in New York's successful seven-play drive.

I looked three hundred and sixty degrees around me and saw nothing but Giants fans erupting with joy. A few sections over, my cousin Jason watched mostly New England loyalists sink in their seats. To his amazement, a handful of those seats were already about to empty. Over eleven minutes remained in the game.

New England was far from finished.

After the teams traded possessions without a first down, the Patriots took over at their twenty-four with just under eight minutes left. Sensing the series could be their last stand, the New England offensive front stiffened and gave their field general the needed protection to advance the ball. Tom Brady completed a throw to Welker for five yards, then another to Moss for ten more. Laurence Maroney, held by the Giants to less than two-and-a-half-yards a carry, managed to burst forward for nine.

Manning Jersey rose from his seat and waved his arms up like a fire and brimstone preacher madly exhorting his congregation.

"Come on! It's not just another game! It's the Super Bowl!" he screamed.

And a hell of a Super Bowl it had already been, no matter what the outcome.

Welker's second catch of the drive took the Patriots over the midfield stripe with just over six minutes to play. The New York linebackers and secondary had shut down the sidelines for most of the game. Brady took what yards he could get by sending his receivers across the middle of the field. This also kept the clock rolling. Welker and Moss each pulled in another reception to bring the ball to the Giants' nineteen.

Once again, Kevin Faulk stepped out from the New England backfield and into the Giants secondary where he snagged a short pass at the fifteen and slid forward to the seven-yard line. The Patriots looked at a first and goal and prospects for a fourth Lombardi trophy with three minutes and twenty-two seconds left on the clock.

Two plays later, on third and goal from the six, Randy Moss lined up to Brady's right against cornerback Corey Webster. Webster backed up and slipped as Brady wound up and threw a high bullet to Moss. The ten-year veteran, who had a tumultuous past in Minnesota and Oakland, temporarily gave New England the lead and a seemingly bright future as he leaped and caught the pass in the corner of the end zone.

Gostkowski converted a crucial extra point to put the Patriots up 14–10 and deflate the Giants' supporters before my eyes. By now, I was one of them and one with them. Each New York advance lifted me up. I died a bit inside with every setback.

Though I felt like something of an interloper in a long and strong love affair between the New York Football Giants' season ticket holders and their team, I was still a native New Yorker. I still had family living within an hour of the city, including a relative currently cheering from the nearby end zone corner.

The Giants would have to come across the field straight towards us to win.

As the Patriots' offense tentatively celebrated in the end zone, Manning Jersey slumped in his chair in front of me with his head between his hands. To my right, Michael Hochman and his son Justin stared dejectedly at the field below. Michael measured his hope at that juncture as perhaps a two or three on a scale of ten.

Two thoughts raced one after the other through my mind as the special teams jogged onto the field for the change of possession kickoff. Something dawned on me as, in the company of strangers in the stands, I watched the equally strange men below clad in blue and white. For all the passion I had I invested in this contest, I had personally met only one the people on the field.

Over the years, radio advertising sales had taken me to places both exciting and odd. I had briefly rubbed shoulders with pro athletes at various business and client functions. I dined with the 49ers during a training camp session. I made small talk with the Oakland A's coaching staff at a fan appreciation event. I recommended Sacramento area restaurants to my boyhood New York Yankee idol, Roy White, when he came to California's capital as a minor league coach. I have met a handful of Olympic legends and even held a gold medal in my hand. However, in all of these encounters, I was a guest on the athlete's turf, every time except once.

In the late nineties, a Lake Tahoe hotel casino client wanted promotional consideration to support their Sacramento radio-time buy. Such value-added opportunities can run the gamut from substantive to ridiculous. These gimmicks are often no more than smoke and mirrors linked together to pass off a host of unrelated activities as a cohesive promotion. Celebrity appearances, silly contests, and random-draw giveaways are the primary tools of this trade.

In this particular instance, my client had scheduled Tony Bennett for a concert appearance in Tahoe. Our station received free tickets with the expectation I would find a more creative way to award the tickets to lucky Sacramento listeners rather than through the typical fifth-caller, on-air giveaway.

One of our afternoon news anchors, a charming woman who also had a modest singing career, happened to have an upcoming engagement at a small Sacramento nightclub. I persuaded her and the nightclub owner to incorporate into the evening's performance a sing-along of Tony Bennett standards. We would offer Bennett concert tickets to patrons willing to join the band on stage. In exchange, I agreed to make certain at least a couple of station staff "ringers," myself included, would join the band on stage if, as expected, no one from the audience volunteered to join in. I enjoy few things less than singing.

The club happened to be popular with both hometown and visiting athletes. One of my radio associates tipped me off to the fact that his brother was friends with Junior Seau. The three of them would coincidentally be meeting at the club the evening my half-baked promotional idea would be executed. My consolation prize for making a fool of myself as a reluctant backup singer was getting to meet Junior, who kept a low profile at a far end of the dimly lit main bar.

For about ten minutes after the performance, I huddled with my former coworker, his brother, and Seau. For a change, a star athlete had shown up in a corner of my world and not the other way around. We chatted about radio, Tony Bennett, and anything other than football. I consciously divided my attention among the noncelebrities and Seau who continued to go unrecognized and unfettered by club patrons. Clearly, he appreciated not being the center of attention as he comfortably engaged our group in small talk.

Before I excused myself, I shook Seau's hand, wished him a pleasant stay in town, and in the first and only acknowledgement of his profession, said I thought he played with great heart and determination. He thanked me and I left him to his friends, impressed by his lack of pretense and genuinely pleasant demeanor.

I had not thought of that meeting for a long time until I saw number fifty-five gallop out to the field for the Patriots' final defensive series of Super Bowl XLII. If the Giants fell, at least a deserving player with whom I had a brief and positive experience would finally be a champion.

A second thought came to me as I glanced up to the game clock.

The Giants lined up for their first play from scrimmage and my memory banks lined up almost twenty years behind them.

Since 2001, I had admired Tom Brady's cool steadiness and total field awareness through the prism of a San Francisco 49er fan. In 1989, the similarly unflappable Joe Montana found himself in the position I thought Brady might arrive at in Super Bowl XLII, behind in a tight game with time running out. Brady had so far amassed twenty-eight, fourth-quarter comebacks in his storied career. Before retiring to the bucolic Napa Valley wine country, Joe Montana produced vintage fourth-quarter comebacks. All week long, I assumed, if the Patriots did not blow the Giants out, it would be Tom Brady, not Eli Manning, with the ball, a slim deficit, a long field, and a short clock.

With two minutes and thirty-nine seconds remaining, I touched the bill of my San Francisco 49er Radio Network cap and wondered if Manning would march his Giants downfield in much the same manner as Montana did in Super Bowl XXIII. I could not know, but I felt a strange sense of destiny.

I had not watched the Giants closely over the years, but as Manning called signals at his own seventeen-yard line, Bill Sharples, who knew the team well, watched from over my shoulder with quiet confidence.

"Eli's going to be OK," Headset Guy said.

Jay Himmelstein sat below me thoroughly subdued. He turned to his sister Bree moments before the snap and raised a finger to his lip to signal quiet. Manning Jersey's gentle appeal for silence was his way of deferring to the real Manning's signal calls on the field. I read his gesture differently, as a possibly superstitious suspension of his wild enthusiasm. Section 430 had temporarily lost its loudest voice. The collective consciousness surrounding us sensed it. I made it my personal goal to get Manning Jersey back on his feet.

With the Giants facing a fourth and one at their own thirty-seven and one minute and thirty-three seconds left on the clock, the tension was nearly unbearable.

I leaned over, summoned every decibel from my already strained vocal chords, and echoed the earlier banshee scream of the now seated fan clad in the red number ten in front of me.

"Get up! It's not just another game. It's the Super Bowl!"

The fans around us knew immediately I was pleading for the self-described "borderline obsessed" Jay Himmelstein to show us all he still believed in his Giants.

Manning Jersey soon complied. He turned back to me, smiled, and gave me a little fist bump as Brandon Jacobs powered ahead for the necessary yard to keep the New York Giants' championship dreams alive.

"Holy shit, I'm goin' bananas," another spectator cried out from the rafters during a measurement confirming the first down.

Thousands of Giants fans under the bubble and millions more glued to television screens were about to go bananas as well. Yawner Super Bowls have come, gone, and will come again, but not on this day.

With one minute and fifteen seconds left, and the Giants looking at third and five from their own forty-three, Eli Manning laid back several yards in shotgun formation. Shaun O'Hara's center snap then launched the signature play of Super Bowl XLII.

Manning collected the ball and dropped back to the thirty-five. The space separating the quarterback and his four frontline defenders rapidly closed in eerie synchronicity. Eli stepped forward to the thirty-seven to find an open gap just as Jarvis Green climbed over Giants' guard Rick Seubert. Green reached out and yanked the back of Manning's jersey at the nametag pulling the passer off balance. Richard Seymour also grasped a handful of the red number ten on Manning's back. Both defenders anticipated a certain sack.

Manning grimaced. He covered the ball up in his gut, hunched over, and bent his knees.

As Manning twisted to his right, a third pursuer, eleven-year linebacker Mike Vrabel, closed in from the front to surround the apparently doomed quarterback. Manning leaned out in the only direction promising daylight to elude the hotly pursuing Patriots' defense. Jarvis Green clung to Manning's shirt and stretched it out to comical proportions. For an instant, human traffic surrounded Eli, hiding him from nearly every camera and spectator view.

When he finally snapped free from Green's relentless gloved hand, Manning was violently propelled forward. He popped out from behind two Giant linemen and miraculously cleared himself from the chaotic, collapsed pocket. He took seven more steps back towards the right sideline. With Vrabel chasing him down yet again, Manning let loose a desperate heave.

Downfield at the Giants' twenty-six, David Tyree scrambled and weaved among the New England secondary, trying to create separation from his defender, Rodney Harrison. Harrison was perched right on Tyree's back in tight coverage. Receiver and defender awaited Manning's fly ball descending towards them. Harrison and Tyree each timed their gymnastic leaps perfectly. The prolate spheroid spiraled into the hands of Tyree and edged perilously forward across the tacky surface of his gloves. His back arched and his left leg extended back as he reached the apex of his vault upwards. Harrison hungrily eyed the ball. In a fleeting, airborne instant, he may have deduced an interception was unlikely. All he needed was to place enough pressure on the ball to send it harmlessly to the ground and force a potential game-ending fourth down.

As the entwined adversaries descended back to earth, the Giants' receiver pulled the ball onto the top right half of his blue helmet to anchor whatever stabilizing forces his fingertips could exert on the laced, leather surface. Like the cartoon character Wile E. Coyote suspended over a cliff's edge, Tyree's left leg drew back under his body and his right leg kicked forward contacting only air. Harrison, also still off the ground, extended his right quad upward for leverage and tried to tug Tyree backwards. His right foot briefly met Tyree's left before each found separate paths towards the turf. Asante Samuel, Ellis Hobbs and James Sanders all closed in from different angles. They could only watch, not influence, this brief and frantic gridiron ballet.

Harrison's right leg, now planted firmly, met Tyree's lower back as Tyree's left foot set down on the painted word *Super*. The arms and legs of the opponents formed a single body in motion. They flailed like a dropped spider with two legs grounded and six more still falling. At the head, Harrison clawed and Tyree pressed on the pointed end of the ball still facing skyward across the hard protective shell of his helmet. Tyree's fingertips crawled over the ball's surface seeking firm foundation against the momentum of the fall and the prying intrusion of Harrison's hands.

Tyree's back draped over Harrison's upper right leg. As he fell backwards into the defender's lap, his weight pushed Harrison down and away from the ball. Tyree could feel but not see the football still pinned to his helmet between his outstretched fingertips and his skull. The last floating limb of the spider, Tyree's right foot, found the turf as the receiver rolled across Harrison's midsection. The exposed point of the ball met the ground. Even as Harrison tried to roll to his left and throw the receiver off him, he could not dislodge the football from Tyree's tenuous but sufficient grasp.

While over seventy thousand can say they were present, a spectator could only truly savor the brilliance of Manning to Tyree with super slow motion, pause, and rewind. As such, it was fitting that Steve Sabol, President of the iconic NFL Films and the game's chronicler for decades, dubbed the play the greatest single Super Bowl play ever, even though it did not win or decide the contest.

Tyree, the fifth-year Giants' wide receiver, had been a Syracuse Orangeman. He had played his college ball in the Carrier Dome where I had logged countless hours in near total solitude, offsetting tuition with my campus security job. I had also spent many days and nights in the Dome as a fan among record collegiate crowds. At the university level, Syracuse, as much as any NCAA institution, made the game bigger. In a few months, the most accomplished player at SU during my time there, Art Monk, would finally be inducted into the Pro Football Hall of Fame.

My wife, on her feet and cheering next to me, was wearing a Syracuse University jacket. I had purchased the garment for Mindy a year earlier. I picked it up on campus on my first return visit with both her and my mother, to the very same school I left behind a quarter century ago as a restless, uncertain young man. It had taken me that long to reconcile and come to peace with a formative but turbulent phase in my life.

Much earlier in the game, Jay Himmelstein had nudged another neighboring fan also wearing a Syracuse shirt. Perhaps he was an alumnus or had a child enrolled. Himmelstein was slightly puzzled and mildly curious about the choice of college over pro insignia apparel on this particular occasion. He asked the fellow seated next to him, "Why Syracuse?"

The fan looked at Himmelstein for a moment refocusing his attention from the action on the field to his row mate. Then he glanced down at his shirt and gave it a slight tug.

"Oh, right," he answered, "It's my *lucky* shirt."

The Giants could use whatever skill, luck, determination, and karma they could get to move twenty-four yards farther. Steve Smith helped them get almost half way there when two plays later he caught another Manning pass.

At the outset of this increasingly familiar drive, Michael Strahan had urged his teammates to believe along with him. "Seventeen to fourteen is the final," Strahan said emphatically to his counterparts assigned to the offensive trenches. As the offense readied to take the field, Strahan added, "One touchdown and we are the world champions. Believe it and it will happen." Michael Strahan's comments were beginning to appear prophetic.

With the ball resting on the thirteen-yard line and thirty-nine seconds left on the clock, my voice was hoarse, raspy, and possibly louder than I had ever made it. It was first down. The Giants had time. Even with no time-outs left, they could waste a play to stop the clock if needed. Logic and reason held that New York had not yet reached the all-in, all or nothing point.

I expect a few who were not there will insist, or at least secretly harbor doubt, that blurred hindsight, revisionism, creative license, or even self-delusion drives the following excerpt of my game day account. There is no point pleading a case for detractors. The recollection is too vivid, the moment too surreal and too stunning to fabricate. Besides, I had witnesses.

Never at a sporting event had I ever felt so certain of an outcome. I can only be thankful that no betting agent could have taken a real-time wager from me at that moment for fear of what extraordinary sum I would have laid down. As an East Coast transplant to Northern California, West Coast roots now extended for half my life. I had long since sprouted a San Francisco 49er branch on my family tree of football loyalties. If the Manning to Tyree play owed a debt to luck, as Tyree himself later implied, perhaps the next play owed a debt to California karma.

I had seen this drama unfold once before, on a tiny screen, in a packed room, in a feverishly expectant City by the Bay. I would revel with friends in San Francisco until nearly dawn the next day after the 49ers defeated the Cincinnati Bengals following a ninety-two yard game-winning drive culminating in a Joe Montana touchdown pass to John Taylor. On January 22, 1989, Eli was eight years old, around the age when young boys and girls begin to archive a mental highlight reel. He was likely watching Super Bowl XXIII with father Archie and big brother Peyton. I knew the highlights of that final drive well. Certainly young Eli did also.

The numbers lined up closely and fired through my memory banks. The 49ers had been on the ten with thirty-nine seconds and down 16–13. The Giants were on the thirteen with thirty-nine seconds behind, 14–10. At this moment in my mind, Manning *was* Montana. About four hours had passed since Ronnie Lott had stood at midfield and tossed a golden coin skyward in tribute to the late architect of a 49er dynasty, head coach Bill Walsh. Maybe Walsh was watching.

I had no idea who, but someone was going into the end zone right now. I just felt an overwhelming certainty, a sense of destiny thoroughly different from hope. As it would unfold, Plaxico Burress, number seventeen, was about to become the John Taylor of Super Bowl XLII. To be sure, this would be a Giants' moment, but I was living that moment in a magical parallel universe. I let anyone within the sound of my maniacal scream know it.

"This is the play! This is the play! It's coming right at us! It happens right now, right here!"

I lifted my seemingly incongruent 49ers cap and raised it amidst utter bedlam. Manning crouched under center. The Giants stacked three receivers to the right facing directly at us. In the stands over the opposite end zone corner, my cousin Jason was on his feet and pulling for his home team amongst mostly wary New England supporters. He had a bird's eye view of Burress, the lone receiver set to the left of Manning.

Eli received the snap standing back at the eighteen. Burress faked an inside slant to the middle then darted for the left corner of the end zone, exactly the way he had practiced with Manning in pregame warm-ups. Once Ellis Hobbs leaned inside, he had no chance in single coverage to make up lost ground. Manning floated a high toss for the six-foot-five-inch Burress, who reached up, easily cradled the ball, and trotted off into Giants history.

Tynes added the seventeenth and final point.

Fittingly, the heroic New York defense would occupy the field for the last meaningful seconds of the game. The Patriots, just like the Bengals of 1989, would get four more shots. Jay Alford, the Giants' rookie defensive tackle and third-round draft pick from Penn State, put Tom Brady on his back one more time with nineteen seconds to go on second down. In much the same fashion, Charles Haley had leveled Boomer Esiason on second down nineteen years earlier. The Giants knocked Brady down twenty-three times in all.

Gibril Wilson batted the second of two Hail Mary passes to the turf. The Patriots turned the ball over on downs with one second remaining. Manning took a ceremonial snap and dropped a knee to the ground. The Giants were Super Bowl champions. New England was 18–1.

Patriot coach Bill Belichick was already on his way back to the locker room.

I gave every stranger within reach a high five, and then I turned to Mindy and squeezed her tight while wild cheers reverberated through the dome.

Behind me, Headset Guy was on the phone to a friend. His wife Linda beamed with delight next to him. Bill Sharples' early fiftieth birthday present from Linda, a trip to the Super Bowl, was an unforgettable gift. Bill's father had been in Yankee Stadium nearly fifty years ago when the Giants fell to Baltimore in what sports pundits still call the Greatest Game Ever Played.

As he accepted the Lombardi Trophy, Giants owner John Mara, grandson of Tim and son of Wellington, declared, "It's the greatest victory in the history of this franchise, without question."

Jay and Bree Himmelstein were ecstatic. Their father celebrated at the other end of the stadium. He had inherited the family's Giants season tickets at age nine when *his* father, the grandfather Jay and Bree never knew, died unexpectedly. Jay's red and white replica road jersey of Eli Manning fit nicely with the Giants' record eleventh straight NFL road victory.

Next to Mindy and I, Michael and Justin Hochman had a helicopter flight to catch. The exotic transport was the result of another string Michael had pulled to be here after his son pulled the strings attached to his father's heart.

"I have to tell this story, Michael." I said, "Would you mind if I called you after you get back home?"

"Sure, I'd like that," he answered and handed me a business card from the firm of Kahn, Hoffman, and Hochman.

"That's strange," I said looking down at the card, "The reason my wife and I are even here today is because of somebody named Hoffman."

Mindy leaned in and yelled over the noise of the crowd to Michael's son Justin, two seats over.

"Great game, wasn't it?"

"Yeah!" Justin responded blissfully.

"You're going to remember this for the rest of your life!" she continued, straining over the crowd's roar in the stadium.

"What?" Justin asked nudging closer. I was a couple feet nearer so I amplified and amended my wife's words for him.

"You're going to remember this *forever.*"

XI. Nobody is Perfect

We are all imperfect creatures infatuated with an unattainable standard of perfection.

The printed evidence littering the local newsstands and gathering places around Phoenix all week suggested our nominally neutral hosts and civic image-makers had a rooting interest in a Perfect Patriots season. What city booster would not want a lasting association with perfection?

The custom publishing house *944* printed the Official Lifestyle Publication of the Arizona Super Bowl Host Committee, a thick, ad-ladened, glossy magazine simply called *Game*. In the fashion-conscious cover shot, Tom Brady struck a Clark Kent style pose by pulling at his suit lapel and dress shirt to reveal his Patriots jersey like Superman's hidden garb.

Ultimately, the New York Giants came to the desert packing kryptonite.

Coach Bill Belichick and owner Robert Kraft built the Patriots to overcome all foes. New England followed their own upset Super Bowl win over the Rams in 2002 by winning again as favorites over Carolina in 2004 and Philadelphia the next season. They pursued a fourth title with the stated objective of a perfect record. For the chase, the organization continued to stress the team over individuals, and, not unlike the 49er dynasty of the 1980s, the 2007–2008 Patriots attracted veteran players already sated by salaried riches but starved for a title. Junior Seau and Randy Moss both walked off the field after Super Bowl XLII still hungry, each stung by defeat in the biggest of games. Seau's former Chargers lost a Super Bowl to the 49ers in 1995. Moss' 15-1 Vikings were upset by Atlanta in the NFC title game in 1999.

However, even if the New England Patriots had reached the mystical 19–0 mark, history may still not have judged the campaign blemish-free. The Spygate flap both motivated and dogged the team throughout the year. The video surveillance of opposing team drills finally drew punitive sanction from the league's commissioner during what was supposed to have been the Patriots' coronation week. Had New England emerged victorious as anticipated, the silver Lombardi trophy of 2008 would have forever borne a clouded lining. No measure of talent and determination could have completely silenced the critics who were eager to apply the label of *cheater*.

Our attraction to a standard of perfection competes with our desire to locate flaws in the seemingly flawless. The Dolphins I had first followed as a child wrote the perfect NFL script in the 1972–1973 season. Miami very nearly wrapped their 17–0 campaign in the perfect, symbolic package.

With just over two minutes remaining in Super Bowl VII, Dolphins kicker Garo Yepremian lined up for a forty-two-yard field goal. At that point, Miami led the Washington Redskins 14–0. A successful kick and a Dolphins' defensive stand would have poetically capped the first ever 17–0 NFL campaign with a 17–0 Super Bowl victory.

Yepremian's low kick bounced off Redskins' defensive tackle Bill Brundige and back towards the kicker's right. The trailing veteran quarterback and placeholder Earl Morrall tried chasing down the ball but Garo was closer. The smart play would have been to fall on the ball and relinquish possession to Washington just shy of midfield. Instead, Yepremian tried to make a play. He scooped up the bouncing ball and attempted a pass to Larry Csonka, *attempt* being the operative word.

Reeling back against hot pursuit, the kicker lost his grip of the ball just as he tried to fling it forward. The football flew straight up and landed directly in the hands of Redskins' cornerback Mike Bass, who sped forty-nine yards downfield for a Washington touchdown. The Dolphins narrowly averted a Redskins' comeback and sealed their place in league history along with possibly the most famous sports blooper highlight since video began capturing the game. Whenever television recounts the Dolphins' unprecedented march to perfection, the path nearly always runs through images of Garo Yepremian's anything but perfect record as a would-be quarterback. Garo's inconsequential gaffe, not the Dolphins 17–0 season, defines Super Bowl VII.

Conversely, the Patriots' consequential loss more than the Giants' upset or the even the image of David Tyree battling off Rodney Harrison, may define Super Bowl LXII. I watched the definition take shape as the New York faithful took up a spirited chant of "eighteen and one" in the dwindling moments of the game.

The notion of the second-place finisher exiled to obscurity crumbles under the weight of the New England Patriots' rising road to Phoenix.

The game site itself had been meticulously prepared and polished to welcome and honor perfection. As we headed jubilantly for the stadium exit, a simple event reminded us that our daily exchanges and interactions as humans are consistently imperfect.

While tens of thousands of spectators filed out of the massive, otherworldly dome in Glendale, we joined the many departing guests that raised cell phones or tapped hands-free earpieces. For nearly an hour after the game, callers made entirely futile attempts to connect with friends, family, and fellow fans.

For several hours, we had resided in a bubble. Millions across the nation and around the planet peered in from the outside through a high-definition eyehole. Meanwhile, we were immersed in the carnival and high drama of the game. We hovered with the privileged over one of the sporting world's greatest stages. After the clock finally ticked to zero, we were present while confetti rained, grown men wept, fans embraced, and all among us slowly prepared to return to the outside world.

In the concrete and steel womb, daylight had passed into darkness largely without notice. Mindy and I joined the massive procession snaking out along the concourse and twisting ramps. We each tried unsuccessfully to contact Jason. We had not seen my cousin since splitting up prior to kickoff. Jason watched the game from a largely Patriots' partisan section in the seat we had finally chased down the previous day. Now, under the desert night sky and dim parking lot lights, we squinted at small, unresponsive screens and clicked the saved number for Jason to no avail. With our cord, or at least our wireless connection, temporarily severed, reality beyond football seeped back into our consciousness.

Cellular communications in Glendale and in selected areas of New York, New Jersey, and Foxboro, Massachusetts, failed as thousands of call attempts hit the same set of towers and relay points. The bottleneck affected multiple carriers.

As an advertising professional, I have never understood why any phone company would adopt a phrase most routinely uttered in moments of anxiety or frustration. The one-time Verizon Wireless commercial tagline, "Can you hear me now?" comes to mind.

Mobile phone users ask this question most often when they are vexed by poor reception or an erratic signal caused by the slightest physical movement. Shrewd marketers regularly import and recycle common conversational expressions or slang into advertising campaigns in the hopes everyday vernacular will trigger a product impression. Nike effectively branded the once generic action command, Just Do It. Chevy trucks project the image of durability with the refrain, Like a Rock. Anheuser Busch built a whimsical series of television spots around nothing but the overused word, *dude*. After the words, "Can you hear me now?" assumed a new and generally less-than-positive association in the mobile phone era, an advertiser inexplicably enlisted the question commercially.

During this particular post-game communication breakdown, the pervasive question asked among departing fans was, "Is anyone getting a signal?"

We eventually reached Jason's voice mail and just after ten, we reunited inside the sprawling Glendale Exposition Hall and Media Center.

Along the wide corridor connecting the main lobby, spacious conference halls, and ground-level lounges, a crowd gathered around a large, makeshift retail stand. Fans rummaged through New York Giants Super Bowl Champion souvenirs. Shirts, caps, pennants and every imaginable trinket covered tables and pegboards. The merchandisers struck while the iron was hot and sales were reflected accordingly. A consigned allotment of comparable New England Patriots Super Bowl XLII championship gear awaited a different fate.

As part of an arrangement in place since 1994, the league would ship preprinted New England Patriots Super Bowl Champion apparel to a warehouse in Pittsburgh. From there, representatives of the nonprofit aid group World Vision forwarded the clothing to villages and towns throughout as many as twenty-five African nations that were impacted by extreme poverty.

With the Patriots post-game attire safely en route to sub-Saharan Africa, I plucked a Giants championship pennant off the table. I handed the pennant along with a youth-sized shirt for Howard's young son, Marshall, to one of the besieged clerks staffing the stand.

A gaggle of Giants' fans congregated on the front steps of the media center. I recruited one to snap a photo of Jason, Mindy, and me holding the banner proclaiming a title as unlikely as our entire trip had been.

Our reassembled trio then shuffled from the exposition center to the Westgate retail village. The mall still teemed with both game spectators and thousands of other people watchers and partygoers overflowing the stores, bars, and eateries. We scouted the walking avenues of the commercial district for a late and quick dinner. Since we were more hungry than fussy, we settled on a modest and bright quick-serve sandwich shop where we huddled in a cramped corner underneath a small television screen.

The adrenaline that coursed through all of us since dawn was finally dissipating. We slumped into functional plastic chairs with our food. During the game, highlights had flashed only briefly on the jumbo-sized stadium screen. Those images had lacked full detail, context and grandeur during the rapidly unfolding action. Nearly two hours after the game, sitting once again shoulder to shoulder with other fans, the adrenaline returned.

We finally got our first true view of Eli Manning's escape artistry and

David Tyree's acrobatic show. From our upper deck vantage points earlier, we could not gather the nuances of the multiple-angle playbacks. Tyree pinning the wobbling football to his helmet as Rodney Harrison clawed in vain would become the quintessential freeze-framed moment of Super Bowl XLII.

A week following the game, editorial cartoonist Gary Brookins of the *Richmond Times Dispatch* ingeniously co-opted the image of the Tyree-Harrison duel for political parody. Brookins depicted Tyree as Barack Obama snatching victory from the outstretched hands of defeated Democratic contender Hilary Clinton. From under her facemask, Clinton cried, "Nooo! That's mine! I'm supposed to win! I'm entitled!" The analogy of unheralded underdog pulling the prize from an anointed one fit seamlessly.

Jason, Mindy, and I cleared off our table. We stepped back out into the night under the twinkling lights of the outdoor mall. Like everything else in the expansive Glendale Sports and Entertainment Complex, the Westgate City Center gleamed. The utter newness of the entire area was almost unsettling. Every walkway, every fixture, every LED and neon display formed a perfect palette seemingly constructed for this specific day. In a manner of speaking, it had been. The stadium and the surrounding complex were key facets of the campaign to bring the Super Bowl back to Phoenix after a twelve-year hiatus.

Other communities readied similar master plans to attract a future Super Bowl or comparable marquee event. In a matter of months, the Summer Olympics would unfold in Beijing, China, with a much larger-scale construction footprint, including a spectacular national stadium, an architectural achievement introduced to the world as The Bird's Nest.

The New York Giants would soon join the New York Jets in a new and shared facility scheduled to open in 2010. The structure would occupy the former parking space of Giants Stadium in the Meadowlands. Special lighting technology and outer aluminum louvers would allow the new building to change colors like a chameleon, from blue to green and back again. The colors will alternate depending on whether the Giants or the Jets are playing. Construction cost estimates have reached $1.4 billion. That's triple the roughly half billion dollar price tags associated with the recently completed University of Phoenix Stadium and Beijing National Stadium. A certain degree of one-upsmanship characterizes the spiraling ascent of these sporting and entertainment palaces. Each seeks to project size, power, and beauty on a more grandiose scale, all in an effort to make the Big Game ever bigger.

In just a few decades, salaries, venues, and corporate associations pervasive in pro football specifically, and in sports generally, have expanded to massive proportions. The current iconic status of the NFL would likely astonish even John Heisman, perhaps the most forward-thinking participant in shaping the game at the dawn of the last century.

What would Tim Mara, who bankrolled the original New York Giants franchise for five hundred dollars, think of present valuations for marquee teams such as the Dallas Cowboys, now estimated in excess of a billion dollars?

Vince Lombardi, the legendary Green Bay Packers head coach, died in 1970 when *Super Bowl* first entered the American lexicon. Lombardi would barely recognize the media circus surrounding today's edition of the game. Multiple sports networks dedicated hundreds of hours of collective coverage to Super Bowl XLII. The record of this exhaustive reporting remains archived in thousands, if not millions, of home digital devices, DVDs and other media. Meanwhile, no complete television broadcast video of the Packers' 1967 victory over the Kansas City Chiefs is known to exist today. Network employees carelessly recorded over the master tapes of Super Bowl I, a game played well before VHS or comparable home recording devices could have archived the event.

Economic, social, and technological forces will certainly continue to advance how the game is documented, marketed, and experienced.

Our trio piled into a cab just before midnight. We left the still electric atmosphere of the Glendale Sports and Entertainment Complex behind. In the morning, Mindy and I would catch a short, direct flight back to Sacramento. Jason's improvised, last-minute flight plan was far more complicated. He would journey from Sky Harbor International in Phoenix to Portland, change planes for the longest connecting leg to Atlanta, and finally board a third aircraft bound for New York. His aerial path would trace a giant *N* across the continental United States, another feat once unimaginable and now taken for granted.

For now, the three of us sped in our steel yellow cocoon along Interstate 10. We were thoroughly spent from the entire chaotic, bizarre, and wondrous events of the past several days. As the dome receded from our view, the illuminated city in the desert unfolded ahead of us. I stared blankly at the shining red digits rolling progressively on the cab meter and imagined how the Big Game might look to the next generation of accidental spectators.

References

Abbott, Mark. Kishner, Irwin. Ruskin, Brad. Vickery, Alan. 2004. The Future of Sports Television. Fordham University Sports Law Forum panel discussion transcript. March 4. http://law.fordham.edu/publications/articles/200flspub6394.pdf (accessed March 1, 2008).

Associated Press, 2008. Coughlin Hopes to Have 80 Percent of Game Plan in Before Trip, ESPN.com. http://sports.espn.go.com/espn/wire?section=nfl&id=3213127 (accessed December 7, 2008).

Attner, Paul. 2005. A 'Have' Who Gave Life to the NFL: Wellington Mara. The Sporting News. November 11. http://findarticles.com/p/articles/mi_m1208/is_/ai_n15786462?tag=artBody;col1 (accessed March 5, 2008).

Bennett, Daviss. 1995.Boob Cube Three-Dimensional Volumetric Television. Discover, December 1. http://discovermagazine.com/1995/dec/boobcube603 (accessed March 10, 2008).

Berberich, Steve. 2007. Two Hours to Tokyo. The Gazette.Net. January 5. http://www.gazette.net/stories/010507/businew174540_31987.shtml (accessed April 8, 2008).

Best, Ben. 1990. Schemers in the Web: A Covert History of the 1960s Era. BenBest.com. http://www.benbest.com/history/schemers.html (accessed July 8, 2008).

Best, Neil. 2008. Prepare to Break the Bank for Super Bowl Tickets. Newsday, January 25. http://www.newsday.com (accessed Feb 15, 2008).

Biathlon Canada. 2004. Olympic Team Nomination Policy for the 2006 Torino Games. Dec 6. www.biathloncanada.ca/selectionprocess2006.pdf (accessed Feb 20, 2008).

Bishop, Greg. Thamel, Pete. 2008. Senator Wants NFL Spying Case Explained. New York Times, Feb1.http://www.nytimes.com/2008/02/01/sports/football/01nfl.html?ex=135952 2000&en=52b09f5fe20888b0&ei=5088&partner=rssnyt&emc=rss (accessed Nov 17, 2008).

Bloom, Howard. 2008. Countdown to Kickoff: Super Bowl XLII Perfect Ticket Storm. Sports Business News, January 30. http://sportsbiznews.blogspot.com/2008/01/countdown-to-kickoff-super-bowl-xlii.html (accessed Nov 17, 2008).

Bosman, Julie. 2006. First Stadiums Now Teams Take a Corporate Identity. New York Times, March 22. http://query.nytimes.com/gst/fullpage.html?res=9F00E5DE1630F931A1 5750C0A9609C8B63 (accessed November 17, 2008).

Burke, Monte. 2003. Turning $500 into a $573 Million NFL Team. Forbes, August 29. http://www.forbes.com/2005/08/31/football-valuations-charts_05nfl.html?index=17 (accessed November 17, 2008).

Business Wire. 2002. Ticket Trader and Master Broker Team Up in Strategic Alliance with Openfield. June 18. http://findarticles.com/p/articles/mi_m0EIN/is_2002_June_18/ai_87415593 (accessed November 17, 2008).

CNN.com. 2003. Limbaugh Resigns Over McNabb Comments. October 2, Entertainment page. http://www.cnn.com/2003/SHOWBIZ/10/02/limbaugh (accessed December 7, 2008).

Deggans, Eric. 2005. Isolating Our Points of Viewing. St. Petersburg Times, July 31. http://www.sptimes.com/2005/07/31/Floridian/Isolating_our_points_.shtml (accessed November 20, 2008).

Davis, David. 2004. Cow Town Cool. Los Angeles Times, March 7. http://www.nba.com/media/kings/CowTown.pdf (accessed December 6, 2008)

Dorfman, Dan. 2008. The Most Expensive Super Bowl. New York Sun, January 28. http://www.nysun.com/business/most-expensive-super-bowl/70314 (accessed November 20, 2008).

Fish, Mike. 2008. Senator Wants to Know why NFL Destroyed Patriot Spy Tapes. ESPN.com News Services, February 2. http://sports.espn.go.com/nfl/news/story?id=3225539 (accessed December 17, 2008)

Glaser, Mark. 2006. DVRs are MVPs for Super Bowl Watchers. Mediashift, February 9. http://www.pbs.org/mediashift/2006/02/super-skipdvrs-are-mvps-for-super-bowl-watchers040.html (accessed November 20, 2008).

Greenberg, Jeff. 2008. Super Bowl Media Day Fun. NBC4 Sports Washington D.C., January 29. http://sportscourt.wordpress.com/2008/01/29/super-bowl-media-day-fun (accessed December 7, 2008).

Happel, Stephen. Jennings, Marianne. 2002. Creating a Futures Market for Major Event Tickets: Problems and Prospects. The Cato Journal, January 1. http://www.cato.org/pubs/journal/cj21n3/cj21n3-6.pdf (accessed November 20, 2008).

Krueger, Alan. 2006. Wait Till Next Year but Lock in Ticket Price Now. New York Times, February 2. http://www.nytimes.com/2006/02/02/business/02scene.html (accessed November 20, 2008).

Lefton, Terry. 2001. Web Firms: Super Bowl Ads Not a Super Idea. The Industry Standard/CNN.com, January 1. http://archives.cnn.com/2001/TECH/computing/01/01/super.bowl.ads.idg/index.html (accessed December 7, 2008).

Massey, Barry. 2008. Bill Clinton Woos Governor Richardson. Associated Press, February 3. http://www.newsvine.com/_news/2008/02/02/1273823-bill-clinton-woos-gov-richardson (accessed November 20, 2008).

Matarese, John. 2006. Bid on Sports Tickets. WCPO-TV Cincinnati, March 15.

http://old.wcpo.com/wcpo/localshows/dontwasteyourmoney/107afae2.html (accessed November 20, 2008).

Moss, Linda. 2008. Puppy Bowl IV Draws 8 Million Dogged Fans. Multichannel News, February 5. http://www.multichannel.com/article/CA6529081.html (accessed November 20, 2008).

Parker, Ev. 2008. A New Vote for 'Greatest Game Ever Played'. Napa Valley Register, March 15. http://www.napavalleyregister.com/articles/2008/03/15/sports/ace_parker/doc47db5fc2a2b77449577443.txt (accessed November 20, 2008).

Pennington, Bill. 2006. John Heisman: The Coach Behind the Trophy. New York Times, December 8. http://www.nytimes.com/2006/12/08/sports/ncaafootball/08heisman.html?_r=1&oref=slogin (accessed November 20, 2008)

Robinson, Joshua. Schwarz, Alan. 2008. Olympic Dream Stays Alive on Synthetic Legs. New York Times, May 17. http://www.nytimes.com/2008/05/17/sports/olympics/17runner.html (accessed November 20, 2008).

Tuohy, John William. 2001. Cal Neva History. American Mafia.com, January. http://www.americanmafia.com/Feature_Articles_109.html (accessed November 20, 2008)

Umphlett, Wiley Lee. 1992. Creating the Big Game: John Heisman and the Invention of American Football, Westport, Connecticut: Greenwood Press.

Wilkinson, Jack. 2000. John Heisman Profile. Georgia Tech Athletics. http://ramblinwreck.cstv.com/sports/m-footbl/mtt/heisman_john00.html (accessed 12/06/08)

Willis, Gerry. 2006. Super Bowl Alternatives: Five Tips, CNN Money.com, February 3.